ECONOMIC EVOLUTION

New institutional economics offers one of the most exciting new agendas in economics – the economic analysis of the evolution of institutions. Yet a careful analysis of what is meant by evolution has been missing. This book fills this lacuna.

It focuses on three of the approaches which are central to the new institutional economics:

- the new theory of the firm, with particular emphasis on Oliver Williamson's transaction cost economics;
- evolutionary economics, taking the work of Nelson and Winter as the benchmark;
- game theoretic accounts of the spontaneous evolution of conventions and institutions inspired by Hayek.

The analysis shows that attempts to group these approaches under the same broad heading conceals many important differences. Not the least of these are the different meanings given to such key concepts as 'institution' and 'evolution'. Despite these differences, the book does identify two evolutionary mechanisms that govern processes of economic change in the approaches that are discussed. Drawing on recent work in biology and philosophy of science the author identifies some unresolved issues in attempts to transfer the concepts of evolutionary biology to economics. The book poses questions which no self-conscious economist working on evolutionary issues can afford to ignore.

Jack J. Vromen is Assistant Professor in the Philosophy of Economics at Erasmus University, Rotterdam and Assistant Professor in the History and Methodology of Economics at the University of Amsterdam. He has co-authored several books in Dutch on the philosophy of economics as well as articles in leading international journals.

ECONOMICS AS SOCIAL THEORY
Series edited by Tony Lawson
University of Cambridge

Social theory is experiencing something of a revival within economics. Critical analyses of the particular nature of the subject matter of social studies and of the types of methods, categories and modes of explanation that can legitimately be endorsed for the scientific study of social objects, are re-emerging. Economists are again addressing such issues as the relationship between agency and structure, between economy and the rest of society, and between enquirer and the object of enquiry. There is renewed interest in elaborating basic categories such as causation, competition, culture, discrimination, evolution, money, need, order, organization, power, probability, process, rationality, technology, time, truth, uncertainty and value, etc.

The objective of this series is to facilitate this revival further. In contemporary economics the label 'theory' has been appropriated by a group that confines itself to largely a-social, a-historical, mathematical 'modelling'. *Economics as Social Theory* thus reclaims the 'theory' label, offering a platform for alternative, rigorous, but broader and more critical conceptions of theorizing.

Published in the series so far

ECONOMICS AND LANGUAGE
Edited by Willie Henderson, Tony Dudley-Evans and Roger Backhouse

RATIONALITY, INSTITUTIONS AND ECONOMIC METHODOLOGY
Edited by Uskali Mäki, Bo Gustafsson and Christian Knudsen

WHO PAYS FOR THE KIDS?
Gender and the structures of constraint
Nancy Folbre

NEW DIRECTIONS IN ECONOMIC METHODOLOGY
Edited by Roger Backhouse

RULES AND CHOICE IN ECONOMICS
Essays in constitutional political economy
Viktor J. Vanberg

ECONOMIC EVOLUTION

An Enquiry into the Foundations
of New Institutional Economics

Jack J. Vromen

London and New York

First published 1995
by Routledge
11 New Fetter Lane, London EC4P 4EE

Simultaneously published in the USA and Canada
by Routledge
29 West 35th Street, New york, NY 10001

© 1995 Jack J. Vromen

Typeset in Garamond by
LaserScript Ltd, Mitcham, Surrey
Printed and bound in Great Britain by
Mackays of Chatham PLC, Chatham, Kent

British Library Cataloguing in Publication Data
A catalogue record for this book is available from the British Library

Library of Congress Cataloging in Publication Data
A catalogue record for this book has been requested

ISBN 0-415-12812-9 (hbk)
ISBN 0-415-12813-7 (pbk)

CONTENTS

PREFACE

This book is a modified, extended and updated version of my dissertation *Evolution and Efficiency* (University of Amsterdam, June 1994). What started all this was my fascination with the relation between realism (as a doctrine in contemporary philosophy of science) and economic science. Although there is a variety of philosophical positions captured under the rubric of 'realism', it seems that they all share the basic supposition that science primarily aims at formulating true, explanatory theories. I was led by the intuition that Milton Friedman's well-known though controversial statement that 'the more significant the theory, the more unrealistic the assumptions' (Friedman 1953: 14) could not be the last word on the subject. At the same time I felt that it would not make sense to superimpose some preconceived philosophical notion of realism on economic theories. If a meaningful connection between realism and economic theories were to be found at all, it would have to square with the self-understanding of practising economists. Indeed, I took this latter requirement to be so important that many, if not all, of the discussions in my dissertation were meant to articulate ways in which economists conceive of their own theoretical endeavours. With hindsight, it must be admitted that as a consequence the realism issue somewhat got out of sight. I thank Tony Lawson and Brian Loasby (as well as several anonymous referees) for alerting me to this. I hope that in the present book the balance is redressed.

I also owe special thanks to Neil De Marchi, who supervised the completion of my dissertation. He never got tired of following and encouraging my 'meanders' through the landscapes of economics, philosophy and biology. Many others have also been of great help to me. I would like to express my gratitude to all of them. In particular, I wish to thank Maarten Janssen, Huib Pellikaan and Herman Vollebergh for their careful reading and their penetrating though always constructive criticism of earlier drafts. I have benefited also from conversations with and comments from Armen Alchian, Marina Bianchi, Harold Demsetz, Sanjeev Goyal, J. Daniel Hammond, Jack Hirshleifer, Elias Khalil, Uskali Mäki and Philippe van Parijs.

The technical and moral support given by Ton Alting and John Dagevos also deserve special mention. Finally, I thank the Netherlands Organization for Scientific Research (NWO) for assigning me a grant that enabled me to visit some of the people mentioned above.

1

INTRODUCTION

1. 'EVOLUTION' IN ECONOMICS: A BIRD'S-EYE VIEW

At the end of the nineteenth century, Veblen proclaimed the end of pre-evolutionary economics. Veblen argued that pre-evolutionary economists were inclined to think that economic events are bound to take a 'natural' course towards a putative equilibrium. In this course of events, 'human nature' was assumed to be unaltered. Veblen believed that the time was ripe for a fundamental reorientation of the discipline. Instead of postulating 'teleological' tendencies in the direction of 'normal' equilibrium situations, Veblen urged economists to develop an up to date, evolutionary 'matter-of-fact' approach. Economists would do better to study unfolding processes in terms of their causes and effects. According to Veblen, the key concept would have to be 'cumulative causation': causal processes engender effects that provide the starting point for subsequent causal processes, which in turn generate effects that provide the material for subsequent causal processes, and so on. Veblen argued that:

> for the purpose of economic science the process of cumulative change that is to be accounted for is the sequence of change in the methods of doing things – the methods of dealing with the material world.
>
> (Veblen 1898: 387)

Far from assuming an inert and immutable human nature, economists were to focus on changes in institutions, in habits of thought in economic communities. Veblen believed that institutions slowly adapt to changing 'exigencies' of industrial society, but he stressed time lags in this process of adaptation. Several institutions were identified by Veblen as hangovers from the past that were maladapted to 'modern' technological life.

At the beginning of the twentieth century, Marshall declared that the Mecca of economists lies in 'economic biology'. In the same spirit as Veblen, Marshall expressed the hope that prevailing statical analysis in economics would be a transitory state that would be superseded by a truly

1

dynamical analysis based on biological conceptions. The central idea of economics, Marshall held, had to be that of 'living force and movement'. Marshall argued that 'the struggle for existence' forces groups of people to change their customs and habits. Like Veblen, Marshall held that many habits survive which are in themselves of no advantage to the human race. Yet, on the whole, Marshall seemed to be convinced that those races survive in which the best habits are developed.

It is not entirely clear whether Marshall subscribed to Veblen's view that in an evolutionary economic theory equilibrium analysis would have no place. Marshall wrote that although 'equilibrium' suggests a statical analogy, really it is part of dynamic analysis:

> in fact it is concerned throughout with the forces that cause movement: and its key-note is that of dynamics, rather than statics.
>
> (Marshall 1920: xiv)

Marshall argued that the forces that are abstracted from statical analysis would have to be studied in an 'economic biology'. But he seemed to hold that the operation of these forces can be accounted for in terms of marginal analysis. As changes in market conditions are reflected in marginal costs, Marshall seems to argue, their effects can be analysed with the 'dynamical principle' of 'substitution at the margin'. This suggests that Marshall held that consequences of dynamical forces under changed market conditions can be accounted for in comparative statics as the replacement of an old by a new equilibrium.

Towards the end of the twentieth century, 'evolutionary economics' is gaining momentum. If the titles of newly appearing books, papers, journals and societies are reliable indicators of current trends in the economics profession, engaging in evolutionary analyses may even be called fashionable among economists nowadays.[1] Much of 'evolutionary economics' that has surfaced over the last two decades is part of, or has been inspired by, what has been labelled 'new institutional economics' (or 'neo-institutionalist economics').[2] 'New institutional economics' analyses *processes* in which *institutions* evolve (see Langlois 1986b). New institutional economists have put institutions firmly on the research agenda of economics. More and more economists appear to be persuaded that institutions matter to economic analysis. New institutional economics seems to be exempted from the 'teleological' overtones of the pre-evolutionary economics Veblen was fulminating against. The course of economic processes is not assumed to be predetermined in the 'nature of things', or to be designed by some divine Creator. Institutions are rather taken to be the unintended outcome of the behaviour of myriad interacting individuals.

Has Veblen's plea been answered at last? The above characterization of new institutional economics suggests an affirmative answer. New institutional economists appear to be doing just what Veblen urged economists to do:

analysing unfolding causal processes in which institutions are generated. But the merits of new institutionalist economics are vehemently disputed by the so-called old institutionalists who present themselves as the only legitimate heirs of Veblen. Old institutionalists criticize new institutionalists for sticking to dubious neoclassical presuppositions. New institutional economists are said to retain methodological individualism (see, for example, Dugger 1983). Institutions, old institutionalists argue, are taken by new institutionalist economists to be the outgrowth of individuals minding their own business. What is more, new institutionalists are said to view institutions as optimal solutions to recurrent problems individuals find themselves in (see, for example, Field 1984 and Mirowski 1986). Old institutionalists maintain that Veblen endorsed methodological holism. Veblen is said to have stressed processes in which the 'arrow of causation' is reversed. Instead of taking institutions to be the effects of the behaviour of atomistically acting individuals, as new institutionalists typically do, Veblen focused on the impact social institutions have on the behaviour of individuals by moulding their ways of thinking and handling things (see, for example, Neale 1987). In addition to this it is argued by old institutionalists that Veblen held that institutions tend to be maladapted to prevailing circumstances. Although Veblen believed that institutions adapt to changing environmental conditions, he emphasized that such processes of adaptation are slow and that time lags are to be expected.

Old institutionalists view new institutionalists as heirs of Marshall. One of the main thrusts of this book is that old institutionalists are right to some extent. The economic worlds of new institutionalists will be seen to be inhabited by individuals who, in the end (after having gone through some evolutionary process), behave *as if* they maximize their utility by equalizing costs and benefits at the margin. In other words, individuals populating new institutionalist worlds can be said to display 'Marshallian' behaviour. But new institutionalists are not heirs of the Marshall that old institutionalists have in mind: Marshall as one of the founders of neoclassical economics with its emphasis on individual 'rational choice'. If there is a Marshall that is the ancestor of present day new institutional economics, it is the visionary Marshall, the Marshall that envisaged the 'Mecca' of economics. To be more precise, their precursor is the Marshall who can be said to have hinted at an evolutionary reinterpretation of marginalist equilibrium analysis. A lot of preliminary 'groundwork' has to be done, however, before we will be able to draw this conclusion.

2. A DOWN-TO-EARTH PERSPECTIVE ON NEW INSTITUTIONAL ECONOMICS

The foregoing history of ideas from a bird's-eye view gives a neat and compendious overview. But its weakness is that it is too stylized. Too many relevant facets are left out. For one thing, the use of the label 'new institutional economics' is far from unequivocal. Often-mentioned candidates for being labelled as such are Nelson and Winter's evolutionary theory, Williamson's transaction cost economics and Schotter's and Sugden's game-theoretic treatments of institutions. They can all be said to be concerned with 'evolution of institutions'. But 'institution' comprises many different phenomena. As we will see, Nelson and Winter focus on evolutionary processes in which routines of firms change. Williamson seems to be preoccupied with explanations of the replacement of markets by prevailing types of organization forms. And Schotter and Sugden analyse processes of spontaneous evolution in which institutions are established and maintained.

Differences between the candidates mentioned pertain not only to the notion of institution. They extend to the meaning of 'evolution'. Special attention will be paid to the notions of evolution that are involved in either candidate. Indeed, one of the major goals of the book is to get a clear understanding of what exactly 'evolution' may signify in economics. In ordinary language, 'evolution' refers to processes of *gradual* change and development (in contradistinction to 'revolution' that refers to disruptive radical change). In this book, 'economic evolution' will not be taken in the broadest sense of comprising all types of gradual change. A 'catchall' definition of 'evolution', such as 'evolution is the changing of something into something else over time' (Faber and Proops 1991: 59), fails to discriminate between different sources of change. One possible source of gradual change is the one that is accounted for in 'standard' neoclassical theory: instantaneous and optimal responses of all individuals to changes in an exogenous environment.

As we will see, in none of the 'new institutional' theories mentioned above is it assumed that gradual change is produced in this perfectly rational way. It is maintained that not all individuals are capable of making prompt and optimal responses. Proponents of new institutional economics hold that gradual economic change originates from other sources. At the other extreme, the definition of 'economic evolution' that will be given here is not so narrow as to exclude all other possible sources but one: technological innovation. Some 'evolutionary economists' seem to reserve the notion of economic evolution to denote transformations of technological 'regimes' or 'paradigms' (see, for example, Allen 1988 and Clark and Juma 1988). They seem to focus exclusively on endogenous 'variety-inducing mechanisms', mechanisms that continuously produce new innovations. A major source of inspiration here is provided by Schumpeter's work.

In this book this narrow definition of 'economic evolution' will be discarded too. New institutional economists will be seen to concentrate on selection mechanisms as sources of economic change. We will see that selection mechanisms tend to reduce rather than induce variety. Hence we can say that the emphasis of new institutional economists is more on variety-reducing mechanisms than on variety-generating mechanisms. The notions of economic evolution that will be discerned in new institutional economics should therefore not be confused with those in 'evolutionary economics'. Indeed, if evolutionary economics is identified by an exclusive focus on variety-inducing mechanisms, this book is not about evolutionary economics at all.[3]

Selection mechanisms will be one of the main topics of this book. It will be argued that selection mechanisms involve *feedback loops*. Selection mechanisms are crucial parts of what will be called *evolutionary mechanisms*. On the basis of a selective though penetrating analysis of the theories mentioned, I shall distinguish between two evolutionary mechanisms: economic 'natural selection' and adaptive learning.

Another recurrent theme in the book is *levels of analysis*. It will be argued that in the theories under consideration, changes in higher-level aggregate phenomena typically are accounted for in terms of lower-level units of analysis. But what are aggregate phenomena and what are elementary units of analysis? Answers to this question again appear to differ from theory to theory. Nelson and Winter, for example, account for changes at the level of the industry. The elementary unit of analysis in their theory is the firm. Williamson's transaction cost economics seems to deal with phenomena 'one level below'. The evolution of organization forms is accounted for in terms of the endeavours of individuals. Here, the individual human agent is the elementary unit of analysis.

This multi-layered structure of theories can be observed also in evolutionary biology. It will be pointed out that Darwinian natural selection deals with evolution at the population level, thereby taking the individual organism as the unit of selection. Frequent excursions will be made into evolutionary biology. These excursions are meant to enhance our understanding of the peculiarities of evolutionary theorizing. One of the things that the present study intends to bring out is that economics and biology have much in common. Indeed, in my opinion the relation that economics has with biology is at least as intimate as its often-discussed relation with physics (see, for example, Mirowski 1989). This is first of all reflected in an unceasing cross fertilization of ideas between economics and biology. Darwin's indebtedness to T. Malthus and the moral philosophers D. Hume and A. Smith is well documented. Conversely, many economists have been inspired by Darwinian (and Lamarckian) evolutionary theory. The group of economists who are influenced by evolutionary biology extends far beyond the economists who are discussed in this book.

The relationship between economics and biology goes deeper, I shall argue, than just some occasional transfers of ideas. The modes of explanation that are entertained in both disciplines show striking similarities. Only recently has it been observed by economists that their explanations resemble the type of explanation that seems to be characteristic of bio-logical theory: *functional* explanation. Crudely put, in functional explanation some (physiological or behavioural) trait is explained by the function that it serves, that is by the useful or beneficial unintended consequences that it has. As we will see, it is argued by Williamson, for example, that the explanations given in his transaction cost economics are of a functional type.

A related mode of explanation that is typical of both disciplines is *equilibrium* explanation. In equilibrium explanations, some specified dynamical process, in which the elementary units (of analysis) are involved, is shown to come to rest in a stable configuration at the systems (or aggregate) level. In evolutionary biological theory, the notion of a stable equilibrium is sometimes expressed by saying that 'fitness is equal at the margin'. It is *as if* individual organisms are maximizing their own fitness. In stable equilibrium, no individual organism could improve its fitness by changing its behaviour. Is this not close to what the visionary Marshall seemed to have in mind?

The foregoing preliminary remarks already indicate that I shall be engaged first and foremost in conceptual and philosophical analysis. The book is meant to be an enquiry into the foundations of new institutional economics. The contribution I want to make to the ongoing discussion in this field is primarily one of clarification. I am aware that this makes my approach vulnerable to obvious objections. The book will be inevitably incomplete, as it is practically impossible to incorporate all the literature that is relevant. And it runs the danger of being obsolete even before it is published. In a sense, I am trying to hit several 'moving targets'. There is 'work in progress' not only in the economic theories that are dealt with, but also in the philosophical discussion of the theories (see, for example, Mäki *et al.* 1993 and Hodgson 1993b). Nevertheless, I believe that I have identified some interesting and promising lines of economic research. Moreover, I am convinced that there is a need for careful philosophical analysis that has not yet been satisfied. I hope to have succeeded in developing a view on 'evolution' in economics that is both clear and comprehensive.

I shall not engage in a 'traditional' type of philosophical analysis in which preconceived philosophical standards (concerning 'genuine science' versus 'pseudo-science', or 'valid' versus 'invalid' explanation) are imposed on scientific theories. I shall rather try to make sense of (developments in) economic theories from an inside and historical point of view (see Diesing 1971). Economic theories will be viewed from the perspective of their 'originators'. What are the phenomena (or problems) that economists account for (or address) and what are the standards that they impose (either explicitly or implicitly) upon themselves? Thus stated, the point of view that I adopt may appear to be similar to the currently fashionable *rhetorical* point of view. Rhetoricians like D. McCloskey and A. Klamer also opt for an inside and historical perspective (see McCloskey 1985 and Klamer 1983). The appearance of similarity may be reinforced by the fact that throughout the book I shall deal extensively with analogies and metaphors devised by economists. Indeed, the book is replete with thought-provoking analogies. It is precisely such 'figures of speech' that rhetoricians focus on.

My approach differs nonetheless from the rhetoricians' one in at least two respects. First, I shall not treat all analogies and metaphors on a par as 'strategic' rhetorical devices employed by economists to persuade other economists. Some analogies will be seen to serve illustrative or expository purposes only. Others will be shown to reflect basic background beliefs of economists about the mode of operation of generative mechanisms in economic processes.[4] In particular, I shall argue that the 'natural selection analogy' is of the latter type. Second, it will be examined whether analogies and metaphors are convincing by the economists' *own* standards. Some analogies will be judged to be misleading, others to entail tacit assumptions that are not explicitly argued for. Some analogies will be shown to be *non sequiturs* in arguments for which counterexamples can readily be provided. In short, unlike the rhetoricians I do not eschew any form of criticism. I shall not rest content with observing that analogies are persuasive to some subset of the scientific community of economists. The type of immanent criticism that will be espoused here is meant to delve deeper into 'what economists do'. I am convinced that genuine understanding of what is going on in economics can be obtained only if we are prepared to press hard questions upon economists, their theories and their arguments.

3. PLAN OF THE BOOK

The book is organized in three parts. The first part deals with firms and industries. All the arguments and theories that are discussed in this part turn out to bear a clear *family resemblance* to Marshall's evolutionary reinterpretation of marginal analysis. In Chapter 2, the 'selection arguments' of A. Alchian, M. Friedman and G. Becker will be discussed against the background of the 'marginalism controversy'. Alchian, Friedman and Becker will be seen to argue that industries behave *as if* they were populated by firms that are infallibly conducting marginalist calculations. 'Neoclassical' tendencies in industry behaviour are argued to be produced *really* by external selection forces impinging on individual firms.

Chapter 3 is about the 'new theory of the firm'. Whereas the old 'neoclassical' theory of the firm is concerned with industry (or market) behaviour, the new theory of the firm focuses on contractual relations within firms. The new theory of the firm will be seen to comprise several approaches, such as the property rights, the agency costs, and Williamson's transaction costs approach. Although these approaches differ from each other in important respects, it will be argued that they all share the supposition that prevailing organization forms are efficient. Special attention will be paid to the 'general background' way in which the approaches are said to rely on the efficacy of market selection.

In Chapter 4, Nelson and Winter's evolutionary theory is subjected to a critical analysis. Nelson and Winter tend to present their theory as an antagonist to 'orthodox' neoclassical analysis. I shall emphasize the 'ancestral thread' that connects their theory via Alchian's selection argument back to Marshall's evolutionary speculations. Nelson and Winter's theory is treated as an attempt to model 'basic background beliefs' about market selection. The discussion will concentrate on Nelson and Winter's contention that firms are engaged in routine behaviour rather than in deliberate choice.

Part II deals with philosophical issues. In Chapter 5, types of explanation are analysed that are associated with evolutionary theorizing. Chapter 5 includes a digression into the notion of Darwinian natural selection in evolutionary biology. The discussion will focus on Elster's influential account of valid functional explanation in the social sciences. Functional explanation will be compared with other types of explanation, such as intentional explanation, causal explanation, Sober's notion of equilibrium explanation and Ullmann-Margalit's notion of invisible hand explanation. It will be examined whether the arguments, approaches and theories that are treated in Chapters 2 to 4 correspond to Elster's notion of 'full functionalism'.

Elster's crucial condition for a valid functional explanation is dealt with in Chapter 6: the demonstration of a causal *feedback* loop. It will be argued that of the theories considered, Nelson and Winter's theory is the only one that meets this condition. It will also be argued, however, that their theory entails the working of two feedback loops rather than one: economic 'natural selection' and adaptive learning. Their notion of adaptive learning is based on H.A. Simon's notions of procedural rationality and satisficing. I shall follow Simon in arguing that as adaptive learning resembles natural selection in relevant respects, it can also be called an evolutionary mechanism. Both evolutionary mechanisms are analysed in detail. Emphasis will be put on their dissimilarities and on problems with studying their combined, simultaneous operation.

In Part III the level of analysis is shifted to individuals and groups. In the theories that will be dealt with here, changes in group behaviour are accounted for in terms of evolutionary forces working on individual organisms. In Chapter 7, human beings are treated from a sociobiological perspective as organisms with inheritable behavioural dispositions. Several attempts by biologists are discussed to explain the natural selection of the socially optimal 'altruistic' behaviour. Maynard Smith's evolutionary game theory is used to demonstrate how *sub*optimal behavioural traits can be selected. Attention will be paid to 'group selection' and (Dawkins') 'gene selection' that figure in the units of selection controversy in biology. Houthakker's comparison of the economic notion of division of labour with the biological notion of speciation is discussed to illustrate what happens when different levels of analysis are confused. Finally, I shall analyse the peculiar way in which economic analysis and sociobiological presuppositions are blended in Becker's, Hirshleifer's and Frank's accounts of altruism.

Chapter 8 is concerned with *cultural* evolution. The chapter starts with the 'Popper–Hayek connection'. It will be argued that appearances notwithstanding, Popper's view on trial and error learning, and the notion of blind search that is entailed in it, is compatible with Simon's notions of selective search. In Hayek's view, as we will see, the spontaneous cultural evolution of 'social order' is taken to be the unintended result of interacting, interdependent, learning and rule-following individuals. Hayek's claim that the rules that evolve spontaneously are optimal to the group as a whole will be attributed to his 'organicistic' notion of groups. I shall argue that game-theoretic notions and approaches capture essential elements of Hayek's view. I shall also argue, however, that game theory is suited to explicate why Hayek's claim is problematic in so-called cooperation games. The chapter will be completed with an examination of attempts by Ullmann-Margalit, Schotter, Axelrod and Sugden to show that Hayek's claim can be sustained also in cooperation games.

In Chapter 9 a realist Millian framework is developed to clarify the explanatory structure of the evolutionary arguments and approaches that are discussed in Chapters 2 to 8. The framework will turn out to be fruitful also for identifying differences between different strands in current evolutionary theorizing in economics and for formulating an agenda for further research.

Part I

FIRMS AND INDUSTRIES

2

SELECTION ARGUMENTS *PRO* AND *CONTRA* THE NEOCLASSICAL THEORY OF THE FIRM

1. INTRODUCTION

The 'marginalism controversy' in economics is commonly regarded to be well-documented. And yet there is an aspect to the controversy, I venture, that has received relatively little attention. Both adversaries in the controversy advanced *selection arguments* to underline their position. In this chapter, I shall focus on these arguments. It is not my aim to give a balanced 'final' judgement as to what side had the better arguments. I shall rather attempt to arrive at a thorough understanding of what the economists involved were up to. In particular, I shall argue that we can learn several things about the economists' own understanding of marginalism from considering the selection arguments that were put forward by the marginalists. Far from being mere afterthoughts, designed to defend marginal analysis against antimarginalist criticisms in an *ad hoc* way, these arguments reveal basic background beliefs of marginalists about the way market economies function.

We will see that the proponents of marginalism that are discussed in this chapter advanced slightly different selection arguments. Yet a common theme can be discerned. The marginalists all argue that the antimarginalist criticism, if not false outright, is at any rate misdirected. The antimarginalist criticism is that, because of the 'fact' that entrepreneurs do not go through the calculations and deliberations that are ascribed to them in marginal analysis, marginal analysis is to be discarded. The claim that the respective selection arguments of the marginalists have in common is that even if the antimarginalists' 'fact' is granted, the hypotheses (and implications) of marginal analysis still hold. Therefore marginal analysis need not be rejected. I shall argue that none of the selection arguments advanced is 'airtight'. The most that can be claimed on the basis of these arguments is that implications of marginal analysis *can* hold (not that they always *do* hold) even if entrepreneurs are not rational profit maximizers.

The chapter is organized as follows. I start with an exposition of some

13

of the elements in the antimarginalist criticism. I shall pay some attention to the evolutionary speculations Harrod entertained to account for the empirical findings of the antimarginalists. Next, I shall deal with F. Machlup's early rejoinder. In section 4, we will see that A. Alchian put forward his selection argument because he took both the antimarginalist criticism and Machlup's rejoinder to be beside the point. Subsequently, it will be argued that M. Friedman gave a twist to Alchian's argument ('another F-twist') in his famous '*as if* methodology'. Finally, in section 6, I shall discuss G.S. Becker's version of the argument. Becker gives his own twist to the argument. He is more explicit on how (market) selection is supposed to work than his predecessors are. As will be argued, however, Becker does not succeed in giving an airtight argument either.

2. THE ANTIMARGINALIST CRITICISM

Antimarginalist criticism showed up in the 1930s in the UK and in the 1940s in the USA. The main target of criticism of the antimarginalists was the neoclassical theory of the firm. Marginalism (or marginal analysis) is part and parcel of the neoclassical theory of the firm. In this theory it is assumed that entrepreneurs, who are supposed to determine the behaviour of firms single-handedly,[1] are profit maximizers. Profit is maximized if marginal revenue and marginal cost are equal. To see why 'profit maximization' can be translated in marginal quantities in this way, consider the following. If marginal revenue were to exceed marginal cost, it would be possible to gain extra profit by expanding production (output) with one unit. Hence, profits would not be maximized in such a situation. Under the (additional) usual assumptions that the marginal revenue curve is negatively sloping and the marginal cost curve is U-shaped, the assumption of profit maximization implies that the price and output policy of entrepreneurs is that they expand production up to the point where marginal revenue and marginal cost are equal. As we will see, the antimarginalist criticism is inspired by empirical findings that are taken to show that entrepreneurs do not adopt such a price and output policy based on marginalist deliberations. I shall confine myself to a discussion of the work of the Oxford Research Group in the UK and that of the American economist Lester.

The Oxford Research Group was a group of economists who studied problems with the trade cycle for several years in the 1930s. Some of its results are presented by Hall and Hitch (1939) in the *Oxford Economic Papers*, accompanied by some comments of Harrod (1939). The Oxford economists questioned the 'applicability' of current doctrine (Hall and Hitch 1939: 112). By current doctrine they meant the neoclassical theory of the firm. They wondered whether entrepreneurs did in fact conduct the price and output policy that was ascribed to them in neoclassical theory. The Oxford economists chose to use the 'method of direct question'

(Harrod 1939: 2) to find this out. Questionnaires were sent to 'practising' business men, followed by discussions with them (Hall and Hitch 1939: 107).

The results were clearly negative. Business men appeared not to think of their pricing decisions in terms of marginal revenue and marginal cost. Instead, Hall and Hitch found that almost all business men followed a 'full cost' pricing rule:

> the larger part of the explanation, we think, is that they are thinking in altogether different terms; that in pricing they try to apply a rule of thumb which we shall call 'full cost', and that maximum profits, if they result at all from the application of this rule, do so as an accidental (or possibly evolutionary) by-product.
>
> (Hall and Hitch 1939: 113)

Business men following the 'full cost' rule took prime (or 'direct') cost per unit as the base, added a percentage to cover overheads (or 'indirect' cost), and made a further conventional addition (frequently 10 per cent) for profit.

Hall and Hitch continued to argue that the pricing policy depicted by current theory of the firm is not only *de facto* seldom applied by practising business men, it is often inapplicable *in principle*. According to Hall and Hitch, the main reason for this is that in actual situations entrepreneurs often cannot know their marginal revenue. Most of the time entrepreneurs do not face purely competitive markets, but markets that are a mixture of monopolistic competition with substantial elements of oligopoly. In a situation of pure competition, in which no single producer can significantly affect the market price, marginal revenue is equal to price, so that there are no principled obstacles to applying the marginal calculus. But according to the Oxford economists it is pure competition that is to be considered as a special case, and not situations in which oligopoly elements are present, as current doctrine would have it. In situations with substantial oligopoly elements the price and output policies of the firms are interdependent. Because of this, the demand curve for the product of the *individual* firm is indeterminate.[2] In turn, this implies that entrepreneurs do not know their marginal revenues. In other words, entrepreneurs often lack the information (or 'material') that is needed to apply the marginalist calculus.[3]

The work of the American economist Lester is in some ways similar to that of the Oxford Group. Lester also mailed a detailed questionnaire to the presidents or executive officers of firms. This questionnaire was also designed to find out whether the neoclassical theory of the firm gives a realistic representation of the deliberations that practising business men go through when making decisions. Again, the results were clearly negative. And Lester also conjectured that the neoclassical theory of the firm is invalid because the information is often lacking that business men require to conduct the marginalist calculations. But whereas Hall and Hitch point out difficulties for entrepreneurs to calculate marginal *revenues*, a good deal of

Lester's paper is devoted to difficulties (if not 'hopeless complexity', Lester 1946: 75) with calculating marginal *costs*. In this sense, Lester's project can be said to be complementary to that of Hall and Hitch's.

In particular, Lester is concerned with wage–employment relationships in individual firms. Lester states that marginal analysis treats (the height of) wage rates as the most important determinant of the employment policies of firms. An increase in wage rates will lead to higher marginal costs of labour. The neoclassical theory of the firm therefore predicts that employment (and the labour–capital ratio) will fall if wages rise *ceteris paribus*. According to Lester, this prediction holds only when entrepreneurs consider wage rates to be a more important factor in determining their employment policies than other factors such as present and prospective market demand for their products and the level of material costs. Lester listed several factors in his questionnaire and asked entrepreneurs to rate them in order of their importance. The answers were unequivocal: 'overwhelming emphasis' was put on current and prospective market demand. Changes in wage rates, a factor stressed by marginal analysis, were rated 'surprisingly low' (Lester 1946: 65).

To Lester, the empirical findings that are presented in his paper cast grave doubts on the validity of conventional marginal theory and the assumptions on which it rests. In his eyes they clearly demonstrated that a new theory of the individual firm is to be developed. As Lester clarified in a response to comments by Machlup (1946) and Stigler (1947): 'at the heart of economic theory should be an adequate analysis and understanding of the psychology, policies, and practices of business management in modern industry' (Lester 1947: 146). In sum, antimarginalists took the fact that entrepreneurs do not think in terms of marginal quantities when devising their price, output and employment policy to be ample reason to reject the neoclassical theory of the firm. Couched in somewhat more general terms, they held that since entrepreneurs do not apply marginalist calculations, marginal analysis is not applicable. In the next section, we will see that the marginalists' rejoinders were more directed against Lester's criticism than against the criticism of the Oxford Group. I will end this section, however, with a brief discussion of the evolutionary ideas Harrod (1939) expressed in order to make sense of the empirical findings of the Oxford Group.

Harrod does not challenge the marginalists' idea that in their actions entrepreneurs are driven by the profit motive. Harrod remarks that anyone who would seriously doubt this would rightly be regarded as a hopeless sentimentalist. What Harrod does challenge is that entrepreneurs normally have the information that they need to conduct the marginalist calculations. The notion of 'profit maximizing' entails more than just the assumption that business men pursue profits. Business men pursuing profits may end up with less than maximum profits because of informational deficiencies. Without perfect information, entrepreneurs may resort to rule-governed behaviour. This is not to say, however, that rule-governed behaviour will lead to less than maximum profits by definition. There may be some evolutionary process going on in which better, more profitable rules replace others. This is a possibility Hall and Hitch also allude to in their interpretation of their empirical findings: it is possible (in principle, at least) that maximum profits are an evolutionary 'by-product' of the application of the 'full cost' rule.

Harrod elaborates on this idea as follows:

> It may be that certain procedures, of which application of the full cost principle is one example, are thrown up purely by chance in the first instance and survive by a process akin to natural selection in biology. New business procedures would then be analogous to new mutations in nature. Of a number of procedures, none of which can be shown either at the time or subsequently to be truly rational, some may supplant others because they do in fact lead to better results. Thus while they may have originated by accident, it would not be by accident that they are still used. For this reason, if an economist finds a procedure widely established in fact, he ought to regard it with more respect than he would be inclined to give in the light of his own analytic method.
>
> (Harrod 1939: 7)

The general idea seems to be here that as entrepreneurs normally are confronted with uncertainty, each new 'way of handling things' is a stab in the dark. It may be impossible to tell in advance which (new) procedures or rules will be more profitable than others. But there may be some evolutionary process going on in which the best rules are selected while other rules are eliminated, so that we can tell in retrospect, with hindsight, what rules turned out to be the best.

Harrod's remarks leave several issues unaddressed. It remains unclear, for example, how the alleged evolutionary process is supposed to be going on. How do better rules supplant other rules? What are the mechanisms that steer this process? And: under what circumstances can we expect such an evolutionary process to be going on? But it must be said to the credit of Harrod, I think, that he presents a general outline of the basic ingredients of an economic evolutionary theory. In the chapters to come, we will see that Harrod was way ahead of his time. The evolutionary theories and models that will be discussed can be regarded as further elaborations of Harrod's evolutionary speculations.[4]

3. MACHLUP'S DEFENCE OF MARGINALISM

Machlup was one of the first, and certainly one of the most prominent and sophisticated, proponents of marginalism who responded to the antimarginalist criticism. In Machlup (1946), marginal analysis is interpreted as an analysis of the single firm. This means that Machlup is prepared to meet the antimarginalists' criticism 'head on', on their own home ground of analysing the deliberations that go into the decision making of entrepreneurs. Machlup argues that the antimarginalists wrongly take testimonies of entrepreneurs at face value. Hall and Hitch and Lester are said to have erred in inferring from their findings that entrepreneurs do not think in terms of marginal magnitudes, that the actual deliberations of entrepreneurs differ from the ones that are depicted in marginal analysis. Machlup argues to the contrary that the empirical findings of the antimarginalists are compatible with marginal analysis.

Machlup criticizes the antimarginalists for having used the unreliable method of direct question (the mailing of questionnaires). Of course, this could have been sufficient reason for Machlup not to discuss the antimarginalists' empirical findings at all. Machlup does not dismiss the findings altogether, however. He only disregards answers to questions that he takes to be ill posed. To Machlup, Lester's question about the rate of importance of several factors in the wage–employment policies of firms is an example of an ill-posed question. Machlup argues quite convincingly that all the factors that are listed by Lester are essential variables in marginal analysis, and not only two of them (changes in wage rates and variations in profits or losses), as Lester appears to think.[5] Consequently, Machlup does not see any reason to deal with Lester's findings on this point. It is a mystery to Machlup how Lester came to think that answers to this question could disprove the neoclassical theory of the firm.

Machlup treats the questions and empirical findings of Hall and Hitch with more respect. He tries to translate their findings into the vocabulary of marginalism. In particular, he tries to come to terms with their supposition that entrepreneurs often behave in a routine way. Machlup seems even to be convinced that this is a fact of 'entrepreneurial life': 'their actions are frequently routine' (Machlup 1946: 524). Hall and Hitch and Harrod viewed routine (or rule-following) behaviour and profit-maximizing behaviour as two mutually excluding opposites. As a consequence, they took their observance of routine entrepreneurial behaviour as conclusive evidence for the inapplicability of marginal analysis. Machlup attempts to show that their view is mistaken. Routine behaviour does not invalidate marginal analysis. The two can be reconciled, for example, when:

> routine is based on principles which were once considered and decided upon and have then been frequently applied with decreasing need for conscious choices.
>
> (Machlup 1946: 524–5)

Apparently, Machlup believes that the principles alluded to either are the marginalist principles or are compatible with the marginalist principles. It is not clear, however, whether Machlup believes that all routine behaviour that can be observed grew out of such conscious principles. But even if not all routine-like behaviour did develop this way, Machlup seems to argue, it is possible to reformulate all observances of routine behaviour in marginalist terms. Each description of behaviour in terms of routines, rules of thumb and the like can be translated into an equivalent statement that is couched in terms of the marginal calculus. This possibility of translation allows Machlup to state that: 'the marginal calculus may be followed without pronouncing or knowing any of the terms in question' (Machlup 1946: 539).

Machlup illustrates this point by constructing the following analogy of an automobile driver. The driver of the automobile faces the alternatives of either overtaking a slower truck proceeding ahead of the driver, or slowing down and staying behind. According to Machlup an experienced driver will take several factors somehow into account (among them: the driver's own speed, the speed of the truck, the distance between the automobile and the truck, the possible acceleration of the automobile; when another automobile is approaching from the other way, its speed, the weather conditions), without taking them into consideration separately and without trying to measure the numerical values of these factors. An experienced driver will rather in one swift moment 'size up' the whole situation in a routine way.

However, if we want to develop a *theory* of overtaking, Machlup argues, we would have to include all these elements (and perhaps others besides) and would have to state how changes in any of the factors were likely to affect the decisions or actions of the driver. In principle, such a theory could be formulated in terms of maximization of a well-specified mathematical function. A theory in which decision making is represented in terms of maximization can thus be seen to be compatible with the idea that actual decision making rarely if ever involves calculations of several factors.

Another point that Machlup makes is that the assumption that entrepreneurs maximize their profits, and hence apply the marginalist principle, does not imply that we have to assume that entrepreneurs know the 'objective' values of the relevant factors (or even that entrepreneurs can get to know the 'objective' values). Marginal analysis is consistent with empirical findings that business men do not know the 'real' marginal costs and revenues. To Machlup, it is clear that the things with which business men reckon are 'subjective':

it should hardly be necessary to mention that all the relevant magnitudes involved – cost, revenue, profit – are subjective – that is, perceived or fancied by the men whose decisions or actions are to be explained (the business men) – rather than 'objective' – that is, calculated by disinterested men who are observing these actions from

19

the outside and are explaining them (statisticians and economists as theorists – not as consultants).

(Machlup 1946: 521)

Machlup goes on to argue that the subjective estimates of business men may differ from the objective figures a disinterested outside observer would come up with. This raises a problem of interpretation, however. What are 'economists as theorists' who apply marginal analysis supposed to do in Machlup's view? One interpretation may be that they are to explain what business men actually do. As Machlup explicitly allows for the possibility that business men get the relevant figures wrong, however, their actions may not lead to maximum profits. Another possible reading is that economists as theorists are to explain what perfectly rational business men would do if they knew the relevant objective magnitudes. The actions of such perfectly rational business men would result in maximum profits. But the problem with this reading is that there may not be any such business man around.

Machlup seems to opt for the first interpretation (see, for example, Machlup 1946: 522). On this interpretation, we can still make a distinction between an 'insiders', agents' point of view and an 'outsiders', theorist's point of view. Behaviour that is perceived from the agents' own point of view as being routinized or rule governed, may be analysed from a theorist's point of view as maximizing behaviour. As Machlup shows in his reply to Hall and Hitch, this can be done by translating routines or rules into *subjective* marginal magnitudes. This is analogous to developing a theory of overtaking in which the routinized 'sizing up' of the whole situation by an experienced driver is analysed as a conscious attempt to take several separate elements into account. But an experienced driver need not be a perfect driver. The driver may make mistakes. Analogous to this, rule-following business men may end up with losses instead of (maximum) profits. In an *objective* sense, then, such business men would have failed to maximize their profits.

This implication seems to have escaped Machlup initially. The only provision Machlup makes is that entrepreneurs must pursue pecuniary goals. Machlup remarks that marginal analysis is invalid when firms pursue non-pecuniary goals to a significant degree. This possibility cannot be ruled out a priori. But Machlup seems to have missed the point that marginal analysis may fail to hold even if entrepreneurs are driven solely by the profit motive. Business men who attempt to maximize profits may fail to achieve maximum profits because their subjective guesses and hunches may be inaccurate. It may be objected that Machlup explicitly states that it is not claimed in marginal analysis that firms achieve maximum profits (in the objective sense). In Machlup's view, marginal analysis does not aim to give a detailed prediction of the output, prices and employment of firms. Rather, it intends to explain tendencies in firm behaviour. Marginal analysis

20

predicts how changes in circumstances affect changes in the actions of firms.[6] A typical example is discussed in Lester (1946): if (real) wage rates rise, firms will employ less labour *ceteris paribus*. If we agree with Machlup that this is all what marginal analysis is about, however, the point raised still undermines marginal analysis: even if firms pursue profits, if they derive their employment policy from false premises, they may not respond to changes in wages in the predicted way.[7]

On the basis of the foregoing discussion we may conclude, I think, that Machlup's (1946) defence of marginal analysis is only partially successful. Machlup succeeds in showing that many of the antimarginalists' empirical findings can be translated into the vocabulary of marginalism. In particular, he points out that behaviour that is rule following from the agents' point of view can be analysed as maximizing behaviour from a theorist's point of view. But Machlup does not succeed in demonstrating that the predictions of neoclassical theory hold if they are taken to be predictions about the behaviour of single firms. As we will see in the next sections, later defenders of neoclassical theory argue that Machlup's defence was bound to fail, precisely because Machlup wrongly took the theory to be a theory of the behaviour of individual firms.[8]

4. ALCHIAN'S SELECTION ARGUMENT

Can I just say something? It's very embarrassing; you write an article in response to two misplaced articles, one by a fellow named Lester and one by a guy named Machlup. Lester was arguing that business-men do not think in terms of Marshall's cost calculations and it therefore cannot be right; and Machlup says oh, yes they do and therefore it is right. Both of them [are?, JJV] irrelevant positions and so you simply apply the well-known evolutionary theory, put it on paper, and it becomes a classic. Having said that, I'll say no more.

(Alchian, quoted in Zerbe 1982: 149)

Alchian (1950) takes the positions of Lester and Machlup to be irrelevant, because they both share the presumption that the fate of the neoclassical theory of the firm hinges upon the deliberations that guide the decisions of entrepreneurs. Underlying this presumption is their idea that the theory is about the behaviour of single firms. Alchian considers this idea to be mistaken. In his view the theory of the firm is about the behaviour of industry. As we will see in this section, Alchian argues that the contemplations of entrepreneurs are unimportant if not irrelevant in assessing the usefulness of the theory. The selection argument that Alchian advances is meant to show that impersonal market forces see to it that the theorems of the theory of the firm hold even if its assumption that firms are profit maximizers is false.

21

Alchian starts his argument by pointing out that profit maximization provides an unambiguous guide to action only when we can assume complete information and perfect foresight. Only under this assumption can we determine the outcome of each action that is available. We simply choose the action that then yields maximum profits. But when there is uncertainty, when we have incomplete information and imperfect knowledge, Alchian argues, profit maximization fails to be a guide to action. We can then no longer determine outcomes to each action. The most we can do is to identify a distribution of potential outcomes with each action. It does not make sense to say that firms maximize the distribution of potential outcomes, for it is unclear what firms are supposed to maximize. Firms can be said to optimize the distribution of potential outcomes, but this goal presupposes subjective valuations of the firms in question. Whereas one firm might prefer a distribution with a higher mean or expectation, but also with a higher variance, another firm might prefer a distribution with a lower variance, but also with a lower mean or expectation. In other words, Alchian concludes, we have to know their preference functions (towards risk) in order to give a definite meaning to the optimization of the distribution of outcomes.

What is more important, it is argued, we cannot know in advance, *ex ante factum*, what subjective preference function towards risk will have the best results. Only with hindsight, only *ex post factum*, can we tell what actions have yielded the highest profits. Under pervasive uncertainty, maximum profits may be achieved by firms that base their attempts to maximize profits on facts they have gathered. As Alchian remarks, however, maximum profits may also go to the more venturesome or the more lucky firms. In short, the link between rational decision and the realization of maximum profits that is directly ascertainable under certainty is cut loose under uncertainty.

Alchian now goes on to argue that what matters in the prevailing economic system is not the deliberations of business men that go into their decision making, but the profits (or losses) that they realize. In the prevailing economic system, impersonal market forces see to it that 'those who realize *positive profits* are the survivors; those who suffer losses disappear' (Alchian 1950: 213). Firms that happen to achieve positive profits in one way or another thrive and prosper, whereas firms that do not succeed in doing so are eliminated sooner or later. As the relation between attempts to maximize profits and realizing positive profits is hard if not impossible to tell under uncertainty, Alchian proposes to focus directly on actual results:

> by backing away from the trees – the optimization calculus by individual units – we can better discern the forest of impersonal market forces.
>
> (Alchian 1950: 213)

Alchian sketches the outlines of a theory (a chance-dominated model) in which it is assumed that behaviour is determined by sheer chance. Nobody is assumed to act deliberately and consciously (let alone rationally). When the environment changes, nobody is supposed to be adapting one's self to the new situation. There is assumed to be only a process of *adoption*: the (new) environment adopts survivors whose behaviour turns out to be 'appropriate'. The purpose of this (sketch of a) theory is to show that regular aggregate behaviour can emerge even if individuals behave irregularly. Alchian develops the following 'travellers' analogy to illustrate this point:

> Assume that thousands of travelers set out from Chicago, selecting their roads completely at random and without foresight. Only our 'economist' knows that on but one road are there any gasoline stations. He can state categorically that travelers will *continue* to travel only on that road; those on other roads will soon run out of gas . . . . If gasoline supplies were now moved to a new road, some formerly luckless travelers again would be able to move; and a new pattern of travel would be observed, although none of the travelers had changed his particular path. The really possible paths have changed with the changing environment. All that is needed is a set of varied, risk-taking (adoptable) travelers. The correct direction of travel will be established. As circumstances (economic environment) change, the analyst (economist) can select the types of participants (firms) that will now become successful; he may also be able to diagnose the conditions most conducive to a greater probability of survival.
>
> (Alchian 1950: 214–15)

The analyst can thus predict a change in the pattern of travel as a result of a change in environmental factors (here a redistribution of gasoline supplies), even when no particular traveller adjusts his or her path to the new circumstances. Likewise, Alchian argues, a marginal analyst can predict adequately in what direction aggregate prices and quantities will change as a result of environmental changes, even if business men do not adjust their decisions to these changes. For example, if real wages rise, an industry's average labour–capital ratio will fall even if no firm adjusts its labour force,[9] for firms with a lower labour–capital ratio will have relatively lower cost positions and, for that matter, a higher probability of survival.

As a matter of fact, Alchian has already driven his main argument home here. The validity of the theorems (the standard results) of marginal analysis is not restricted to cases in which firms can be assumed to be profit maximizers: 'the essential point is that individual motivation and foresight, while sufficient, are not necessary' (Alchian 1950: 217).

Alchian does not believe that the foregoing account of business behaviour is realistic. Its main purpose is expository. Alchian only wanted to show that the assumption of goal-directed behaviour need not be true for the theorems of the theory of the firm to hold. This does not mean that Alchian really thinks that business men do not act purposefully. On the contrary, Alchian subscribes to the view that business men are driven by the profit motive. But, to repeat, he argues that the theorems of the theory of the firm hold even if this view is false.

Alchian emphasizes that the assumption that business men pursue profits should be sharply distinguished from the assumption of 'profit maximization'. Under pervasive uncertainty, Alchian argues, it is quite reasonable for business men to resort to various forms of conscious adaptive behaviour. One of them is imitation. Rules of behaviour, such as the 'full cost pricing' rule, may be the result of imitations of observed success. Imitation need not necessarily result in conformity to already existing patterns of behaviour. When attempts to imitate others fail, new patterns may emerge. Imitation can thus lead to innovation. 'Trial and error' is another form of conscious adaptive behaviour that is mentioned by Alchian. In principle, trial and error may induce a process of convergence to a limit of the perfect 'profit maximization' position. But there are some caveats here. There may be suboptimal local equilibria at which a process of trial and error may get stuck. And trial and error learning is difficult if not impossible when the environment changes. In a changing environment:

> trial and error becomes survival or death . . . . Success is discovered by the economic system through a blanketing shotgun process, not by the individual through a converging search.
>
> (Alchian 1950: 219)

Some may be inclined to argue in any case that the firms that survive do so because they have consciously *adapted* themselves to the environment. But the truth may well be, Alchian argues, that they were so lucky as to be *adopted* by the environment.

The discussion so far might easily give one the impression that Alchian is arguing here for a replacement of marginal analysis by an evolutionary type of analysis, in which impersonal market forces, passive adoption, active adaptation and the like take central stage. After all, it is clear that Alchian takes the latter to be the fundamental forces at work in competitive markets, and not the striving after maximum profits by calculating individuals endowed with perfect foresight. This is not the case, however. What Alchian really argues for is that there is no compelling reason to reject marginal analysis. Marginal analysis is not affected by the antimarginalist criticism, for the applicability of marginal analysis does not rest upon the truth of its assumptions, or of its axioms as Alchian prefers to call them.

Alchian (1953) clarifies his own position in the marginalism controversy. Alchian argues that the antimarginalists and Machlup alike confused axioms with theorems. They assessed marginal analysis by testing its axioms, instead of testing its theorems as they should have done according to Alchian. Whereas the axioms of marginal analysis are about entrepreneurial behaviour, its theorems are about the operations of industries (or about the economic system as a whole). The antimarginalists and Machlup failed to notice that although the theorems of marginal analysis are derived from its axioms, the theorems hold also on less restrictive axioms. Alchian devised his selection argument to show that when the assumptions of the theory of the firm are relaxed, for example by dropping the assumption of perfect foresight, its predictions can still be made. In Alchian's view, marginal analysis is suited to predict industry behaviour that most of the time is not produced by perfectly informed profit maximizers but by evolutionary forces. Or, as Enke aptly puts it:

> the economist can make aggregate predictions *as if* each and every firm knew how to secure maximum long-run profits.
>
> (Enke 1951: 567)

Alchian (1950) is often thought to convey the same message as Enke (1951). This is at least partly incorrect. Alchian and Enke raise the same argument. But they draw opposite conclusions from it. Enke pleads for a replacement of marginal analysis by 'viability analysis'. In viability analysis it is investigated what types of firms are viable in different environmental settings. Enke gives two reasons for drawing this opposite conclusion. The first reason is that Enke is less confident than Alchian that both types of analysis always lead to the same predictions.[10] The second reason that Enke gives is that viability analysis is more realistic than marginal analysis. Even if the two can be expected to yield the same results, viability analysis is to be preferred. For viability analysis does not ascribe the 'quite unreasonable degree of omniscience and prescience to entrepreneurs' that is attributed to them in marginal analysis.

Penrose (1952) is one of the commentators who fails to notice this difference between Alchian and Enke. Her criticism of Alchian (1950) proceeds on the assumption that just like Enke Alchian is arguing for a conversion of the economics profession from marginal analysis to viability analysis. To Penrose, viability analysis tries to provide an explanation of economic processes that does not depend on human motives. Penrose's main point of criticism is that viability analysis cannot do without implicit assumptions about human motives. What is more, Penrose argues that viability analysis tacitly presupposes precisely what it purports to dispense with: profit maximization. Her argument runs as follows. The environment selects the successful only when competition is intense. In biology, intense competition takes the form of an omnipresent struggle for existence. This is due to the fact that reproduction causes excessive '*entry*' all the time. The only plausible economic counterpart of such processes of reproduction Penrose can think of, is the desire of business men to make as much money as possible. Unless we assume this desire to be predominant, competition in economic life cannot be accounted for. The same holds for innovation: we can explain the innovative behaviour of entrepreneurs only on the assumption that they try to maximize profits. To treat innovations as chance mutations, as Alchian is said to do, leaves them essentially unexplained.

I think that Penrose is wrong in arguing that the notion of competition that is at stake in Alchian's selection argument presupposes the desire of business men to make profits. In Alchian's argument, 'competition' seems to refer to the scarcity of positive profits as prerequisites to remain in business. In competitive markets, there is selection for *realized* positive profits, not for *intended* maximum profits. Selection for results, for realized positive profits, does not require that business men pursue profits. Whether business men have this goal or not, no firm can afford to make losses for some lasting period of time. Recall Alchian's analogy of the travellers setting out from Chicago. Like the travellers who are so unfortunate to have picked the wrong road, firms who are on the wrong track sooner or later run out of gas.

Alchian's selection argument goes further, however, than just stating that in competitive markets this type of selection effect obtains. Alchian claims that economists can use marginal analysis to predict the direction of change in aggregate selection effects as a result of environmental changes. For example, economists predict that the labour–capital ratio in an industry decreases as (real) wages rise (*ceteris paribus*). Does this prediction hold irrespective of the motives, deliberations and the like of entrepreneurs? As Alchian himself remarks, what is needed for this prediction to hold is variation in the production techniques of the respective firms in the industry. To see why, consider an industry that is faced with an increase in (real) wages in which all the firms are optimally adapted to the previous wage rate. If no firm changes its labour–capital ratio, nothing will change at the aggregate industry level either. There will be a change in the average industry ratio only if one or more firms change their ratios. But the predicted change will not follow from any change in firm behaviour. Imagine, for example, that the firms that change their ratio do so in an 'irrational' direction: they increase their ratio. Then, if there is selection for realized positive profits, market selection will benefit the firms that did not change their ratio (at the expense of the 'irrational' firms), as they are the ones with the most profitable lowest ratio. Consequently, the initial ratio will be restored. The predicted change in industry behaviour, a decrease of the average industry ratio, will not be forthcoming.

In the example presented so far, entry is left out. Bringing in the possibility of new firms entering the industry, however, only affirms the point I want to make here: the validity of Alchian's claim in his selection argument crucially depends on the existing 'material' on which market selection operates. Yet there is nothing in the argument that tells us what material to expect. To put the same point differently, although the various actions (or lines of behaviour) actually tried by firms determine what selection effects will come about, Alchian's selection argument is silent on what actions firms can be expected to try. I take this to be the kernel of truth in Penrose's criticism: it is more likely that there will be business men who try the 'right' profitable type of actions if we assume that business men are guided by the desire to make profits than if we dispense with this assumption.

In his reply to Penrose's criticism, Alchian (1953) repeats that the desire to make profits should not be confused with profit maximization. Alchian makes clear that his (1950) argument that profit maximization is meaningless under pervasive uncertainty is not to be misinterpreted as an assertion that entrepreneurs do not pursue profits. Alchian repeats that he believes that entrepreneurs are led by the profit motive, but he questions that they are able to find the most profitable actions that are available to them. And in Alchian (1950), economists were already warned that as the most (or even more) profitable actions may not be among those that are actually tried, they may be pushing their luck too far when they apply the standard marginalist tools of analysis (Alchian 1950: 220).[11]

This leaves us with a puzzle. Alchian clearly advanced his selection argument to defend the neoclassical theory of the firm as a theory of industry behaviour. He argues that its theorems (or implications, or predictions) hold even if its restrictive assumption of profit maximizing is false. Alchian's (1953) statements on (more and less) restrictive axioms and theorems might lead one to expect rigorous mathematical proofs of the neoclassical theorems under less restrictive axioms than profit maximization. Such proofs are lacking in Alchian's work, however. Instead, in using a term like luck Alchian appears to weaken his own claim. The neoclassical theorems *may* hold also when entrepreneurs are not profit maximizers, but we cannot be certain that they do. How can economists know when they are pushing their luck too far? It seems that the answer Alchian (1953) finally comes up with is that economists cannot know this in advance. In each particular case, they can only know this with hindsight, by testing its predictive value by empirical investigation (Alchian 1953: 602).

Conceiving marginal analysis as an analysis that is to be understood in an 'as if' fashion, and that is to be judged finally by its predictive power, sounds pretty much like Friedman's celebrated (1953) essay. In the next section we will see that this association is not a whimsical one.

5. FRIEDMAN'S SELECTION ARGUMENT: ANOTHER F-TWIST

Friedman (1953) can be said to be a *pièce de résistance* in economic methodology. Probably, there is no other paper that is so much discussed as Friedman's essay. Although the interpretations and assessments of the essay show an enormous variation, it seems to be acknowledged by all commentators that there are paragraphs in the essay that have a distinct Popperian flavour. Popper's falsificationism appears to be endorsed in Friedman's assertion, for example, that: 'factual evidence can never "prove" a hypothesis; it can only fail to disprove it' (Friedman 1953: 9). Yet it is also observed by many that Friedman gives his own twist to the Popperian story. This so-called 'F-twist' is succinctly summarized in Friedman's statement that: 'the more significant the theory, the more unrealistic the assumptions' (Friedman 1953: 14). Friedman's view here seems to be at odds with Popper's view, for Popper seems to hold that 'significant' theories are to be based on realistic assumptions.

In this section, I do not argue for one more interpretation of Friedman (1953). It is my impression that the essay contains many perspectives and viewpoints, some of which are not, and perhaps even cannot be, reconciled with each other. But I do argue that there is something in the essay that is not given due attention by many commentators: Friedman's selection argument.[12] I argue that a proper understanding of this argument makes Friedman's 'as if methodology' more intelligible. It helps us understand Friedman's view that a theory is useful even though its assumptions are unrealistic. Friedman's selection argument will be seen to have much in common with Alchian's (1950) argument. But, again, just as Friedman gives his own twist to Popperian falsificationism, he presents his own version of Alchian's argument.

Although Friedman (1953) refers to Alchian (1950), it is unlikely that Friedman extracted his selection argument from Alchian's paper. Hammond (1991) points out that an early draft of Friedman's essay, written in 1947/8, already contains a 'natural selection argument'.[13] In this draft, Friedman argues that the profit maximization hypothesis is of no great use in explaining the behaviour of individual firms. The hypothesis is said to work best for industries. Friedman's view can therefore be said to be identical to Alchian's on this point. Hammond traces this view back to the major influence of Marshall on Friedman. Marshall's 'representative firm' was a theoretical construct to analyse processes and tendencies at the level of industries. Indeed, Hammond goes as far as to argue that in retrospect a more apt title of Friedman's essay might have been 'The methodology of Marshallian economics'.[14]

There are other ideas that Friedman shares with Alchian. Friedman gives the same explanation as Alchian for their joint belief that although the profit maximization hypothesis is not suited to analyse the behaviour of individual firms, it is suited to analyse the behaviour of industry: there is a force operating from the outside on firms. Forces working 'inside' firms, the motives and contemplations of business men, may lead individual firms astray. But such aberrations will be corrected in due course by an external force. This force favours firms that manage to make maximum positive profits over firms that fail to do so. The latter types of firms will be wiped out eventually. This process of selection sees to it that in the long run the average behaviour of the firms in the industry will approximate the behaviour that is predicted on the basis of the profit maximization hypothesis.

Friedman also agrees with Alchian that the foregoing account implies that criticizing theories for having false or unrealistic assumptions, as the antimarginalists do, is misguided, for a theory can also hold if its assumptions are false. According to Friedman (1953),

> this point needs emphasis, because the entirely valid use of 'assumptions' in *specifying* the circumstances for which a theory holds is frequently, and erroneously, interpreted to mean that the assumptions can be used to *determine* the circumstances for which a theory holds, and has, in this way, been an important source of the belief that a theory can be tested by its assumptions.
>
> (Friedman 1953: 19)

The antimarginalists wrongly took the theory of the firm's assumptions to determine the conditions under which the theory would hold. The theory's assumptions specify sufficient conditions: if the assumption is true that entrepreneurs are engaged in profit maximization under perfect foresight, then we can infer (with certainty) the truth of the theory's theorems (or its implications, or its predictions). The theory's assumptions do not state necessary conditions for the theory to hold. Showing that the theory's assumptions are false therefore does not imply that the theory is false. The selection argument precisely purports to show that the theory also holds when entrepreneurs are not profit maximizers. This is what Alchian meant in arguing that the theorems hold also under less restrictive axioms.[15]

So much for the ideas that Friedman (1953) has in common with Alchian (1950). In what respects does Friedman's selection argument differ from Alchian's? In order to get this clear, it is useful to quote the relevant paragraph in Friedman (1953) at length. After having established the point that evidence relating to the way business men actually reach their decisions does not bear on our confidence in the 'maximization-of-expected-returns' hypothesis, Friedman goes on to argue that:

> Confidence in the maximization-of-returns hypothesis is justified by evidence of a very different character. This evidence is in part similar to that adduced on behalf of the billiard-player hypothesis – unless the behavior of businessmen in some way or other approximated behavior consistent with the maximization of returns, it seems unlikely that they would remain in business for long. Let the apparent immediate determinant of business behavior be anything at all – habitual reaction, random chance, or whatnot. Whenever this

determinant happens to lead to behavior consistent with rational and informed maximization of returns, the business will prosper and acquire resources with which to expand; whenever it does not, the business will tend to lose resources and can be kept in existence only by the addition of resources from outside. The process of 'natural selection' thus helps to validate the hypothesis or, rather, given natural selection, acceptance of the hypothesis can be based largely on the judgment that it summarizes appropriately the conditions for survival.

(Friedman 1953: 22)

Let us consider this quote carefully. The evidence for the maximization-of-(expected-)returns hypothesis is said to be similar to that adduced on behalf of the billiard-player hypothesis. The 'billiard-player hypothesis' was introduced in Friedman and Savage (1948) to illustrate the point that the realism of a hypothesis is irrelevant when we assess its merits. What is relevant is solely whether the hypothesis yields sufficiently accurate predictions about the class of actions with which the hypothesis deals. The actions with which the billiard-player hypothesis deals are the shots made by an *expert* billiard player. The hypothesis says that the expert billiard player makes the shots that he or she considers to be optimal after having conducted all kinds of calculations and mathematical reasoning properly. The player is assumed to have located the positions of the balls precisely, to have estimated the optimal angles accurately, to have calculated the optimal speed and direction of the ball to be hit, etc.

Of course, Friedman and Savage do not believe that expert billiard players really go through these things before making their shots. Yet they do believe that the hypothesis yields predictions of the observable behaviour of expert billiard players (the shots they actually make) that are fairly accurate. Expert billiard players can be expected to play *as if* they go through the contemplations and calculations that are ascribed to them in the hypothesis. Likewise, the maximization-of-expected-returns hypothesis is not to be understood as a literal description of the decision-making process entrepreneurs go through. It rather predicts that individual firms behave *as if* they knew the relevant cost and demand functions, calculated marginal cost and marginal revenue from all actions open to them, and pushed each line of action to the point at which the relevant marginal cost and marginal revenue were equal.

What is the evidence adduced on behalf of the billiard-player hypothesis? According to Friedman, the answer to this question is to be found in the following proposition:

unless in some way or other they were capable of reaching essentially the same result, they would not in fact be *expert* billiard players.

(Friedman 1953: 21, see also Friedman and Savage 1948: 298)

The type of 'evidence' that seems to be at stake here can hardly be called empirical evidence (or 'factual' evidence, as Friedman himself calls it). The proposition just quoted does *not* suggest that if a billiard player makes shots that are definitely worse than the ones predicted in the hypothesis, this is to be taken in a Popperian vein as empirical evidence that disproves the hypothesis. It rather suggests that the billiard player is not likely to be called an *expert* billiard player. The suggested conclusion is that the billiard player in question does not meet the standards we associate with being an expert billiard player. It is part of the meaning of 'expert' that the player must show he or she is able to make the shots that can be inferred from the hypothesis. In other words, there seems to be a *definitional* rather than an empirical issue involved here.

What about the evidence that Friedman gives in support of the maximization-of-expected-returns hypothesis?:

> unless the behavior of businessmen in some way or other approximated behavior consistent with the maximization of returns, it seems unlikely that they would remain in business for long.
>
> (Friedman 1953: 22)

Here the 'evidence' seems to be quite *dis*similar to the evidence given for the billiard-player hypothesis. The issue at stake here does not seem to be definitional. For it is not part of the meaning of 'business men who remain in business for long' that they achieve maximum profits. But the 'evidence' does not seem to be empirical either. Maybe it is a 'fact' that business men that have remained in business for long have achieved maximum profits throughout. But Friedman does not refer to any *empirical* investigation in which this 'fact' has been established.[16] Instead, Friedman derives the 'evidence' as a conclusion from his *theoretical* natural selection argument: given 'natural selection', only those business men who have achieved maximum profits throughout cannot be outperformed.

But perhaps the notional evidence should not be taken too literally. As I take it, the point Friedman wants to make here is that his confidence in the usefulness of the maximization-of-expected-returns hypothesis is *not* grounded in his belief that business men pursue profits, that they are well informed (or gather the information they need), etc. It is grounded in his belief, first, that there is a process of 'natural selection' going on, and, second, that the maximization-of-expected-returns hypothesis predicts the outcomes of this process. It is not that Friedman questions that business men try to maximize profits. But their 'internal' motives and deliberations are not the crucial forces in market economies. To Friedman, the really important forces at work are external forces that 'correct' firms when they fail to maximize profits. The theory of the firm is not what it seems! Appearances notwithstanding, the theory is not about decisions made by individual firms, but about underlying processes in market economies.

We are now in a position to illuminate differences between Alchian's and Friedman's selection argument. Just as Alchian does in his (1950) paper, Friedman wrote about the 'profit maximization' hypothesis in his earlier drafts of the essay. In his final (1953) version, however, Friedman prefers to use the phrase 'maximization-of-expected-results' hypothesis. According to Friedman, it is better to reserve 'profits' for the difference between *ex post* and *ex ante* receipts (Friedman 1953: 21, footnote 16). Following Alchian, Friedman argues that profits that are a result of uncertainty cannot be deliberately maximized in advance. Friedman prefers 'expected returns' because expected returns can be deliberately maximized in advance. 'Expected returns' is taken by Friedman to be broad enough to cover any of the probability distributions entrepreneurs might choose in the face of uncertainty. According to Friedman, the issue at stake here is not basic to the methodological issues discussed.

It seems, however, that Friedman misses an essential point in Alchian's argument, for Alchian stresses that it is *ex post* profits that are selected for, not *ex ante* receipts. And under uncertainty, positive *ex post* profits may follow from irrational and not from rational decision rules. When uncertainty is pervasive, any *ex ante* expectation may be frustrated. Friedman's selection argument is consistent with Alchian's only if the expectations referred to are '*ex post* expectations': the 'expectations' of business men who have discovered with hindsight what decisions would have brought them positive profits. There are lines in Friedman (1953) that strongly suggest that this is what Friedman has in mind (see, for example, Friedman 1953: 21–2). The lines even suggest that the 'maximization-of-expected-returns' hypothesis predicts behaviour that business men would have chosen had they known all the relevant data, had they conducted the relevant calculations correctly, etc.; in short: if they would have had perfect expectations.

This brings me to a second point. Friedman seems to hold that 'natural selection' eliminates all firms that do not succeed in making maximum profits. Eventually, only those firms survive whose behaviour is (approximately) consistent with profit-maximizing behaviour: the behaviour firms would have displayed if they would have pursued profits with complete information and perfect foresight. This is meant by Friedman, I venture, where he argues that the 'maximization-of-expected-returns' hypothesis summarizes the conditions for survival. In Alchian (1950), we can find similar statements. It is argued by Alchian, for example, that marginal analysis can be used to diagnose the conditions most conducive to a greater probability of survival (Alchian 1950: 215). But Alchian never goes as far as Friedman does in claiming that 'natural selection' ensures that these conditions eventually will be met.

Of course, *if* firms achieve maximum profits, they cannot be outperformed by competitors in a process of selection. One cannot beat the unbeatable. The same idea can be expressed by saying that Friedman's condition is a sufficient condition for survival, just as being a *perfect* billiard player is a sufficient condition for not losing any billiard game. Alchian is more careful than Friedman. Alchian does not assume that unbeatable firms will be among the competitors. In section 4, we have seen that he warns economists against drawing too easily the type of conclusions Friedman draws. It seems that the claim Alchian is arguing for is weaker than Friedman's. Alchian's claim seems to be that 'natural selection' sees to it that the tendencies in *industry* behaviour are forthcoming that are predicted in neoclassical theory, not that each and every *individual* surviving firm achieves maximum profits.

To avoid misunderstanding, I shall henceforth distinguish between profit maximizing (or profit seeking, or the profit motive) and the neoclassical assumption of 'profit maximization'. *'Profit maximizing'* refers to actions that are undertaken with the *desire* to attain maximum profits. *'Profit maximization'* refers to that behaviour that leads to maximum profits. Profit maximizing may result in 'profit maximization'. This will be the case if profit maximizers are perfectly rational and if they are perfectly informed and have perfect foresight. 'Profit maximization' refers to the behaviour that perfectly rational profit maximizers would display if they had perfect information and foresight. Under uncertainty, however, when foresight is imperfect, profit maximizing may well lead to less than maximum profits.

'Profit maximization' can be brought about also by business men who are not engaged in profit maximizing. Business men who are interested in other things than making profits or who are satisfied with less than maximum profits may arrive at maximum profits. This is the point that has to be kept in mind: 'profit maximization' does not presuppose profit maximizing. 'Profit maximization' can have many different 'immediate determinants', as Friedman puts it. Whatever may be the determinants of firm behaviour, I take Friedman to argue that, as long as firms display behaviour that is consistent with 'profit maximization', they cannot be extinguished in market competition.

On the basis of the foregoing analysis, we can make another crucial distinction. Alchian and Friedman seem to concur in the idea that the neoclassical theory of the firm is really, or *ultimately*, a theory about industry behaviour. They both seem to argue for the following *ultimate claim*:

> whether firms are engaged in profit maximizing or not, economic 'natural selection' sees to it that the neoclassical theorems, that are about tendencies at the industry level, hold.

In contrast to Alchian, however, Friedman seems to be arguing also for a stronger claim, a claim that I will henceforth call the *intermediate claim*:[17]

whether firms are engaged in profit maximizing or not, economic 'natural selection' sees to it that each and every surviving individual firm displays behavior that is consistent with 'profit maximization'.

Acceptance of the intermediate claim implies acceptance of the ultimate claim, but not vice versa. In other words, the validity of the intermediate claim is a sufficient, but not a necessary, condition for the validity of the ultimate claim. Consider once again the neoclassical theorem that an industry's labour–capital ratio tends to decrease when real wage rates rise. If each and every firm eventually adopts the labour–capital ratio that is optimal given the new wage rates (that is, all firms arrive at 'profit maximization' behaviour), then of course the industry's ratio settles at the new equilibrium rate. But, conversely, a tendency towards this new equilibrium rate can be forthcoming also if not every individual firm in the industry is optimally adapted to the new situation. There may be some variation among the new ratios of the surviving individual firms and the new optimal ratio may not be tried by any firm. As long as the new ratios decline *on average*, the neoclassical theorem holds.

In the next section, we will see that the difference between the intermediate and the ultimate claim is spelled out in more detail in Becker (1962a).

6. BECKER'S SELECTION ARGUMENT

Becker's (1962a) aim is similar to that of Alchian (1950) and Friedman (1953): to show that the validity of the theorems of neoclassical economics is not restricted to situations in which individuals behave rationally. Becker purports to show that the theorems also hold when individuals exhibit irrational behaviour. The general principle underlying the neoclassical theorems, Becker argues, are shifts in opportunities of individuals. We will see that in Becker's view the 'great achievement' of the selection argument is that it demonstrates how changes in production opportunity sets of firms can explain changes in industry (or market) behaviour without assuming that firms behave rationally. I shall argue that Becker is right in taking shifts in opportunities of firms to be the crux in Alchian's and Friedman's selection arguments. But I shall also argue that just as Alchian and Friedman, Becker does not succeed in validating the ultimate claim.

According to Becker, one of 'the important theorems of modern economics' is that market demand functions are negatively inclined. This theorem holds for demand for outputs (products and services) as well as for demand for inputs. An increase in the real wage rate, for example, will lead to a decrease in the employment of labour (with a given outlay). Becker argues that the 'general principle' behind this theorem is that changes in opportunities (in the example changes in employment opportunities as a result of an increase in the real wage rate) 'force' economic units into rational market responses (in the example a decrease in the employment of labour). Households and firms cannot continually 'live' beyond their means. They are forced to respond to changes in opportunities in the way that is asserted in the theorems of modern economics, regardless and independent of the decision rule they use. Whether they use a rational decision rule or not, that is whether they consistently maximize a well-ordered function (such as a utility or profit function) or not, their response will be the same.

In the case of households, the set of opportunities usually is determined by budget constraints. The budget constraints can change as a result of, for example, a change in relative real prices. Becker shows that the demand for a good X decreases when the relative real price of X increases no matter what decision rules are employed. The result obtains when the households are rational utility maximizers (which is what 'traditional theory' assumes), but also when the households behave irrationally: when they act impulsively or when they exhibit inert or habitual behaviour. Firms are usually considered not to be faced with similar restricted opportunities: 'the traditional analytical distinction between households and firms is that firms are not supposed to be subject to budget constraints' (Becker 1962a: 10).

In Becker's opinion, it is the contribution of Alchian (1950) and Friedman (1953) that has shown that non-profit-maximizing firms in fact are subject to similar constraints:

> In my judgment the great achievement of the 'survival' argument advanced by Alchian and others is not a demonstration that surviving firms must act as if they were trying to maximize profits, for counter-examples can easily be developed, but rather a demonstration that the decisions of irrational firms are limited by a budgetary constraint. [. . .] firms could not continually produce, could not 'survive', outputs yielding negative profits, as eventually all the resources at their disposal would be used up.
>
> (Becker 1962a: 10)

Becker considers the ultimate claim to be the real and valuable point of the selection argument. Friedman's intermediate claim is dismissed on the ground that counterexamples can easily be given. Apparently, Becker does not want to rule out the possibility that firms may survive that do display behaviour that is *in*consistent with 'profit maximization'. Surviving firms may behave irrationally. But that does not imply, Becker argues, that aggregate market behaviour is also 'irrational'. Quite to the contrary, Becker, inspired by the selection ('survival') argument, endeavours to show that changes in 'resource constraints' alone can account for the 'rational market responses' that are predicted in the neoclassical theorems.

His argument rests upon the observation that rational and irrational firms alike cannot afford to ignore significant losses. Firms cannot survive if their total income is less than zero. They must keep their level of operation within their own production opportunity set,[18] for otherwise their resource constraints may shrink to the point of bankruptcy. This being the case, Becker argues that it really does not matter whether firms consistently maximize a well-ordered function, behave in a completely impulsive way, or display total inertia; changes in the firms' environment can cause shifts in their production opportunity set, which in turn will 'force' the firms to change their behaviour in the direction that is predicted in the neoclassical theorems. Becker relates this general result to the marginalism controversy in the following way:

> irrational firms can give very rational market responses, and this seeming paradox offers a solution to the heated and protracted controversy between marginalists and anti-marginalists. Confidence in the irrationality of firms induced the latter to conclude that market responses were also irrational, while confidence in the rationality of markets induced the former to conclude that firms were also rational.
>
> (Becker 1962a: 12)

Antimarginalists may have been right that firm behaviour is not (always) rational, but wrongly took market behaviour to be simply firm behaviour 'writ large'. Marginalists, on the other hand, made the opposite failure to assume that firm behaviour is a microscopic reproduction of market behaviour.

In my opinion, there is no doubt that Becker is right that shifts in opportunities is the principle that underlies the selection arguments of Alchian and Friedman. Their arguments are based on the principle that firms that happen to make positive profits gather the means they can use to expand, whereas firms that confront losses cannot but contract. In competitive markets, this process of selection takes place regardless of the motives, deliberations and the like of business men. But does this process of selection also make industries behave in ways that are predicted in neoclassical theory, regardless of the firms' motives and deliberations? Does Becker succeed where Alchian and Friedman failed?

Kirzner (1962) argues that Becker does not succeed either. Kirzner concentrates on the prime example Becker gives of an environmental change: shifts in real relative prices. Kirzner argues quite convincingly that this shift in relative real prices must be accounted for (and in fact is accounted for in economic theory) in terms of the behaviour of (at least some) market participants. If all market participants were price takers, as Becker in effect assumes, shifts in relative real prices would be a miracle. According to Kirzner, a convergence to equilibrium (relative real) prices and quantities can be explained only if we assume that market participants are rational. It should be noted here that Kirzner does not take 'rational behaviour' to mean consistent maximization of a well-ordered function, as Becker does. To Kirzner rational market participants learn from their past failures:

> The *essence* of this market process, it will be observed, is *the systematic way in which plan revisions are made as a consequence of the disappointment of earlier plans.*
>
> (Kirzner 1962: 381)

Equilibrating market processes presuppose that market participants are engaged in learning by trial and error. Kirzner therefore concludes that shifts in opportunities alone fall short of producing neoclassical results.

I think that Kirzner is right that changes in relative real prices are not accounted for in Becker's argument. But what about Kirzner's claim that adjustment processes in markets can come about *only* when market participants revise their plans in a rational, systematic way? I do not think that this claim is valid. Becker seems to be right in arguing that 'rational market responses' can be forthcoming also when agents do not learn in a systematic way. Learning by trial and error is not a necessary condition for the neoclassical theorems to hold. But perhaps this is not Kirzner's point. Kirzner appears to have a different conception of the 'essence' of market processes than Becker. Becker (and Alchian and Friedman) consider the selection for profits, produced by market forces and leading to differential shifts in opportunities of firms, to be the essence of competitive markets. The neo-Austrian Kirzner is wedded to the Hayekian view that the coordination in markets of individual plans is produced by the interdependent learning processes of individuals.[19]

Becker succeeds in pointing out that the neoclassical tendencies in market behaviour *can* result from differential shifts in opportunities even if firms do not learn from their past mistakes. But he fails to show that these tendencies can be accounted for by shifts in opportunities under any assumption of individual firm behaviour. Counterexamples can easily be constructed. If some environmental change causes the production opportunity sets of all firms in the industry to move to the left, for example, the aggregate market response need not be rational (turn to the left also). For if the new sets sufficiently overlap the old ones, and if all firms are irrational firms that on average move to the right, then market response will also be irrational, for it is possible then that the irrational firms still make positive profits.

The validity of Becker's selection argument can thus be seen to be subject to qualifications.[20] Shifts in opportunities need not force firms to respond in ways that ensure that rational market behaviour is forthcoming. True, diminishing opportunities force firms to operate on a smaller scale. We cannot infer from this fact alone, however, what behaviour firms will display with limited means. Will they hold on to the behaviour they displayed before (on a smaller scale, though), or will they change their behaviour? In order to answer this, we need to know their decision rules. At this point, Kirzner's main point of criticism becomes relevant. If firms really learn systematically from their failures, they will not persist in displaying behaviour that leads to worse results than they were used to. It seems that if firms are rational in this minimal sense, Becker's argument becomes more convincing. Under this assumption of minimal rationality, the counterexamples that can be provided to Becker's argument are less likely to be observed in reality. Or, to put it in different terms, the 'material' (the behaviour displayed by firms) 'natural selection' works on is more likely to be such, then, that neoclassical tendencies come about.

Seen in this light, Kirzner's criticism of Becker's argument amounts to the same thing as Penrose's criticism of Alchian (see section 4). Recall that the main point I extracted from Penrose's criticism was that there is nothing in the selection argument as such that ensures (or that makes it at least plausible) that the 'right' type of entry is forthcoming; the type of entry, that is, that will bring about neoclassical tendencies. Kirzner's criticism makes clear that the same result may obtain if we abstract from the possibility of entry; when firms learn by trial and error. Both Penrose and Kirzner can be taken to argue that selection effects are not as insensitive to the 'behavioural input', to the material that selection forces work on, as the proponents of selection arguments want to make us believe. Neoclassical selection effects are more likely to obtain if we assume that business men are pursuing profits in a minimally rational way after all.

7. CONCLUSIONS

On the basis of the foregoing discussions, it can be concluded that Alchian, Friedman and Becker advanced selection arguments in order to show that the antimarginalist empirical findings, that entrepreneurs are not rational, perfectly informed profit maximizers, can be reconciled with the neoclassical theorems. They all believed that the antimarginalist criticism is misguided, because it rests on the misunderstanding that the neoclassical theory of the firm tries to explain and to predict the behaviour of individual firms. The theory is said to be really about the behaviour of industry. To be more precise, Alchian, Friedman and Becker held that the neoclassical theory of the firm predicts the direction in which aggregate variables in industries change as a consequence of changes in the industry's environment. Their selection arguments purport to point out that the tendencies in industry behaviour that are predicted in neoclassical theorems hold even if the antimarginalists are right that the neoclassical assumption of profit maximization is false.[21]

Appearances notwithstanding, the forces that Alchian, Friedman and Becker take to be producing the predicted tendencies are *not* profit-maximizing actions taken by individual entrepreneurs, but impersonal

38

market forces. They do not deny that business men are led by the profit motive. But their confidence in the neoclassical theorems is rooted in their belief that impersonal market forces 'punish' business men who do not succeed in making positive profits.[22] Competitive markets select for positive profits. Becker is most explicit in arguing that the market forces perform their disciplining function via shifts in opportunities. The opportunities of firms that happen to make profits increase, while the opportunities of firms that fail to make profits decrease.

Alchian, Friedman and Becker concur in the claim that 'selection', thus understood, brings about tendencies as predicted in neoclassical theory regardless of whether firms are profit maximizers. This 'ultimate claim' is to be distinguished from the 'intermediate claim' that is put forward by Friedman: regardless of whether firms are profit maximizers or not, only those firms survive that display behaviour that is consistent with 'profit maximization'. The validity of the intermediate claim is a sufficient but not a necessary condition for the validity of the ultimate claim. Alchian and Becker seem to hold that although economic 'natural selection' does not ensure the validity of the intermediate claim, it does ensure the validity of the ultimate claim.

Both claims are not to be confused with the claim Machlup (1967) advances in his review of the marginalism controversy. Machlup argues that firms are forced to pursue no other goal than maximization of profits when competition is harsh. The pursuit of any other goal is said to be fatal for firms:

> under [this] 'competitive pressure' the firm is constantly compelled to react to actual or potential losses in sales and/or reductions in profits, so much so that the firm will not be able to pursue any objectives other than the maximization of profits for the simple reason that anything less than the highest obtainable profits would be below the rate of return regarded as normal at the time.
>
> (Machlup 1967: 18)

This claim is alien to the selection arguments of Alchian, Friedman and Becker. Alchian (in particular) would discard it for the simple reason that under uncertainty no particular goal, decision rule or whatever guarantees success. Firms that try to maximize profits may be outperformed by firms that do not try to do so. And it is *actual* results that are selected for, not intended results, goals or motives. Firms that suffer losses are forced to lower their scale of operation. They are not forced to pursue particular goals.[23]

It is characteristic of the selection arguments of Alchian, Friedman and Becker that they take the ultimate claim to be valid under many different, if not all different, determinants of firm behaviour. They consider the claim to be valid whether or not business men actually go through the reasoning

39

that is ascribed to them in the profit-maximizing assumption. Hence their conclusion that not too much attention should be paid to the actual determinants of firm behaviour. This conclusion contravenes the conclusion Harrod draws from his evolutionary speculations (see section 2). Harrod argues that if some procedure, or rule of thumb, is widely established in industries (which, in fact, it is), and if this procedure has won out in some evolutionary process akin to natural selection (which is what is speculated by Harrod), then this procedure merits more attention than economists are inclined to give. The remarkable thing is that although Harrod refers to the same process of selection as Alchian, Friedman and Becker, he comes to the opposite conclusion.

This discussion relates to the issue of how much psychology a sound economic theory (about aggregate phenomena) needs. How much do we need to know about 'micromotives' in order to explain and predict 'macrobehaviour'? Alchian's, Friedman's and Becker's radical answer seems to be: nothing at all. Relying in part on the criticisms of Penrose and Kirzner, I have argued that this answer is not convincing. Selection effects are sensitive to 'behavioural input', and hence to the determinants of behaviour. Alchian *cum suis* succeed in showing that consistent patterns in macrobehaviour need not be the result of 'microscopic reproductions' of these patterns. In this respect, their endeavour resembles Schelling (1978), who also points out that macrobehaviour can be consistent with a whole range of micromotives. Schelling argues that there are games like 'musical chairs' that have a determinate (aggregate) outcome under all conceivable micromotives. Predicting tendencies in industry behaviour is not like predicting the outcome of 'musical chairs', however. Alchian *cum suis* do not succeed in showing that the same tendencies in industry behaviour come about no matter what motives and decision rules firms have.

In Chapter 4, we will see that Nelson and Winter developed an evolutionary theory precisely to examine such issues. But before I turn to their theory, we shall first have a closer look at 'the new theory of the firm'. It will turn out that many differences notwithstanding, the new theory also relies in some informal, background way on selection arguments.

3

BREAKING OPEN THE BLACK BOX

The new theory of the firm

1. INTRODUCTION

In the neoclassical theory of the firm the firm is treated as a unitary agent. Or, to put it somewhat more accurately, the entrepreneur is implicitly considered to be the personification of the firm. Firm behaviour is equated with the behaviour of the entrepreneur. What goes on within firms remains in the dark; the firm is analysed as a black box. As a matter of fact, in Chapter 2 we have seen that proponents of the theory argue that the neoclassical theory of the firm does not even purport to be a theory of the behaviour of individual firms. It is a theory (or, better, a building block in the theory) of industries, of markets. Industry behaviour is studied as the outcome of the behaviour of firms.

Meanwhile, a new theory of the firm has surfaced. One of the main purposes of this new theory is to shed light on the internal organization of firms. As a first and crude approximation, we could say that the new theory studies phenomena at one level below the level of analysis in the 'old' neoclassical theory. Whereas the old theory analyses industry behaviour as the result of firm behaviour, the new theory studies firm behaviour as the outcome of the behaviour of individual participants. It is no longer assumed a priori that all participants have the same interest as the entrepreneur. This shift in level of analysis can be called an important breakthrough in the theory of the firm. Yet it must be added immediately that the new theory is in many respects also a continuation of the old theory. For one thing, the assumption of profit-maximizing firms in the old theory has its counterpart in the assumption of utility-maximizing individuals in the new theory.

The crude approximation given above can be refined in a way that is suggested by Williamson (1990), one of the leading pioneers in the new theory of the firm. Williamson also argues that the old and the new theory are complements rather than competitors of each other. The theories address different issues and highlight different aspects of firms. The neoclassical theory is concerned with prices and output. It concentrates on the

41

technological aspects of firms. The new theory, on the other hand, is interested in different ways of organizing transactions. Accordingly, it focuses on contractual aspects of firms (and markets).

In this chapter, I will reconstruct several strands in the new theory of the firm. I will start with a discussion of Coase's path-breaking paper on the nature of the firm. Subsequently, the property rights and agency costs approach will be considered. Next, attention will be paid to Williamson's transaction cost economics. Despite their differences, the approaches will be seen to share the basic theoretical presupposition that in competitive markets efficient organization forms are selected. This presupposition can be regarded as a variation on Friedman's theme that firms exhibiting profit-maximizing behaviour are selected in competitive markets.

2. MULTIPLE MARKETS AS DISCIPLINING DEVICES

Coase (1937) starts with the remark that economists tend to think of the economic system as an organism that is being coordinated by the price mechanism. Yet, Coase argues, this way of thinking is not appropriate when considering what goes on inside organizations like firms. Within firms, voluntary exchange transactions are replaced by obeying the directions of the 'entrepreneur–coordinator'. The agents working within a firm are not guided by price movements but by orders given by the entrepreneur. Coordination within firms is much more akin to economic planning than to market governance. Clearly, then, in market economies two distinct ways of coordinating resources exist side by side.

Coase goes on to argue that this poses a puzzle for economists. If 'organic' coordination is as efficient as it is claimed to be by economists, why then is there also 'organizational' coordination? Why do firms exist at all? Coase points out that the explanations of the emergence of the firm given so far are all defective. In particular, the existence of firms cannot be accounted for in a 'Smithian' way in terms of division of labour. Division of labour certainly creates the need for some integrating force. But since the price mechanism can meet this need, what is entrepreneurial control needed for?[1] The explanation that Coase gives of the displacement of the price mechanism by authoritative direction in firms is that the latter coordination mechanism has cost-saving advantages over the former: 'the main reason why it is profitable to establish a firm would seem to be that there is a cost of using the price mechanism' (Coase 1937: 38). According to Coase, *marketing* (or contract) costs, the costs of using the price mechanism, include among others search and negotiation costs.

Coase claims that his own explanation of the existence of firms is both realistic and tractable. It is realistic in that it stresses the element of direction, which Coase takes to be the essence of the legal relationship between employer and employee. And Coase's account is tractable, because it shows that 'the ordinary technique of economic analysis', marginal analysis, is applicable to 'the whole of the structure of competitive industry' (Coase 1937: 47). Coase can be said to extend the scope of marginal analysis by pointing out that phenomena like the internal organization of firms, that previously were considered to fall outside the scope of marginal analysis, are in fact amenable to it. One could also argue, however, that, given the fact that Coase clings to marginal analysis, he is 'forced' to argue that firm-type coordination has cost-saving advantages over market-type coordination. For within the marginalist framework the existence of firms would otherwise be inexplicable.

The latter argument can be discerned in Alchian and Demsetz (1972). In a reaction to Coase's account, they argue that:

> we do not disagree with the proposition that, *ceteris paribus*, the higher is the cost of transacting across markets, the greater will be the comparative advantage of organizing resources within the firm; it is a difficult proposition to disagree with or to refute. We could with equal ease subscribe to a theory of the firm based on the cost of managing, for surely it is true that, *ceteris paribus*, the lower is the cost of managing the greater will be the comparative advantage of organizing resources within the firm.
>
> (Alchian and Demsetz 1972: 783)

What Alchian and Demsetz object to is not that the existence of firms is explained by Coase in terms of cost advantages over transacting across markets. Alchian and Demsetz subscribe to Coase's claim that marginal analysis can be applied here. What they object to is that Coase fails to specify: 'the circumstances under which the cost of "managing" resources is low relative to the cost of allocating resources through market transaction' (Alchian and Demsetz 1972: 784). Coase does not point out what distinguishing features make firms more efficient than markets.

According to Alchian and Demsetz, firms have two distinguishing features: they are characterized by team production (team use of inputs) and there typically is some party that has a centralized position in the contractual arrangements with all other inputs. Alchian and Demsetz argue that team production will be used only if it yields an output larger than the sum of separable production. 'Team production' is defined here in terms of technological inseparability: when there is team production the contributions of the team members cannot be readily inferred from the team output. Two men jointly lifting cargo into trucks is Alchian and Demsetz' 'paradigmatic' example. In order to determine the individual efforts, *monitoring* costs have to be made. As Alchian and Demsetz show on the basis of marginal analysis, positive monitoring costs make shirking an attractive option to each team member. For the costs of shirking will then not be borne solely by the members who shirk (but also by their colleagues).

43

Given the fact that positive monitoring costs are to be made, what is the most efficient way to do so? How can the (potential) benefits of team production be secured while reducing the costs of organizing and disciplining team members to a minimum? Here we come to the second distinguishing feature of firms. Costs can be reduced by giving one person a centralized position as a monitor in the relations with the other team members. But how can monitors be made to perform their task well? In other words: 'who will monitor the monitor' (Alchian and Demsetz 1972: 782)? Alchian and Demsetz argue that if the monitors are 'residual claimants', that is if they are given title to the net earnings of the team, they have a personal interest in an optimal team performance. This is exactly why the *classical capitalist firm*, in which the net earnings (profits) go to the entrepreneur–monitor, has been so successful.

Coase can be said to have given an account of the economic *rationale* of firms in general. Likewise, Alchian and Demsetz have given an account of the *raison d'être* of the capitalist firm. The capitalist firm can be regarded as a particular organization form, a form in which the entrepreneur–manager has well-defined private *property rights*. The entrepreneur is the only one in the capitalist firm who has the rights to appropriate the residual claim, to renegotiate any input's contract independently of the contracts with others and to sell his or her contractual residual status. Alchian and Demsetz are considered to be the founders of the 'property rights' approach in economics (see also Alchian and Demsetz 1973). Property rights theorists emphasize that different property rights assignments lead to different penalty–reward structures and hence possibly to different outcomes (see Furubotn and Pejovich 1972). They try to figure out in what specific and predictable ways the assignments of property rights affect the allocation and use of resources. In general, they hold that more complete specifications of individual property rights tend to promote the efficient allocation of resources. And in particular, they claim that property rights internalize externalities.[2] Marginalism is not rejected by property right theorists. They merely extend its scope.[3]

All of these tenets of the property rights approach can be found back in Alchian and Demsetz (1972). Marginal analysis is applied to show that with the emergence of the classical firm new private property rights are assigned to entrepreneurs–managers. The new property rights internalize the 'externalities' that stem from the shirking problem in team production. As a consequence, resources are allocated and used more efficiently. Alchian and Demsetz also argue that testable implications can be derived from their general theoretical framework. On the basis of this framework it is possible to predict which types of firms are efficient under different conditions. If the efficient types of firms can be shown to be prevalent under the specified conditions, the predictions can be said to be borne out by the facts.

Alchian and Demsetz clearly diverge from Coase in arguing that it is a delusion to think that the firm is characterized by its power of authority or disciplinary action. Contracts between employers and employees are said by Alchian and Demsetz not to differ in kind from those between buyers and sellers on spot markets. The options available to a dissatisfied employer are exactly the same as those available to a dissatisfied customer: withholding future business or seeking redress in the courts. Alchian and Demsetz' view that there is no authority or direction involved in firm contracts is shared by Jensen and Meckling: 'the "behaviour" of the firm is like the behaviour of the market; i.e., the outcome of a complex equilibrium process' (Jensen and Meckling 1976: 311). And Jensen and Meckling also assume that the agents that partake in this process are utility-maximizing individuals.

Jensen and Meckling endeavour to develop a theory of the ownership structure of the firm. In particular, they focus mainly on a specific ownership structure, the structure in which the ownership and control of the firm is separated: the corporation. Jensen and Meckling try to explain why the corporation has done so well despite the fact that it is acknowledged to be vulnerable to excesses of managerial discretion by eminent scholars such as Adam Smith and Berle and Means (1932).

In Jensen and Meckling's own vocabulary, separation of ownership and control typically engenders a problem of agency: how to bring the behaviour of the managers (the *agents*) in line with the interests of the shareholders (the *principals*). It is an illusion, they argue, to think that this problem can be solved costlessly. Positive *agency costs* have to be incurred. Among the agency costs is the so-called residual loss, the decline in the value of the firm due to the problem of agency. Jensen and Meckling point out that although the value of the firm is not maximized in the corporation, the corporation is an efficient ownership structure.

Their argument that the corporate structure is efficient proceeds from the assumption that the equity market is competitive. It is this assumption that allows Jensen and Meckling to argue that the agency costs are borne completely by the agents, the managers. That is, the benefits of a reduction in the agency costs (because of the managers' reduced consumption of non-pecuniary items) go to the managers, as these benefits are assumed to be capitalized in the equity market into the price of equity claims. For example, consider a manager–owner who initially owns 100 per cent of the residual claims of a firm and who wants to sell 5 per cent (say because the manager–owner's wealth falls short of exploiting some profitable opportunity). At first sight it then seems that it becomes advantageous for the manager–owner to expend more in non-pecuniary items. For it seems that after the 5 per cent is sold one extra dollar expenditure in non-pecuniary items costs the manager–owner only 95 per cent in wealth reduction. But if it is assumed that the equity market is efficient, as Jensen and Meckling do, then the price of the equity claims falls by 5 per cent. This implies that the decline in the total value of the firm that would result from the manager–owner's expenditure in non-pecuniary items is imposed entirely on the manager–owner.

The characteristic feature of the Jensen and Meckling argument is that it is not only in the interest of 'outside' shareholders to monitor the behaviour of the manager(s). It is also in the interest of the manager(s)–owners themselves. A reduction in agency costs is mutually advantageous because both parties profit from a higher firm value. This feature is reflected in Jensen and Meckling's notion of *bonding costs*. Bonding costs are paid by managers–owners, as agents, to let themselves be audited in a public account. Again, it is advantageous for manager–owners to incur these costs because the equity market is assumed to be efficient; malfeasance on their part will lower the price of their own equity claims. Therefore, Putterman seems to be basically right in arguing that, strictly speaking, the behaviour of managers is not monitored here by the principals, but by the efficient equity market (Putterman 1986: 22).[4]

Yet the residual loss, the divergence from profit maximization, that results from the problem of agency, may still be considerable, depending on the tastes of managers, for example, and on the costs of monitoring and bonding activities. Jensen and Meckling remark that this divergence can further be reduced by the market for managers and by the market for the firm itself, that is by capital markets. Fama (1980) elaborates on this remark. Fama praises Alchian and Demsetz and Jensen and Meckling for having developed the insight that the firm is to be seen as a team whose members act from self-interest. But at the same time these authors are criticized by Fama for sticking to the outdated idea of the entrepreneur, the manager–owner, as the residual claimant who has a special interest in the survival of the team. In Fama's view, there really are no owners of the modern corporation. There are only owners of factors of production. Usually there are a lot of capital owners in each corporation, and usually each capital owner has diversified his or her portfolio across the securities of many corporations. Managers are also to be viewed as owners of a factor of production: of human capital. Fama's point is that managers also have a stake in the success of the corporation. The immediate, short-term interest of managers seems to be to shirk or to consume more perquisites than was agreed to in their labour contracts. This may endanger the corporation's survival. But the success or failure of the corporation is likely to have an impact on their future wages:

> rational managerial labour markets understand any shortcomings of available mechanisms for enforcing ex post settling up. Assessments of ex post deviations from contract will be incorporated into contracts on an ex ante basis; for example, through an adjustment of the manager's wage.
>
> (Fama 1980: 295–6)

In effect Fama argues that even if managers do not own equity claims, and hence are not disciplined by the efficient equity market, the managerial labour market provides a supplementary disciplining device. In case the managerial labour market fails to discipline managers sufficiently, Fama argues, there is still the *discipline of last resort* forced upon managers by the market for outside takeovers. The unrestricted inalienability of the residual claims in open corporations implies that corporations that are managed inefficiently can be taken over by those who believe that they (or some agents who they can appoint) can manage the corporation more efficiently.

The standard reference here is Manne (1965). Manne is convinced that the takeover scheme provides the primary assurance of competitive efficiency among corporate managers. Fama disavows. Fama states that outside takeover is a relatively expensive mechanism. He argues that the markets for the factors of production are the primary disciplining devices. The market for outside takeover comes into play only if these primary devices do not work well.

The same idea of an interplay of multiple markets as mutually re-inforcing disciplining devices reappears in Fama and Jensen (1983a and b). As teams, corporations have to compete with other teams in product markets. Separation of different functions opens up new opportunities for specialization. But at the same time it creates a problem of agency: the interests of the owners of factors of production may diverge. The costs that are associated with this problem are reduced to a minimum by markets of the factors of production. The same markets for the factors of production that enable the owners of the factors to seize the fruits of their special-ization see to it that it is in their own interests to serve the interests of the team as a whole.

It is precisely this line of thought that Williamson objects to. Williamson does not deny that competitive markets lead to efficient results. What he objects to is the idea that firm relations are nothing but a continuation of market relations. Williamson turns back to Coase, by paraphrasing von Clausewitz's famous dictum that 'war is [. . .] a continuation of political relations by other means' (Williamson 1991a: 162). In Williamson's view, firm relations can be said to serve the same function as market relations: economizing on costs. Firm relations have evolved in situations in which market relations would fail to serve this function well; in situations in which market pressure is insufficient to discipline contractants. In this sense, firm relations are a continuation of market relations. But firm relations econo-mize on costs by other means than market relations: by means of fiat.

3. HIERARCHICAL GOVERNANCE STRUCTURES

Although it may be somewhat premature to take stock of the new theory of the firm, it seems that Oliver Williamson's 'transaction costs economics' has won the day.[5] In some respects Williamson's approach is consonant with Alchian and Demsetz' property rights and Jensen and Meckling's (and Fama's) agency costs approach. Williamson also holds that the success of prevailing organization forms is to be accounted for in terms of their efficiency, an efficiency that these forms are assumed to have demonstrated in competition with other forms. In this sense, Williamson is right that property rights, agency costs and transaction costs theorists all belong to the *Efficiency Branch* (see Williamson 1985: 26). But Williamson differs from the theorists discussed above in arguing that Coase was right in pointing at authority and hierarchy as the essential distinguishing features of *intra*firm transactions as opposed to *inter*firm transactions.

As documented in several publications, Williamson's transaction costs economics rests on two behavioural assumptions: *opportunism* and *bounded rationality*. Williamson regards opportunism as an extension of the conventional assumption that economic agents are guided by considerations of self-interest. Opportunistic behaviour often is strategic behaviour in which agents pursue selfish goals with guile. Of special interest are the possible consequences of such opportunistic behaviour in the *post-*contractual period, that is in the period after contracts are signed. Once contracts are signed, it may be tempting for contractants to deviate from what was agreed upon. This may lead to several types of transaction costs. There may be information and monitoring costs involved in the execution and enforcement of contracts, for example.

So far, Williamson's account closely resembles that of the theorists discussed in the previous section. 'Opportunism' and 'transaction costs' are similar, if not identical, to Alchian and Demsetz' 'shirking problem' and 'monitoring costs' and to Jensen and Meckling's 'problem of agency' and 'agency costs'.[6] Or, to put it in Fama's phrase, the problem is how to reduce *ex post* deviations from contract to a minimum. As we have seen, Fama is quite confident that *ex post* deviations are mitigated because actual deviations will be translated into new contracts on an *ex ante* basis. Williamson is much more sceptical about this possibility. Here we arrive at Williamson's second behavioural assumption: bounded rationality precludes the *ex ante* design of complete contracts. Because of the fact that individuals are assumed to be '*intendedly* rational, but only *limitedly* so', they cannot foresee all contingencies that may obtain once contracts are signed. This makes complete (or comprehensive) contracting, which the agency costs theorists rely on, infeasible (see Williamson 1985: 27 and Williamson 1990: 68).

Williamson agrees with the agency costs theorists that opportunism is attenuated in competitive, large-number situations. Opportunistic inclinations will be curtailed then, for there will be competitors waiting in the wings to replace opportunists at contract renewal intervals by bidding at competitive terms. Things are different, however, when there is *asset specificity*. Assets are specific (or specialized) when they cannot be redeployed to alternative uses or by alternative users without sacrificing productive value. Asset specificity can relate both to physical capital that is especially valuable to an organization or to its especially valuable human capital. Whenever there is asset specificity, *ex ante* bidding competition involving large numbers is followed by an *ex post* situation of monopolistic bargaining. This is Williamson's *Fundamental Transformation*:

> a large numbers bidding condition at the outset is effectively trans-formed into one of bilateral supply thereafter.
>
> (Williamson 1985: 61)

It is precisely because of this 'Fundamental Transformation' that oppor-tunism would yield high transaction costs if asset specificity were dealt with in the 'usual' market mode. It may be in the interest of all parties then, both of those owning the specialized assets and of those buying or renting the assets, to join each other in *vertical integration*.

This is the main thesis also in Klein *et al.* (1978). They also stress the ('contracting') costs, due to post-contractual opportunistic behaviour, of using the market system when there is asset specificity. The contracting costs that are at stake here do not relate to the transaction and information costs of reaching agreements, but to the enforcement costs involved in assuring compliance with the agreements. For when assets are specialized, it is tempting for both contractants to renege on the initial contract. The owner of the assets may try to get a higher rental price while the renting contractant may try to get a lower rental price than specified in the initial contract. They have the opportunity to do so because they are in a sense wedded to each other in the post-contractual period. Or, as Williamson puts it, a situation of *bi*lateral dependency emerges after the contracts are signed.

Klein *et al.* argue that there may be appropriable *quasi rents* then to both contractants. Quasi rents are not to be confused with monopoly rents. There are appropriable monopoly rents when market *entry* is barred or at least restricted. Appropriable quasi rents occur when specialized assets, once installed with a particular user, can be transferred to some other user only at high cost.

As Williamson observes, this is a special case of *sunk costs*. The presence of sunk costs implies that *exit* is costly, and, in Baumol's (1982) vocabulary, that the prevailing market structure is not *contestable*. Baumol's notion of a contestable market entails that exit is absolutely costless (and entry ab-solutely free). It is argued by Baumol that his notion of a contestable market provides a generalization of the notion of the perfectly competitive market. Firms need not be small or numerous, for example, for markets to be contestable. What is crucial is that firms in contestable markets are vul-nerable to 'hit-and-run' entry because entry is absolutely free and exit absolutely costless. This ensures that the domain in which Smith's invisible hand holds sway is not restricted to the domain that is specified by the notion of the perfectly competitive market, but is extended to the domain that is specified by the notion of the contestable market.

If Williamson and Klein *et al.* are right, the transformation of an *ex ante* contestable market situation into an *ex post* uncontestable one (when there is asset specificity) implies that in the post-contractual period the contractants are not vulnerable to hit-and-run entry. In other words, the contractants are shielded to some extent from effective market pressure. Besides effective market pressure, the replacement of market contracts by vertical integration is an efficient way to suppress the opportunistic inclinations of both parties. Efficiency is enhanced when 'the invisible hand' is supplanted by 'the visible hand'; when spontaneous market governance is replaced by hierarchical governance.[7] A point that is also emphasized by Williamson is that public courts are not the only courts of appeal when conflicts arise within organizations. Public courts may not even be accessible to settle some intraorganizational disputes like disputes between one internal division and another. It is characteristic of organizations that they entail *private* orderings that are their own court of appeal for the settlement of conflicts and disputes.[8]

Likewise, external capital and labour markets are supplemented by internal markets in hierarchical organizations. Again the main idea is that because external capital and labour markets cannot prevent costly opportunistic behaviour from happening (in post-contractual intervals when there is asset specificity), internal markets as intraorganizational devices have arisen as an extra safeguard to economize on transaction costs. One of the main advantages of the *M-form* (multi-divisional) firm over the *U-form* (large, functionally organized) firm is precisely that the former takes over the key disciplining function of the external capital market in situations where the latter fails to perform this function well.[9] As Williamson (1975) argues, the M-form firm can itself be regarded as a miniature capital market. The general management in M-form firms can allocate capital more efficiently over the divisions than the external capital market could have done, because the general management has more means of detecting and punishing opportunistic behaviour (of division managers, for example) than outsiders.

It seems that Williamson's elaboration of Coase's (1937) insight that there is conscious control involved in handling intraorganizational transactions is generally acknowledged and accepted nowadays. The thesis of property rights and agency costs theorists that contracts among members of an organization do not differ in kind from spot market contracts, seems to be rejected. There seems to be a *communis opinio* that intraorganizational relations are long term rather than short term. But beyond this shared understanding there seem to be several disagreements left. To name just a few: what is the precise nature of intraorganizational contracts (and contract laws)?[10] Are transaction costs the most important category of costs that are economized on in organizations (see, for example, Demsetz 1991)?[11] Is asset specificity as crucial in explaining hierarchies as Williamson supposes it to be (see Coase 1991)? I will not go into these questions here. Rather than dealing with disagreements, I will focus on the theoretical suppositions that the approaches discussed so far seem to have in common.

4. 'SURVIVAL OF THE FITTEST' AS A USEFUL TAUTOLOGY

Jensen (1983) argues that the choice of tautologies and definitions is of crucial importance in the early stages of research. It is said to have a large impact on the success or failure of further research efforts. Jensen points at two tautologies that in his opinion are solid building blocks for creating a theory of organizations: 'agency costs are minimized' and 'survival of the fittest'. Before I discuss these 'tautologies' in detail, some remarks will be made as to how tautologies can serve as building blocks for a positive, empirical theory of organizations.

For an elaboration of his view that the choice of tautologies and definitions may determine whether research is successful, Jensen refers to Whitehead and Russell's *Principia Mathematica* (1910). At first sight, this work does not seem to be especially suited to make Jensen's point. For Whitehead and Russell subscribe to the logical positivist doctrine that tautologies are analytic statements that are devoid of empirical content. According to the logical positivists, tautologies have nothing to say about states of affairs in reality. Tautologies are always true, irrespective of the prevailing state of affairs. They are true by virtue of their grammatical form (as in 'it either rains or it does not rain') or by virtue of the meanings of the concepts that are expressed (as in 'squares are rectangular'). From a logical positivist standpoint, the problem with the view that tautologies can be building blocks for a positive, empirical theory is that in a positive, empirical theory synthetic statements must be expressed that do have empirical content.[12] It is only synthetic statements that can tell us something about states of affairs in reality. How then can synthetic statements be based on (or erected upon) empirically empty tautologies?

Not surprisingly, Jensen concentrates on Whitehead and Russell's remarks on definitions. Whitehead and Russell note that although definitions are theoretically superfluous, they often convey important information. First of all, the *definiens* (the concepts that are used to define the *definiendum*, the concept to be defined) indicates what subjects are taken to be worthy of careful consideration. Furthermore, a definition may give definite meaning to an already familiar idea that previously was more or less vague. Probably, Jensen takes his own definition of an organization as a 'legal entity that serves as a nexus for a complex set of contracts (written and unwritten) among disparate individuals' (Jensen 1983: 326) as an illustration of 'making definite' a familiar notion. What interests me more here is the first sense in which a definition is said to convey important information. Jensen's own definition suggests that the subjects worthy of careful consideration when studying organizations are nexuses of contracts. But this tells us neither what kinds of nexuses are to be considered nor how they are to be studied. I believe that the two 'tautologies' that are already mentioned provide the answer to these questions.

Jensen seems to consider his first 'tautology', that agency costs are minimized, as an implication of another 'tautology' that is standard in economic theory: individuals are utility maximizers. Jensen does not explain why the latter is a tautology. But it seems safe to assume that his reason for believing so is that any (consistent) individual behaviour can be 'rationalized' by ascribing some utility function to the individual. As Becker (1957) has shown, seemingly irrational behaviour can be accounted for in terms of rational, utility-maximizing action by assuming that individuals have utility functions with several components (like pecuniary and non-pecuniary gains). Presumably Jensen thinks of analyses like Becker's when he argues that 'individuals are utility maximizers' is a tautology that has proved useful in understanding human behaviour and markets. The usefulness of the tautology apparently depends crucially on how skilfully the specification of the utility functions (and the opportunity sets) is made. Jensen and Meckling's specifications of the utility functions of principals and agents allow them to conclude that agency costs are minimized:

> Recognizing that one or more of the contracting parties can capture the benefits from reducing the agency costs in any relationship provides the analytical device, the tautology, that yields implications for the forms of the contracts that evolve – maximizing agents minimize the agency costs in any contracting relationship.
>
> (Jensen and Meckling 1976: 331)

Jensen's reason for believing that 'survival of the fittest' is a tautology is straightforward: 'because the fit is defined to be that which survives' (Jensen 1983: 330). If this is correct,[13] the problem with this tautology as a building block of a positive theory is, I gather, that, as it stands, it is uninformative. First of all, it does not tell us what surviving phenomena to look for. Numerous phenomena exist and persist, but which phenomena deserve our special attention? And, second, it does not say anything about the phenomena except that they have survived. It gives us no clue as to what features are responsible for their survival. For the purpose of developing a positive theory of organization, Jensen argues that the phenomena that merit our special attention are organizational forms and that the organizational forms that survive do so because they are efficient, that is cost minimizing:

competition is a general phenomenon that takes place over many dimensions, including organizational form [. . .]. Those organizations survive that are able to deliver the activities or products at the lowest price while covering costs. Understanding the survival process involves understanding how the contracts of particular organizations achieve low cost control of agency problems and how they combine with the production technology of an activity to enable the organization to survive.

(Jensen 1983: 331–2)

It seems that the empirical content that Jensen gives to the two tautologies ensures that they both lead independently of each other to the same result: organizational forms prevail that minimize agency costs. If this is the case, why does Jensen need two tautologies instead of one? If maximizing individuals are capable of devising contracting relations that minimize agency costs, then references to survival processes seem to be redundant. What I want to argue here is that if there is a tautology that is redundant, it is rather the first one, that individuals are utility maximizers. Or, to put it more accurately, Jensen assumes that individuals are capable of arriving at cost-minimizing relationships because they too (and not only the organizations of which they are part) are involved in survival processes.

When writing about survival processes in economies, Jensen refers to Alchian (1950) 'for the use of the natural selection principle in economic analysis' (Jensen 1983: 331). But Alchian (1950) is also referred to when Jensen discusses the status of the 'utility-maximizing' assumption in positive economic theory. Jensen argues that individuals need not consciously carry out the 'maximization' calculations that are attributed to them in economic theory. Individuals need not even be engaged in purposeful action at all. They may randomly choose actions. The only condition for the 'maximizing' assumption to be applicable is that markets are competitive:

Suppose [also] that the environment rewards with survival those who happen to select strategies that are closer to optimal and grants extinction to those who are unlucky enough to choose dominated strategies or actions. In such an environment, observed behaviour and institutions will tend toward the optimal because those far from it will continually tend towards extinction.

(Jensen 1983: 322)

In section 2 we have seen that Jensen, Meckling and Fama assume that all agents are disciplined by a variety of competitive markets. Hence, *given* the competitive pressure imposed on agents, Jensen relies on Alchian's argument in assuming that the agents' observed behaviour is close to optimal, utility-maximizing behaviour.[14]

We are now in a position to reconstruct the role that Jensen's 'tautologies' play in the development of his positive theory of organization. The 'tautology' of the survival of the fittest serves to identify the *explananda*, the phenomena to be explained, in Jensen's theory of organizations. What has to be explained are the organizational forms that have proved to have survival value, that can be observed frequently over a considerable period of time. What is more, the explanations given must come to terms with what is implied in both 'tautologies': that the organizational forms to be explained are *efficient*. In other words, the two tautologies not only define the research agenda of the theory of organizations, they also delineate the type of explanation that is regarded as 'admissible'.

Thus understood, Jensen's definitions and tautologies show some resemblance with 'hard core' propositions in Lakatos' methodology of scientific research programmes. Jensen's definitions and tautologies imply both 'positive heuristics' and 'negative heuristics'. They indicate not only the kind of phenomena to address, but also the way to proceed when tackling them. The two tautologies suggest that the 'proper' task of researchers is 'to develop propositions about the important aspects of the environment and their relation to traits contributing to survival' (Jensen 1983: 331). Jensen's remarks about the success and fruitfulness of further research can be rephrased in Lakatos' terms of the theoretical and empirical progressiveness of a research programme. Just like Lakatos does Jensen insist that a theory of organization must have refutable implications. The propositions to be developed must enable researchers to make qualitative predictions about what types of organizational forms are likely to survive in different environmental circumstances. In the end, the 'fate' of Jensen's building blocks depends on the predictive power of the theory that can be built on them.

As to the 'negative heuristics', it seems that Jensen wants to cling to his conventional economic building blocks as long as possible. Why subvert to *ad hoc* theorizing, Jensen seems to think, when the analytical framework of economic theory seems flexible enough to deal with organizational forms? It may turn out that this 'conventional' economic approach is not fruitful, but only after this has become clear does it make sense to have recourse to altogether different core propositions. So Jensen does not want to rule out the possibility that the two 'tautologies' happen to be unsuccessful building blocks. They may have to be replaced by others. But what Jensen does not question is that his building blocks are true. They can be an inappropriate starting point for further research, but they cannot possibly be false.

In sum, the research programme that Jensen advocates can be characterized as follows. Research should focus on organizational forms that are quite common. The fact that they are quite common is taken to testify to their efficiency. They are assumed to have proved their efficiency in survival processes that go on in competitive markets. The first task to be carried out is to figure out what features of the forms are responsible for their efficiency. Once this first task is fulfilled, the second task is to derive refutable implications concerning the organizational forms that are expected to evolve in different environmental settings. The work of Alchian and Demsetz, Jensen and Meckling (and Fama), and Williamson can all be said to be part of this research programme.[15]

Alchian and Demsetz (1972) try to explain the success of the traditional capitalist firm. To them, teamwork is one of the distinctive features of firm-like organizations in general. In principle, teamwork allows for efficiency advantages, but the problem is that teamwork invites shirking because, as Demsetz puts it, 'the revenues of the firm must be shared by the various owners of inputs used by the firm without the full guidance or protection normally offered by intervening competitive markets' (Demsetz 1988: 153–4). The solution that the capitalist firm offers is that the controllers are made the residual claimants. In effect, this means that the controllers are controlled by competitive markets. Jensen and Meckling's (1976) attempt to explain the success of the giant corporation is very similar. The separation of ownership and control can be regarded as an example of the division of labour with potential efficiency advantages. The problem is that managerial discretion leads to agency costs. The 'puzzle' that Jensen and Meckling try to solve is: 'Why, given the existence of positive costs of the agency relationship, do we find the usual corporate form of organization with widely diffuse ownership so widely prevalent?' (Jensen and Meckling 1976: 330). The solution that the corporation offers is that the separation of ownership and control leads to a multiplication of competitive markets (among them the capital market and the market for managers) that see to it that the advantages of the division of labour are secured at minimal cost.

In the analyses of Alchian, Demsetz, Jensen, Meckling and Fama, the agents are disciplined ultimately by an interplay of competitive markets. Williamson's account of vertical integration differs from theirs in that he argues that vertical integration evolves when there is asset specificity precisely because competitive market pressure is relieved (or may even fall away) in contract execution and renewal. Firm-like organization does not lead to new external market pressure. Quite to the contrary, firm-like organization entails internal governance structures that replace external market governance. But Williamson also seems to subscribe to the idea that the evolving organization forms are efficient. He is part of the *Efficiency Branch* (as he calls it) as well. The governance structures that can be observed are efficient not just because the individuals involved are assumed to be pursuing efficiency. After all, the actions of individuals may have unintended and possibly counterproductive consequences. The structures are efficient first and foremost because they have proven to be so in competition with other structures in the market. The organization forms that manage to produce at low *costs* (including notably transaction costs) are assumed to outcompete and to supplant forms that produce at higher costs. To put it somewhat paradoxically, the organization forms that emerge because (after the 'Fundamental Transformation') market pressure is insufficient to curtail opportunism, must demonstrate their efficiency in competitive markets.

What all the authors of the new theory of the firm discussed here have in common is the idea that prevailing types of organization forms are so common because they have proven their efficiency in 'survival processes' in competitive (or contestable) markets. This idea is one of the hard core propositions, if not *the* core proposition, that characterize their shared research programme. The fact that Jensen speaks in terms of tautologies clearly suggests that he takes its truth to be self-evident. Yet part of the criticism of the new theory of the firm (voiced especially by non-economists and economists alike) has challenged this idea. In the next section, I will discuss two papers in which this type of criticism is related to the charge of 'Panglossian functionalism'.

5. THE EVOLUTION OF EFFICIENT ORGANIZATION FORMS

The sociologist Granovetter (1985) argues that the 'tone' of the 'new institutional economics' is similar to that of 'structural–functional sociology of the 1940s to the 1960s'. According to Granovetter, the general story told by members of the school of new institutional economics is that:

> social institutions and arrangements previously thought to be the adventitious result of legal, historical, social or political forces are better viewed as the efficient solution to certain economic problems.
> (Granovetter 1985: 488)

Granovetter ranks Alchian and Demsetz and the game theorist Schotter among the members of this school. But Granovetter's main target is Williamson. Granovetter focuses on the functionalism implicit in Williamson's assumption that 'whatever organization form is most efficient will be the one observed' (Granovetter 1985: 503). Granovetter argues that as it stands this assumption is unwarranted. Williamson invokes Darwinian arguments to substantiate this assumption, but he does so in a 'cavalier fashion': 'the operation of alleged selection pressures is here neither an object of study nor even a falsifiable proposition but rather an article of faith' (ibid.). Treating Darwinian arguments in this way leads to a 'Panglossian view' according to which all institutions and arrangements that exist are elevated to the status of the best possible ones.

Although the economist Dow (1987) makes no reference to Granovetter (1985), his criticism of Williamson shows a striking similarity with

Granovetter's. Dow also objects to the inference that Williamson makes from existence to efficiency. By itself mere existence does not testify to efficiency, Dow argues. Williamson's functionalism is said to be deficient because it lacks a 'causal grounding'. Williamson does not offer a causal account of the emergence of organization forms, in which it is shown that the organization forms that exist are efficient. According to Dow, three arguments can be traced in Williamson's writings that could in principle provide the required causal account. The first argument relies on the 'intentionality' of the individuals involved. This argument in effect says that efficient organization forms emerge because individuals designed them to be efficient. As Dow points out, however, this argument does not square with Williamson's emphasis on bounded rationality:

> if agents cannot cope with contracts featuring complex contingencies [. . .], it is doubtful that they can select in advance an efficient decision making procedure to use in adapting to future circumstances.
>
> (Dow 1987: 27)

The second argument that could provide the required causal grounding is based on 'organizational learning'. Individuals cannot foresee all complex contingencies in the future. But they can learn from the experience that accumulates within an organization over time, so that, in the end, they could arrive at an efficient adaptation to the organization's environment. Dow mentions several problems with this argument, one of which seems to be implied in Williamson's assumption of opportunism: 'the information which is needed for adaptation may be suppressed or distorted by organizational participants, and those who have the authority to restructure the organization may suffer from opportunistic propensities' (Dow 1987: 29).

This leaves us with the third and last argument. This argument refers to 'competitive market pressures'. Here we come to Williamson's Darwinian argument already hinted at by Granovetter: market competition considered as a suitable analogue to natural selection. Dow argues that this analogue can be elaborated upon in two distinct claims:

> (a) that competition from successful firms will induce imitation and learning among others, encouraging the diffusion of efficient organizational forms, or
> (b) that firms with efficient structures will simply eliminate firms having inefficient ones.
>
> (Dow 1987: 30)

Dow remarks that both claims are used by Williamson to explain the spread of the multi-divisional structure.

Dow sets out to argue that this third argument is not convincing either. One of his points is that a more explicit treatment of selection processes may reveal that selection outcomes can be *in*efficient. This would run counter to the 'Panglossian logic' that Dow takes Williamson to share with Jensen and Meckling: what exists (that is, what is selected) must be efficient. Dow makes his point by assuming that just as in natural selection the units which are selected are not organizations as a whole but their individual members. If this assumption is correct, then what is relevant in selection processes is not only the aggregate transaction costs of a governance structure (as Williamson tacitly assumes), but also the distribution of these costs (and the benefits of economizing on them) among agents.

Dow suggests that taking the latter into account may explain why capital-managed firms (CMFs) survive even though labour-managed firms (LMFs) may be more efficient. For if we assume that the governance benefits of any structure, CMF or LMF, flow to the agents who have managerial authority in that structure, the few managers of CMFs may outcompete the many 'managers' of LMFs even when the latter have a higher (aggregate) sum to share. Appropriation differences in CMFs and LMFs may thus break the link between (aggregate) efficiency and selection results.

Williamson has replied both to Granovetter and to Dow. Although Williamson does not deny that there are instances of functionalism to be found in his work, he accuses Granovetter and Dow of downplaying the important role that intentionality plays in his account of the emergence of governance structures. Williamson emphasizes that his claim that departures from the classical market exchange model serve economizing purposes is based first and foremost on the behavioural assumption that individuals wish to behave economically. Individuals try to seize cost-saving opportunities whenever they show up. The assumption of bounded rationality, Williamson argues, does not diminish the role that is played by intentionality. In Williamson's account, bounded rationality refers to behaviour that is '*intendedly* rational, but only *limitedly* so' (Williamson 1987: 618). 'Bounded rationality' does not imply myopia. Boundedly rational individuals can be farsighted (see Williamson 1991b: 174). Williamson also argues that the assumption of bounded rationality does not imply satisficing behaviour. He accepts the former notion but rejects the latter (see Williamson 1991a: 92). Bounded rationality is said to appeal to economics, whereas satisficing is said to imply irrationality and to appeal to psychology.

According to Williamson, what is implied in the notion of bounded rationality is only that all forms of comprehensive (or complete) contracting are infeasible. This is why *ex post* governance is necessary: *ex ante* agreement cannot sufficiently attenuate opportunism in contract execution and renewal stages. To Williamson, the limitations that are entailed in the notion of bounded rationality do not seem to pertain to the choice of a *particular* efficient governance structure. Dow's criticism at this point is that if individuals cannot draw comprehensive contracts because they cannot foresee future contingencies, then it is unlikely that they can know in advance that some governance structure will be the most efficient one. Williamson seems to hold that individuals are capable of foreseeing this. Williamson's boundedly rational individuals do not seem to be so limited after all!

This impression seems to be confirmed in Williamson (1991a). Here, Williamson argues that although 'thin' rational accounts carry the day, there is a need for developing 'thick' rational accounts. Williamson associates thin rational accounts with accounts in which the efficacy of spontaneous 'hands-off' governance in market economies is emphasized. On the other hand, thick rationality is associated with intentional (hierarchical) 'hands-on' governance. As Williamson observes, the association of thin rationality with a plea for spontaneous governance can perhaps be seen most clearly in Hayek's work. Hayek's celebrated argument for free market economies is that free markets utilize 'dispersed' information most efficiently. Central planning is inferior, because the central planning agency can gather the required dispersed information only at high cost (if it can gather the required information at all). Williamson does not want to challenge Hayek's argument for the efficacy of spontaneous governance. But he argues that partly because of the influence of the Hayekian argument the importance of intentional governance within organizations tends to be undervalued in the economics profession.

What Williamson does not point out, however, is how intentional governance relates to thick rationality. The foregoing discussion suggests that Williamson holds that at least within firms the 'private governments' can gather all the information that is needed to design the optimally efficient organization form. Yet this is not borne out by reading the remainder of his paper. It turns out that Williamson criticizes accounts of firm-like phenomena in terms of spontaneous governance precisely for being based on assumptions of *hyper*rationality. Many 'thin' accounts are said to be infeasible 'in that they place impossible demands on bounded rationality' (Williamson 1991b: 160). In particular, game-theoretic accounts of reputation-building and organizational culture are dismissed because their assumption of 'common knowledge' is said to be too expansive. Apparently, then, in Williamson's view the assumption of 'thick rationality' has a peculiar meaning. It does not imply that individuals have all the relevant information (which would allow them to make optimal choices). It implies that in private governance structures some individuals have the authority to make decisions that other individuals have to obey.[16]

We can safely conclude, therefore, that in Williamson's view individuals do not and cannot foresee what specific governance structure will be most efficient. True, it is assumed that individuals intend to bring about efficient structures. But their information and knowledge may fall short of singling out the most efficient ones. It is possible that some of them are convinced that they have spotted efficient structures. And maybe they do actually hit upon them. But it is also possible that structures that appear to be efficient turn out to be not as efficient as was hoped for. Williamson acknowledges that there may be *unanticipated* consequences of intentional actions. He argues that his behavioural framework allows for the analysis of such consequences:

> the bounded rationality/opportunism framework comes to terms easily with and helps to inform the study of unintended consequences. Regimes of hyperrationality and promise, by contrast, disallow these or regard unintended outcomes as aberrations.
>
> (Williamson 1988: 166)

It is also possible that none of the individuals involved perceive of opportunities that are, in principle, open to them, or that they fail to respond faultlessly to them. As Granovetter rightly observes, this is exactly where selection arguments come in in Williamson's account. Given the infeasibility of infallible decision making, what is and what is not efficient is decided upon by market selection. Under competitive market pressure, efficient organization forms are assumed to drive out inefficient ones. Williamson emphasizes that what survives and what is driven out of existence depends on the organization forms that are *actually tried*. Following Simon (1983), he argues that only a weak form of selectionism is tenable. A strong form of selectionism would hold that the most efficient form possible will of necessity be established. Weak-form selectionism entails 'survival of the *fitter*', not 'survival of the *fittest*'. It is on this ground that Williamson can legitimately disqualify references to Panglossianism as a 'red herring' (see Williamson 1987: 623).[17]

In my opinion, the charge of Panglossianism is more appropriate to property rights and agency costs theorists. They seem to endorse strong-form selectionism: it is the most efficient organization forms that survive. Demsetz (1967) argues, for example, that new property rights can be expected to emerge when new opportunities arise because of changes in technology or market values. The existing regime of property rights determines the gains of trade that can be made at that time, but if there are potential additional benefits to be gained by introducing new rights, the new rights are likely to be established: 'property rights develop to internalize externalities' (Demsetz 1967: 350). Likewise, Jensen and Meckling (1976) seem pretty sure that the most efficient organization forms come about:

> If we could establish the existence of a feasible set of alternative institutional arrangements which would yield net benefits from the reduction of these costs [i.e. agency costs, JJV] we could legitimately conclude the agency relationship engendered by the corporation was

not Pareto optimal. However, we would then be left with the problem of explaining why these alternative institutional arrangements have not replaced the corporate form of organization.

(Jensen and Meckling 1976: 328, footnote 28)

Apparently, Jensen and Meckling take the prevalence of the corporate organization form as evidence for its efficiency. If some other feasible organization form were more efficient, so it is argued, it would certainly have supplanted the corporate form. It can therefore be concluded that, contrary to Williamson, Demsetz and Jensen and Meckling seem to rule out the possibility that hitherto unperceived opportunities remain unperceived and hence untried.

Williamson holds that market selection ensures that the most efficient structure that is tried will be the one that is prevalent. He does not hold that market selection ensures that the ideally efficient structure is among those that are tried. But exactly how are less efficient structures replaced by more efficient ones in the process of market selection? Williamson (1988) gives an illustration of this process in a discussion of the replacement of the U-form firm by the M-form.

Williamson follows Chandler (1962) in arguing that the M-form innovation was developed mainly to lessen the administrative and communication overload on the senior executives in the U-form. The innovators hoped to create an organization form that would enable the executives to handle their entrepreneurial responsibilities more efficiently. In Williamson's vocabulary they tried to economize on bounded rationality. They succeeded. The innovators can therefore be said to have anticipated these consequences correctly. The results were even better than they expected them to be. According to Williamson, this was due to the fact that their innovation in addition had beneficial unexpected and unanticipated consequences: it attenuated subgoal pursuit. This meant that opportunism was reduced. Once the success of the M-form innovation was appreciated, it became clear to many also that this structure could be used to support the *takeover* of firms in which managerial discretion excesses were occurring. Thus formerly inefficient independent firms were incorporated as divisions in larger encompassing and more efficient M-form firms. Resources were shifted to more efficient modes. Takeover, as a selection mechanism, lead to a rapid spread of the M-form over the economy.

Williamson cherishes this account of the spread of the M-form firm as one of the rare satisfactory instances of functional explanation in social science. Williamson claims that his account fulfils all the conditions of 'full functionalism' that are stated in Elster (1983). In Chapter 4, I will deal more extensively with this claim. For now, it is sufficient to note that Williamson strongly recommends economists to engage in process analyses of this type. He concedes to sociologists like Granovetter that the importance of process to economic organization is widely neglected and undervalued by economists. Economists are urged to go beyond 'structure and incentive and control instruments' (Williamson 1988: 163). Greater attention to the 'spontaneous process of organization', Williamson argues, is sorely needed. In Williamson's view, his account of the replacement of the U-form by the M-form contains the essential ingredients of process analysis: intentional, purposeful innovation, the possible occurrence of unintended consequences (either beneficial or harmful) and the working of selection mechanisms.

The importance of further study of the last ingredient, selection processes, is stressed especially by Williamson. Williamson acknowledges that his transaction cost approach relies in a background way on the efficacy of market selection (see Williamson 1985: 22–3). He refers to Nelson and Winter (1982) as a valuable study of market selection. But their work is not the end of the story:

> To be sure, a more well-developed theory of weak-form selection – when it works well and poorly – is greatly needed. The important work of Richard Nelson and Sidney Winter notwithstanding, much remains to be done to assess the efficacy of the selection process.
> (Williamson 1988: 177)

Williamson does not seem to dispute Nelson and Winter's assumption that market selection works upon firms. In Williamson's view, selection sees to it that firms with less efficient organization forms give way to firms with more efficient forms. Therefore, Dow's 'appropriability' critique, which is based on the assumption that selection works upon individual agents (managers, to be more precise), seems to be misplaced. Maybe Dow is right that it should be investigated which individual agents bear the (reduction in) transaction costs. Maybe the distribution of these costs among the individuals involved affects the organization forms that come about.[18] But this does not mean that it is the performances of individual agents that are decisive in the market selection of organization forms. It is the 'aggregate' performance of the comprising firms that is decisive.

Williamson does not want to rule out the possibility that Dow is right in his general point that less efficient (instead of more efficient) organization forms can be selected. But again he argues that only further study can settle the issue:

> transaction cost economics . . . asks that selection arguments be applied symmetrically. If efficiency outcomes are purportedly defeated, what is the selection process by which this defeat is realized?
> (Williamson 1987: 623)

6. CONCLUSIONS

In Chapter 2, we have seen that the selection arguments advanced by Alchian, Friedman and Becker were meant to show that neoclassical theorems hold even if firms are not profit maximizers. Entrepreneurs need not have the information and foresight that are required for profit maximization. 'Natural selection' in competitive markets will see to it that the tendencies in industry behaviour that are predicted in neoclassical theory are forthcoming anyway. I have argued in Chapter 2 that the validity of this argument is far from self-evident.

In this chapter we have seen, however, that pioneers of the new theory of the firm take the validity of the selection argument for granted. They proceed from the assumption that as competitive markets select for the most efficient organization forms, prevalent organizations are efficient. The individuals involved in organization need not have known in advance what organization form was efficient; market selection takes care of it in that inefficient forms are eliminated in due time. I have argued that this assumption, 'widely observed organization forms are efficient because they are selected for', can be regarded as a hard core proposition in the research programme of the new theory of the firm. I venture that this proposition lies at the heart of the new theory of the firm that is discussed here. It determines the identity of the basic research programme of which the two distinct approaches discussed are offshoots.

We have seen that there are non-negligible differences between the approaches. Proponents of the property rights and agency costs approach argue that certain organization forms are very common because they have led to new markets and, hence, to an amplification of market pressure. On the other hand, Williamson holds that organizations as hierarchies imply a departure of the 'classical norm' of market exchange. Rather than multiplying markets, hierarchies replace markets. But this does not mean that Williamson questions that competitive markets select efficient organization forms.[19] Quite to the contrary, in his view hierarchies have evolved precisely (*and could have evolved only*) in situations in which market pressure is relieved. And, again, competitive productive markets are assumed to select the most efficient types of hierarchies.

It is demanded by all that the hard core proposition should yield not only explanations of commonly observed organization forms, but also qualitative refutable implications. Not only should specific features of common forms be identified that ensure their success in certain environmental circumstances, it should also be possible on the basis of the core proposition to predict what particular form is to be expected in some circumstances. Or, to use Williamson's words, theories in this programme should assign transactions to governance structures in discriminating ways (depending on environmental circumstances). The predictions that could be made then should be borne out by the facts. In other words, the core proposition should be fruitful in the Lakatosian sense of being theoretically and empirically progressive.

This also explains why Williamson presses his critics to develop alternative '*main case*' propositions. Williamson expresses his own main case proposition as follows:

> economic organization has the main purpose and effect of economizing on transaction costs. According to this hypothesis, governance structures are aligned with transactions in such a way as to effect a transaction cost economizing result.
>
> (Williamson 1993: 17)

Transaction cost economics predicts that economic organization is adapted to prevailing environmental circumstances. Williamson argues that instead of raising 'isolated' objections, critics would do better to develop competing research programmes and derive refutable implications from them. As Williamson puts it, it takes a theory to beat a theory.[20]

It would have been perfectly in accordance with the Lakatosian framework if Williamson had left it at that. Hard core propositions of a research programme are not to be criticized directly, on their truthfulness or falsity, but only indirectly, on their theoretical and empirical progressiveness. Hence, it would have been legitimate for Williamson just to challenge his critics to show that they can produce better explanations and predictions, without giving any further defence of his own core (main case) proposition. This is not what Williamson did, however.[21] Williamson seems to concede to his critics that a direct substantiation is required of his main case proposition. Apparently, Williamson is not as confident that he is on the right track as theorists like Jensen. He grants that his transaction cost economics is open to the same objections that evolutionary economists such as Nelson and Winter (1982) have made of orthodoxy. Let us have a closer look at Nelson and Winter's work, then, and see what they have to say about orthodox economic theory.

4

MODELLING THE SELECTION ARGUMENT

Nelson and Winter's evolutionary theory

Evolutionary Economics relates to Armen Alchian's classic paper, 'Uncertainty, Evolution and Economic Theory', in much the same way that transaction cost economics relates to Coase and 'The Nature of the Firm'.

(Winter 1991: 186–7)

1. INTRODUCTION

In Chapter 2 I argued that Alchian, Friedman and Becker advanced natural selection arguments in order to defend marginal analysis in general, and the neoclassical theory of the firm in particular, against antimarginalist criticisms. I pointed out that they all argued for the so-called ultimate claim: the tendencies in industry behaviour that are predicted by neoclassical theory come about even if its assumption of 'profit maximization' is false. Friedman is the only one who argued also for the 'intermediate claim': surviving firms display behaviour that is consistent with 'profit maximization' even if this assumption is false. In Chapter 3 we have seen that pioneers of the new theory of the firm are engaged in a research programme that is characterized by its 'hard core' proposition that prevailing organization forms are efficient. In turn, this hard core proposition was seen to be based on a variant of Friedman's claim: even if those who introduced organization forms did not know (and perhaps could not have known) in advance what forms would be efficient, economic 'natural selection' in competitive markets has seen to it that efficient organization forms survive.

Winter (1964) is generally acknowledged to contain a thorough and systematic examination of Friedman's selection argument. Many commentators take it that Winter offers a conclusive refutation of his argument. What is more, Winter's later work with Nelson, culminating in Nelson and Winter (1982), is praised by some for its sustained criticism of the theoretical foundations of 'orthodox' neoclassical theory. The foundations of Nelson and Winter's own evolutionary theory are considered to be far more realistic than, and at any rate radically different from, those of neoclassical theory. No doubt, Nelson and Winter's professed self-understanding has contributed to this popular view. Their discussions of 'orthodox' theory often have an overtly hostile tone. They present their own foundations in opposition to those of orthodoxy and argue that theirs are more realistic.

In contrast to this popular understanding, I shall argue that Nelson and Winter's evolutionary theory is better viewed as an explication and extension of the basic beliefs of 'orthodox' theorists such as Alchian and Friedman. These basic beliefs pertain especially to the adjustment processes industries are supposed to go through when their environment changes. The mechanisms that are supposed to produce adjustment processes in competitive markets are modelled explicitly by Nelson and Winter. Their denunciation of neoclassical theory notwithstanding,[1] the results that Nelson and Winter derive from their models will be shown (in section 2) to be compatible rather than conflicting with both the intermediate and the ultimate claim. This is not to say, however, that Nelson and Winter's criticism of selection arguments has no bite. Their qualifications to and objections against the argument are convincing. But they do not follow from their formal models. They follow from informally stated arguments that can be regarded also as extensions of qualifications that were already acknowledged by Alchian (and others).

In section 3, I shall argue that the theoretical foundations of Nelson and Winter's own evolutionary theory are consonant with what Nelson and Winter call 'orthodox *appreciative* theory'. Nelson and Winter distinguish orthodox appreciative theory, which is an informal 'theory' about dynamic processes in competitive markets, from textbook orthodox formal theory, which deals with (comparative) statics. We will see that in Winter's writings, emphasis has shifted from 'natural selection' to routine firm behaviour as the cornerstone of his evolutionary perspective. In 'Organizational genetics' (section 4), I shall discuss Nelson and Winter's central claim that firms' prevailing routines are relatively rigid over time, so that they can be treated as the economic counterparts of genes. What evolves in Nelson and Winter's evolutionary theory will be seen to be routines and not organization forms (as is assumed in the new theory of the firm). Nelson and Winter's distinction between 'inert' routine behaviour and flexible deliberate choice is dealt with in section 5. Drawing on Nelson and Winter's own remarks on satisficing and learning rules, I shall introduce several conceptual distinctions to point out that following fixed behavioural rules can lead to flexible, and even optimally flexible, behaviour. In section 6, Nelson and Winter's claim will be discussed that firm behaviour that is consistent over time can better be modelled in terms of routines than in ('orthodox') terms of maximizing choice. I shall argue that the only cogent reason they come up with is that when behaviour is analysed in terms of routines, it is not assumed from the outset that firms respond instantaneously and optimally to environmental changes.

2. A SYSTEMATIC EXAMINATION OF THE SELECTION ARGUMENT

Nelson and Winter's (1982) treatment of the selection argument (in their chapter 6, 'Static Selection Equilibrium') draws heavily on Winter (1964) which is a sustained attempt to examine the validity and significance of the selection argument in a systematic rather than in an *ad hoc* way.[2] According to Winter, it was Friedman's intention to discourage a careful examination of the argument. In Winter's opinion, however:

> something more than a wave of the hand is needed to establish the scope and degree of the support that selection considerations afford to traditional theory. The problem is complex enough to make formal, rigorous analysis a virtual necessity if crucial assumptions are not to remain implicit.
>
> (Winter 1964: 245)

Winter develops a simple set-theoretic model to assess Friedman's argument. He arrives at the conclusion that the argument gives *qualified* support to traditional theory *only*. This result is not proven formally from the model, however. Winter merely asserts, but correctly, I think, that the variables in the model, notably the initial state of the world and the decision rules that are followed by existing firms, can be given specifications for which the argument does not support traditional theory. In this section, I shall argue that the same holds for Nelson and Winter (1982). The techniques of finite Markov chains and computer simulations that Nelson and Winter (1982) apply in their evolutionary models are more sophisticated than set theory. But, again, their 'results' that would prove Friedman's argument invalid are not derived from their model. Their criticism of the argument is rather based on informally stated 'complications and snags'.

Nelson and Winter investigate whether selection processes inevitably will drive a market system to an 'orthodox' static equilibrium ('static' refers to a stable environment). Nelson and Winter acknowledge that neoclassical theory, which they call 'orthodox' theory, attempts to explain the behaviour of industries. Their analysis of the behaviour of industries proceeds in terms of decision rules (routines) that individual firms follow. The behaviour of an industry is analysed as the sum of the behaviour of the individual firms in the industry. And the behaviour of firms is assumed to be determined by decision rules. Nelson and Winter's central question is whether a 'realistic' evolutionary model of selection dynamics yields equilibrium states in which firms adhere to optimal orthodox decision rules. I will postpone a discussion of the main tenets of their evolutionary model to the next sections, and focus on their conclusion here.

Nelson and Winter's conclusion is clearly to the negative. Their overall argument is in two steps. The first step relates to an important qualification that was already anticipated by Alchian: there is nothing in the idea of natural selection as such that gives us reason to believe that optimal actions will be among those tried.[3] In Chapter 3, we have seen that this is the prime reason for Williamson to reject strong selectionism. When optimal actions are not tried, Nelson and Winter argue, an equilibrium will be achieved all the same, but, of course, it will be an unorthodox equilibrium. In the second step, Nelson and Winter argue that even under the assumption 'that the orthodox rule is among those tried, a selection equilibrium does *not* correspond to an orthodox market equilibrium' (Nelson and Winter 1982: 153). As I shall point out now, this conclusion is far too strong. Even if we accept their argument in this second step and their interpretation of 'orthodox market equilibrium', their conclusion is not warranted.

'Orthodox market equilibrium' is roughly described as the state in which all existing firms follow the optimal rules that can be derived from orthodox theory. In particular, firms then follow the following 'capital utilization rule':[4]

> if $P < c$, then $q = 0$;
> if $P = c$, then $q \leq k$;
> if $P > c$, then $q = k$,

where P stands for price, c for unit variable production cost, k for capital (capacity) and q for output.

Intuitively, this rule says that capital is fully utilized if price exceeds unit variable production cost. The rule can be derived from the assumption of 'profit maximization'. Nelson and Winter now go on to argue that in an orthodox market equilibrium, equilibrium price P^* must equal $(\hat{c} + r)$, where $\hat{c}$ is the lowest unit variable cost and r is the cost of capital services (for 'else profit maximizing firms would see incentives to change capacity', Nelson and Winter 1982: 146). In such an orthodox equilibrium, since $P^* > \hat{c}$, all firms will use their capital fully.

Nelson and Winter then show that under certain 'evolutionary' assumptions concerning the selection process involved (instead of 'under orthodox assumptions'), the industry will also ultimately (in the long run) settle in such an equilibrium if it is not there initially. That is, the same equilibrium price P^* will emerge. But they are at pains to argue that in such an equilibrium firms may be following other capital utilization rules than the orthodox one formulated above. That is, they show that although firms *must* be using their capital fully in equilibrium (just as the orthodox rule prescribes), firms *may* display non-orthodox behaviour in disequilibrium situations.[5] When the latter is the case, firms can be said to follow non-orthodox capital utilization rules, and hence, Nelson and Winter conclude, the equilibrium is not an orthodox market equilibrium.

The proper conclusion of their argument here would therefore be that a selection equilibrium *need* not (and not *does* not, as Nelson and Winter assert) correspond to an orthodox market equilibrium. Their argument shows only that in selection equilibrium the sole requirement on firm behaviour is that firms must use their capital fully, and that there are many capital utilization rules besides the orthodox rule that meet this requirement. Nelson and Winter call the set of rules that meets this requirement the set of '*eligible*' rules. For example, Nelson and Winter regard the capital utilization counterpart of 'full cost pricing' as one among the many eligible rules that are not optimal (see Nelson and Winter 1982: 154). As we have seen in Chapter 2, the antimarginalists Hall and Hitch argued on the basis of the responses to their questionnaires that the full cost pricing rule was prevalent among firms. According to Nelson and Winter, full cost pricing implies that:

if $P < \hat{c} + r$, then $q = 0$;
if $P \geq \hat{c} + r$, then $q = k$.

If Nelson and Winter are right about the behavioural consequences of full cost pricing, it would lead to exactly the same firm behaviour as profit maximizing at selection equilibrium!

What is the implication of Nelson and Winter's 'proper' conclusion for an assessment of Friedman's selection argument? It seems that it underwrites, rather than undermines, Friedman's *intermediate* claim. Selection is shown to induce movements in the direction of an 'orthodox' equilibrium. In the long run, the 'orthodox' equilibrium price will come about and the behaviour of all surviving firms will be consistent with the profit maximization hypothesis. The only proviso is that there is at least one eligible decision rule among the set of rules that is actually followed by firms. This result seems to reconcile antimarginalists' empirical findings with 'orthodox' marginal analysis. Maximum profits can be 'evolutionary by-products' of rule-governed behaviour of firms, as Hall and Hitch speculated.

Nelson and Winter's formal analysis is followed by a list of informally stated 'complications and snags'. Nelson and Winter remark that the main purpose of their evolutionary model here is to explicate the restrictiveness of the assumptions that are needed to generate strictly orthodox conclusions. It is argued that many assumptions in the model are not realistic. For example, it is assumed in the model that firms can sustain themselves only by the profits that they make. The possibility that firms might be sustained by resources from the outside is ruled out. Another complication to their own model that they mention is that the firms' environment is determined to some degree by the decision rules of extant firms. This means that the assumption in Nelson and Winter's model that decision rules are selected by the '*natural*' environment only is too restrictive. The environment that firms have to cope with has a '*social*' component also: firms are part of each other's environment. This last complication will be the main topic of Chapters 7 and 8. For now, it suffices to remark that Nelson and Winter do not hold that their simple static selection model serves expository purposes only. They maintain that more realistic evolutionary models would have to contain assumptions that bear a 'family resemblance' to those incorporated in the simple model. As a matter of fact, we will see that Nelson and Winter do not replace the particular assumptions that are mentioned above by less restrictive ones in the evolutionary models that they take to be more realistic than their simple static selection model.

Nelson and Winter admit that the result of their formal analysis, that surviving rules may yield non-optimal behaviour out of equilibrium, is of no consequence when orthodox theory would be concerned only or primarily with static equilibrium. But they then go on to argue that:

> orthodoxy is much concerned, and properly so, with the analysis of *displacements* of equilibrium – the problem of what happens if some parameter of the equilibrium position changes.
>
> (Nelson and Winter 1982: 154)

And for this purpose, they argue, it matters that non-optimal eligible rules may survive in selection equilibrium. These remarks suggest that Nelson and Winter hold that selection will *not* (or at least not necessarily) cause an industry, which initially is in orthodox equilibrium and in which firms follow non-optimal eligible rules, to move in the direction of a new orthodox equilibrium when it is confronted with environmental change. This would imply, for example, that the intensity of use of labour in an industry need not decrease if (real) wages rise.[6] If Nelson and Winter had proven this, they would indeed have shown Friedman's (and Alchian's) *ultimate* claim to be invalid. But they did not prove this. On the contrary, what they show is that 'standard' neoclassical industry responses (the intensity of use of labour decreases) are predicted also by evolutionary theory. Nelson and Winter's evolutionary model vindicates rather than demolishes the ultimate claim.

Comparative statics is discussed under the title 'Firm and Industry Response to Changed Market Conditions' in Nelson and Winter (1982). It is clear from the outset that Nelson and Winter hold that 'orthodox' (neoclassical) theory deals inadequately with change. But it is also clear that they take 'standard' 'orthodox' results of neoclassical comparative static analysis to be correct. Nelson and Winter argue that:

to be credible as a general theory of firm and industry behavior, an evolutionary theory must show itself capable of similarly predicting the standard responses.

(Nelson and Winter 1982: 164)[7]

Why, then, is neoclassical theory said to deal inadequately with change? Basically, Nelson and Winter argue, because neoclassical theory does not highlight the real underlying causal mechanisms that produce the change.[8] Here we get to the heart of Nelson and Winter's evolutionary project. Their disagreement with 'orthodoxy' does not so much concern 'orthodox' results as 'orthodox' behavioural assumptions. 'Orthodoxy' is said to assume that firms are responding instantaneously and optimally to unexpected environmental changes. Nelson and Winter argue that this assumption is unrealistic. A closer look at their evolutionary model reveals that Nelson and Winter believe that a more realistic treatment of economic change accounts for the following basic mechanisms. First, there is selection for profits. A firm's profitability is regarded as a *sine qua non* for its growth. Second, firms are assumed to follow rigid, self-sustaining routines. Firms cannot adapt their routines rapidly to changed circumstances. And third, if firms face dissatisfactory results they will engage in time-consuming search. Firms are said to satisfice. The three mechanisms will be discussed in turn in the next three sections.

3. SELECTION AS A REAL GENERATIVE MECHANISM

The simple evolutionary model Nelson and Winter employ to assess Friedman's (and Alchian's) selection argument is not designed to serve destructive purposes only. The unrealisticness of its assumptions notwithstanding, the model is said to be realistic in that it captures basic insights in the workings of market economies. In particular, it is realistic in that it deals with *selection* effects. Selection effects pertain to the possibilities for growth of individual firms in industries. Profitable firms gain resources that they can use for investment. They can expand, whereas firms that make losses cannot but contract. In Nelson and Winter's evolutionary models, this implies at the industry level that the industry's capital share weights change in favour of profitable firms.

For all their hostility towards 'orthodox' theory, Nelson and Winter acknowledge that they have this basic insight in common with 'orthodox' *appreciative* theory.[9] Orthodox appreciative theory is contrasted with textbook orthodox formal theory. The latter is concerned with (comparative) statics. It attempts to give rigorous mathematical treatments of (displacements of) equilibria. In contrast, 'orthodox' appreciative theory deals with adjustment processes. It is focused on dynamics and its style is informal. Its view on 'competition' is basically evolutionary in that it is stressed in appreciative theory that competition serves two functions: it allows for diversity in economic behaviour and at the same time it evaluates economic behaviour. Competition rewards and enhances behaviour that proves good in practice and suppresses behaviour that turns out to be unsuccessful. Nelson and Winter approvingly quote Marshall who explicitly stated in his *Principles* that his real interest was in economic dynamics. Marshall's 'Mecca' was 'dynamic' 'economic biology', and not 'static' 'mechanics' (see also Hodgson 1993a). Nelson and Winter argue that Marshall lacked the mathematics that is needed to arrive at his Mecca. They conceive of themselves as heirs of Marshall in that they use the modern mathematical techniques that have become available to model the evolutionary processes Marshall presumably had in mind: the theory of stochastic processes and computer simulations. I think that this self-conception of Nelson and Winter is correct in another respect as well. They follow Marshall in arguing that an economic theory of the firm is not about the behaviour of individual firms. Nelson and Winter's characterization of individual firms is reminiscent of Marshall's 'representative firm' in that it is primarily a step towards analysing the behaviour of industries.

In Chapter 2, I have argued that these 'Marshallian' beliefs are reflected in the respective selection arguments of the 'orthodox' theorists Alchian, Friedman and Becker. Their arguments are based on the belief that market forces generate the type of selection effects that are modelled in Nelson and Winter's evolutionary theory. And, indeed, Nelson and Winter consider Friedman, Becker and especially Alchian to be 'intellectual antecedents' of their own evolutionary theory. Where they differ from Alchian *cum suis* is where they argue that this correct belief of 'orthodox' appreciative theory should be at the basis of a formal evolutionary theory rather than at the background of formal 'orthodox' theory. In this, they follow early comments on Friedman's selection argument such as Koopmans (1957) and Nagel (1963). Koopmans argued that if 'market selection' is indeed the basis for the belief in profit maximization, then we should postulate that basis itself and not profit maximization which it is said to imply in certain circumstances. And Nagel also maintains that explanatory scientific theories should specify the mechanisms involved in the occurrence of phenomena.

Nelson and Winter's repeated insistence on a realistic account of firm and industry behaviour can be related to the philosophical doctrine of *realism*. Nelson and Winter agree with Koopmans and Nagel that a sound economic theory should explicitly analyse the workings and effects of the mechanisms that are believed to govern economic events. In this they differ from those who advanced selection arguments to defend the neoclassical theory of the firm. Alchian, Friedman, Becker and Nelson and Winter also believe, I ventured in Chapter 2, that 'natural selection' governs industry behaviour. But they do not subject this mechanism to explicit analysis. They rather argue that the effects produced by this mechanism coincide with the effects that are predicted by neoclassical theory. Only Nelson and Winter base their evolutionary approach explicitly on the belief that what really governs industry behaviour is 'natural selection'. The realist 'inclination' of Nelson and Winter is already transparent in a series of papers Winter wrote before Nelson and Winter (1982) appeared. In Winter (1975: 95), for example, it is argued that an economic theory is, and ought to be, 'an attempt to state what the causal factors are'. Winter makes clear that the selection arguments Friedman *cum suis* gave to defend 'orthodox' theory hints at a 'true explanation'.

The mechanism of 'natural selection' is not the only generative mechanism that is modelled in Nelson and Winter's evolutionary theory. Nelson and Winter argue that firm behaviour is best understood as *routine* behaviour. This additional 'mechanism' was first introduced in Winter's (1964) examination of the selection argument. Winter's main reason for assuming that firms follow routines seemed to be that definite results can be derived from his simple evolutionary model only under this assumption. To understand this, recall our discussion of Alchian's selection argument in Chapter 2, section 4. Alchian argues that selection sees to it that neoclassical tendencies are forthcoming also if firms were to display random behaviour. Winter rightly points out that if firms really were to display such irregular behaviour, anything could happen. For example, firms could change behaviour that turned out to be successful for unsuccessful behaviour in the next moment. No general statement could then be made about the direction of change in industry behaviour. In order to avoid theoretical inconclusiveness and to achieve theoretical 'closure', some consistency over time in firm behaviour must be assumed. Winter assumes that firms have *organization forms*.

Winter's 'organization forms' are not to be confused with the 'organization forms' that are central to the 'new theory of the firm'. The latter type of organization forms relates to particular types of contractual relations between the suppliers of inputs within firms. Winter's organization forms, on the other hand, relate to decision rules that are followed by firms. Nelson and Winter and proponents of the new theory of the firm share with each other the basic belief that firms are involved in selection processes. It is the actual and 'overall' performance of firms which determines their viability. But Nelson and Winter and the proponents of the new theory of the firm differ on exactly what features of firms are decisive for their performance. The proponents of the new theory of the firm hold that organization forms in the sense of structures of internal organization are decisive. Nelson and Winter argue that the firms' fate depends predominantly on the decision rules that they follow. In Chapter 5 I shall return to this discussion.

Later on, Winter replaces the notion of organization form by the notion of *routine*. Firms are said to follow routines only if doing so brings them satisfactory results. This suggests that firms always have the option at hand to change their routines if they want to. This is not what Winter (and Nelson and Winter) seem to have in mind, however. As we will see in the next section, Nelson and Winter stress that routines are rigid. They are taken to be more or less resistant to environmental change. This alleged crucial feature of routines make Nelson and Winter think that routines are the economic counterpart of genes.

For now, I want to complete this section by making one last remark. In Winter (1964) it is doubted by Winter that Alchian and Friedman would subscribe to his discussion of their selection argument in terms of organization forms as fixed decision rules. But in Nelson and Winter (1982), it is boldly stated that in addition to 'natural selection' this mechanism would also be alluded to in the selection arguments advanced by Friedman *cum suis*. As I have argued in Chapter 2, neither Alchian nor Friedman hold any particular view on the 'actual determinants' of firm behaviour. In their view, selection works directly on actually displayed behaviour, and not on organization forms or any other possible determinant of firm behaviour. Winter (1964) may be right that selection leads to predictable results only when firm behaviour shows some consistency over time. But behavioural consistency is not required for the process of selection to take place.

4. ORGANIZATIONAL GENETICS

The notion that firm behaviour is rule governed is elevated to a 'first principle' in evolutionary theory in Nelson and Winter (1982). What started as an *ad hoc* assumption that was introduced in Winter (1964) to achieve theoretical conclusiveness, grew out to be a 'real causal mechanism' distinct from and at least as important as selection. The role that routines play in Nelson and Winter's evolutionary theory is said to be similar (if not identical) to the role genes play in biological evolution. Routines are supposed to account for stability in firm behaviour. Routines are supposed to provide the stable material economic 'natural selection' works on just as genes do in biological natural selection. In this section, I shall first discuss Nelson and Winter's main reasons for believing that routines followed by firms are relatively rigid and 'inert' to environmental change. Subsequently, I shall deal with Nelson and Winter's contention that firms are satisficers. I shall argue that the two strands in Nelson and Winter's account of firm behaviour, that firms follow stable routines and that firms are satisficers, do not fit in as nicely with each other as Nelson and Winter appear to think.

Nelson and Winter treat routines as the organizational analogue of skills. Routine behaviour of firms is compared with skilful behaviour exercised by individuals. Nelson and Winter argue that skilful behaviour of individuals has three characteristic features. First, skilled performance is *automatic*. Most of the details are executed without conscious volition. Second, the knowledge underlying a skilful performance often is *tacit knowledge*, that is knowledge that cannot be articulated explicitly. Skilful behaviour presupposes the mastering of a set of rules that are not known to the individual who follows them. Learning these rules requires instruction, imitation and laborious trial and error search. And third, though the exercise of a skill can be said to involve the making of numerous choices, to a considerable extent the options are selected automatically. The 'choice' that is involved here is choice without deliberation. Nelson and Winter contrast skilful behaviour with maximizing choice. 'Orthodox' formal theory is said to be based on the behavioural assumption that individuals make maximizing choices. Individuals making maximizing choices pick out the best option from a choice set of available options. According to Nelson and Winter, this not only means that maximizing choice involves deliberation and conscious volition. Maximizing choice entails more than just deliberate choice. In addition to deliberation, maximizing choice presupposes that choice sets are well defined and exogenously given.

Individuals may switch relatively freely between skilful behaviour and deliberate choice. But at the level of organizational behaviour, Nelson and Winter argue, things are different. As centralized control in organizations is relatively weak compared with individuals, the possibilities for organizations to change their 'ways of handling things' are limited (Nelson and Winter 1982: 126). Nelson and Winter appear to be convinced that firms are not engaged in deliberate choice (let alone maximizing choice). Indeed, they are quite pertinent on this:

> knowledge of the routines is the heart of understanding behavior. Modelling the firm means modelling the routines and how they change over time.
>
> (Nelson and Winter 1982: 128)

The assumption that firms quasi-automatically follow rigid routines lies at the heart of Nelson and Winter's evolutionary theory. Nelson and Winter advance the following theoretical considerations to vindicate this central assumption.[10] One of the major effects of routinized behaviour in organizations, Nelson and Winter argue, is that it keeps latent and manifest intraorganizational conflict within predictable bounds. Routinized behaviour involves a *truce* in this conflict. By leaving organization members content to play their roles, it prevents the ongoing routine from being disturbed. Another important function that routinized behaviour is said to serve is that it facilitates the storage of the organization's specific operational *knowledge*. When activities were not routinized, there would be a fair chance that the operational knowledge would get lost. As Nelson and Winter put it: 'organizations *remember* by *doing*' (Nelson and Winter 1982: 99). Without frequent exercise, organizational memory would not be refreshed and coordination would not be preserved, just like individual skills that become rusty when not exercised.[11]

Nelson and Winter thus hold that routinized behaviour in firms has both a motivational aspect ('routine as a firm's truce') and a cognitive aspect ('routine as a firm's memory'). The two aspects account for the stability of a firm's routines. The general idea seems to be here that once certain 'ways of doing things' come about that serve the two functions reasonably well, these 'ways' will be self-sustaining. In other words, these 'ways of doing things' become part of the firm's routines. In particular, their function as a truce, which is related to intraorganizational affairs, may explain why routines may persist even though they are not optimally adapted to the firm's environment.[12] The two aspects also account for the 'quasi-automaticity' with which routines are followed. Routines can have a life of their own. They can serve their functions well without being observed by any organization member. Routines can be considered to be part of a firm's core competencies or basic capabilities. They are as much part of a firm's production opportunity set as their material resources (see also Loasby 1991).

In Nelson and Winter's view, the function that routines have as a firm's repository of productive and technological knowledge (its memory) cannot be reduced to the memories of its individual members. A firm's memory is taken to be more than just the sum of the memories of its members. The shared experiences of the firm members in the past, and the specific communication system that these experiences have established, are said to be also part of a firm's memory. The 'evidence' that Nelson and Winter allude to in order to substantiate this point is that a firm's memory can survive replacements of firm members. This is not to say, however, that Nelson and Winter hold that any replacement between firm members leaves the prevailing routines intact. A new role occupant can induce a *mutation* in routines. And such mutations, Nelson and Winter contend, tend to be deleterious on the average.

Nelson and Winter are right, I think, that the view that is presented here of firms and their routines resembles the view of organisms and their genes in evolutionary biology in some important respects. Routines 'instruct' firms to handle things in much the same way as genes instruct organisms. The 'instructions' need not be followed consciously by any firm member. Indeed, the members may not even be aware of the 'instructions'. What is more important, in this view routines seem to exhibit the persistence that Nelson and Winter are looking for. Routines seem to provide the stable genetic material economic 'natural selection' works on. The analogy between firms and organisms seems to be appropriate also in the respect that prevailing routines of firms are seen as a result of a process of 'spontaneous evolution'. The 'instructions' that routines give are not supposed to be designed by some central authority within the firm. They are rather supposed to evolve gradually in ongoing interactions between firm members and their environment.

There is another view on firm behaviour in Nelson and Winter (1982), however, that does not match with the one discussed so far. That is the view that firms satisfice. In this view, it is assumed that there is a central authority in firms that decides whether to prolong routines or not. Keeping existing routines running smoothly, or replacing them by others, is seen as a target for managerial effort. The general idea here is that managers stick to routines as long as doing so yields satisfactory results. If following routines leads to dissatisfactory results, search for better routines is triggered. In this view, 'replication' of existing routines is optional and 'mutations' are failure induced. What is more, firm behaviour is not quasi-automatic in this view. Firm behaviour is goal directed. It is this view that is modelled in the formal representations of their evolutionary theory. In the evolutionary models that Nelson and Winter present 'profit seeking' is assumed to be the managers' objective (Nelson and Winter 1982: 30; see also Winter 1991: 189).

The 'black box' that proponents of the new theory of the firm tried to open seems to be closed again in this latter view of Nelson and Winter. Instead of modelling firm behaviour as the resultant of the interaction between input owners who possibly have divergent interests, the manager (–entrepreneur) is restored as the personification of the firm. I think that Williamson (1990) is right in arguing that the view on the firm that is modelled in Nelson and Winter (1982) is technological and non-contractual. In this respect it resembles the neoclassical view of the firm. Nelson and Winter acknowledge that the view of the firm that they model lies closer to 'textbook orthodoxy' than to the contractual view advocated in the new theory of the firm. They admit that a contractual view of the firm would be more realistic. But they doubt that a contractual approach is of much use in empirical applications. There is a trade-off between realisticness and tractability here. Nelson and Winter prefer a simple and tractable approximation that relates directly to the questions of interest over a realistic account that is inconclusive. As we have seen in section 3, Nelson and Winter's 'questions of interest' concern industry behaviour and not firm behaviour. This seems to be precisely how 'orthodox' economists try to defend their approach, a type of defence that is criticized by Nelson and Winter.

Nevertheless, Nelson and Winter hold that their models are far more realistic than neoclassical models. And they also hold that their models are more realistic than a strictly 'Darwinian' economic evolutionary theory would be. In a strictly 'Darwinian' theory, gene mutations are 'blind' and only those properties of organisms are transmitted to subsequent generations that are genetically encoded. Nelson and Winter argue that these assumptions do not seem to be very realistic in an economic context. They state that their evolutionary theory is 'unabashedly Lamarckian':

it contemplates both the 'inheritance' of acquired characteristics and the timely appearance of variation under the stimulus of adversity.

(Nelson and Winter 1982: 11)

I shall postpone further discussion of the 'Lamarckian' character of Nelson and Winter's theory to Chapter 6. In the next section, I shall reconsider the alleged contrast between the behavioural foundations of Nelson and Winter's models and 'orthodox' foundations. If firms satisfice, are they engaged in rigid rule following or in flexible deliberate choice?

5. RIGID RULE FOLLOWING VERSUS FLEXIBLE DELIBERATE CHOICE

In the previous section, we have seen that Nelson and Winter argue that firm behaviour is best understood as routine behaviour. They take this insight to be as essential in their evolutionary theory as the notion that selection effects are produced. Indeed, they seem to believe that it is an indispensable integral part of an economic evolutionary theory. As Winter puts it: 'it is, of course, a fundamental commitment of evolutionary theory that routines do tend to persist' (Winter 1986: 166). We have also seen that Nelson and Winter contrast routine behaviour with deliberate choice. Whereas routine behaviour is said to be displayed quasi-automatically or mechanically, deliberate choice is taken to imply conscious volition and deliberation. Furthermore, it is suggested by Nelson and Winter that adherence to routines leads to relatively rigid or even inert behaviour, and that engaging in deliberate choice would enable firms to display flexible behaviour. In this section, it will be examined whether Nelson and Winter's account of firm behaviour in terms of satisficing is able to meet Winter's 'fundamental commitment'. I shall argue that satisficing can be called routine behaviour only if search is governed by fixed higher-order learning routines. If we accept the view that routines of satisficing firms are part of stable hierarchies of rules, however, then following routines may lead to flexible rather than inert behaviour.

On the face of it, H.A. Simon's conception of satisficing seems to entail deliberate choice and not routine behaviour. Satisficing behaviour is goal directed. Satisficers intend to achieve satisfactory results. This seems to entail conscious volition. Satisficing also seems to entail deliberation. Satisficers are assumed to contemplate whether to continue some line of behaviour or to engage in search for better lines of behaviour. This type of contemplation is referred to in Nelson and Winter's account of the 'replication' of routines. Routines are not assumed to be replicated in the same automatic or mechanical way as genes are inherited. The exercise of a routine in a following period is acknowledged to involve an element of choice.

Nelson and Winter recognize an asymmetry in their own evolutionary theory: whereas contraction is a *mandatory* response to failure – as it becomes impossible to acquire the inputs that are necessary to continue the routine – replication is an *optional* response to success. There is always the option to go on in quite another direction. It is said to be basically an issue of investment analysis whether replication attempts will actually be made. Managers will only invest in efforts to copy existing routines when they expect the benefits to be obtained to exceed the expected costs (Nelson and Winter 1982: 120). Search for better lines of behaviour also seems to imply moments of deliberation and contemplation. It seems to imply the choice, for example, where, in which direction, to search.

The conclusion appears to be therefore that satisficing is a species of deliberate choice and not of routine behaviour. Yet drawing this conclusion may be premature, for there are also paragraphs in Nelson and Winter (1982) that indicate that satisficing can be conceived of as a sequence of mechanical, automatic steps of rule following. In this conception, the first step is a mechanical reaction to realized results. If realized results exceed some aspiration level, the satisficer continues the 'rewarding' line of behaviour. The satisfier is reinforced to stick to his or her previous behaviour. If realized results lie below the aspiration level, however, the satisficer is set in motion. Search is triggered. Here we come to the second step. Dissatisfied satisficers are not supposed to search 'at random'. Their search activities are supposed to show regularity and consistency. Search of satisficers is assumed to be governed by second-order 'meta' rules: search or learning rules. Triggering the second-order rules may lead to a replacement of the 'old' first-order rules by new ones. There may also be third-order rules that instruct satisficers how 'to learn to learn'. If second-order learning rules continually fail to bring about satisfactory results, then third-order rules may be triggered in search for better second-order rules. In short, in this 'mechanical' conception of satisficing, routines and procedures of firms are ordered hierarchically.

The key reference here is Cyert and March (1963). Nelson and Winter follow Cyert and March, colleagues of Simon at Carnegie Mellon, in arguing that searches of firms that may lead to changes in their (first-order) routines are themselves routine guided. Even innovating activities are said to be rule governed. This 'mechanical' conception differs from the 'deliberative' one discussed above in that while satisficing is *forward looking* in the latter conception, it is '*backward looking*' in the former. In the 'mechanical' conception, it is *realized* results that count, not *expected* (or anticipated) results. Firm behaviour is thought of as being determined by feedback mechanisms. Cyert and March argue that:

> any organization as complex as a firm adapts to its environment at many different (but interrelated) levels. It changes its behavior in response to short-run feedback from the environment according to

some fairly well-defined rules. It changes rules in response to longer-run feedback according to some more general rules, and so on. At some point in this hierarchy of rule change, we describe the rules involved as 'learning rules'.

(Cyert and March 1963: 101–2)

In this 'mechanical' conception, satisficing can thus be seen to be consistent with Winter's 'fundamental commitment'. Satisficing can account both for the stability of the routines that firms follow and for the automaticity with which they are followed.

But in this conception there is no reason to think that satisficing cannot lead to flexible behaviour, the type of behaviour Nelson and Winter invariably associate with deliberate choice. In one of their discussions about the distinction between routine behaviour and deliberate choice,[13] Nelson and Winter argue that routine behaviour and deliberate choice both have advantages and disadvantages. There is said to be a trade-off. The potential advantage of routine behaviour is that it is cost saving: one can rely on standard procedures without engaging in time-consuming deliberations. But its potential disadvantage is its inflexibility when environmental conditions change unexpectedly. In contrast, deliberate choice is flexible. But its potential disadvantage is that a conscious overriding of habitual response by deliberate choice in unexpected situations can result in poor coordination and, in general, ineffective action. The price that is paid for routines that are highly effective in standard situations, Nelson and Winter argue, is their incapability to cope with environmental change.

If firms possess hierarchies of routines, including learning rules, however, environmental change is likely to induce changes in (first-order) routines. Environmental change that makes existing first-order routines ineffective will trigger higher-order routines so that firms are likely to end up with other, more effective first-order routines. Firms that automatically follow fixed rules can thus adapt to new, unanticipated circumstances. As a matter of fact, it is possible that firms adapt to environmental change even if they do not dispose of learning rules. If firms possess fixed (first-order) rules only that they follow automatically, they may respond in a flexible and even optimal way to environmental change. This is illustrated by Nelson and Winter themselves in their discussion of the selection argument. The rule that is identified by Nelson and Winter as the optimal capital utilization rule is consistent with 'profit maximization'. This rule prescribes flexible behaviour; the degree in which capital is used is conditional on the prevailing price (as the key environmental variable).

What this discussion makes clear, I think, is that the contrast drawn by Nelson and Winter between rigid rule following and flexible deliberate choice is misleading. To be more precise, I think that the assertion that firms follow fixed rules does not tell us very much about the (in)flexibility or (sub)optimality of firm behaviour. On the basis of the foregoing discussion two illuminating distinctions can be made. The first distinction relates to different kinds of rules that may be followed. An *unconditional* rule gives an unequivocal prescription of the thing to do regardless of the 'environmental' conditions that obtain. In contrast, a *conditional* rule discriminates between different environmental conditions that may obtain and relates these to possibly different things to do under these different conditions. An example of an unconditional rule is: use capital fully regardless of prevailing circumstances. The optimal capital utilization rule that Nelson and Winter discuss is an example of a conditional rule. The point of making this distinction is that rigid adherence to a conditional rule may result in flexible and even optimal responses to changes in environmental conditions.[14]

The second distinction concerns different modes of rule following. Rules can be followed either *success-dependently*, or *success-independently*. A rule is followed success-dependently when an agent continues to follow a rule only when following that rule has yielded successful results so far. In contrast, a rule is followed success-independently when the agent in question keeps following it regardless of whether following that rule in the past was successful. Satisficing clearly entails success-dependent rule following. If following some rule leads to dissatisfactory results, satisficers will search for a better one. Success-dependent rule following may thus lead to changes in rules and in behaviour. It may induce a process of convergence towards optimal behaviour. Satisficers may find optimal rules, for example. Of course, such a process of convergence cannot take place when rules are followed success-independently. But we have just seen that success-independent rule following need not necessarily result in inert or suboptimal behaviour when the rule in question is conditional.

There are four possible combinations here and it can easily be checked that optimal behaviour (in a given situation) can, at least in principle, be the outcome of rule following in any combination. What all these combinations have in common is that the behaviour that is produced shows some consistency over time. Whether agents are assumed to be 'simple-minded' agents who follow unconditional rules success-independently, or are assumed to be more sophisticated success-dependent followers of conditional rules, to say that agents follow rules implies that some regular pattern can be discerned in their behaviour. In Chapter 2 we have seen that 'orthodox' theorists like Machlup and Friedman hold that behaviour that shows consistency over time can be accounted for also in theories in which agents are assumed to maximize some utility function. If they are right, the question arises whether there are good 'non-question-begging' grounds to choose either to model rule-governed behaviour as maximizing behaviour, as Friedman and Machlup do, or to model it as routinized behaviour, as Nelson and Winter do.

6. HOW CAN FIRM BEHAVIOUR BE MODELLED?

In the preceding section the question was how Nelson and Winter's notion that firms satisfice fits in with their contention that firms 'quasi-automatically' follow stable rules. Is satisficing in their view a 'mechanical' affair, involving higher-order routines, or does it entail making conscious deliberate choices? This section deals with the question of how firm and industry behaviour is to be modelled theoretically. Attention thus shifts from the *agent's* (firm's) point of view to the *theorist's* point of view. Nelson and Winter seem to argue as follows. Firm behaviour is routine behaviour. This being the case, it is preferable to model firm behaviour as such, that is *as* routinized behaviour. This argument is not convincing, however, for routine behaviour can be modelled also as maximizing behaviour. I shall argue that a more convincing reason for modelling firm behaviour as routine behaviour is that it allows us to examine the effects evolutionary forces have on industry behaviour. Indeed, this seems to be a main task of an evolutionary theory à la Nelson and Winter: rather than assuming from the outset that firms will arrive at optimal equilibrium behaviour, to investigate whether they will do so if their behaviour is moulded by evolutionary forces.

Nelson and Winter argue that their evolutionary theory is to be preferred over neoclassical theory for two reasons. At the level of their *explanandum*, the level of industry behaviour, it covers more phenomena and at the level of their *explanans*, the level of firm behaviour, its microfoundation is more realistic. Evolutionary theory covers the phenomena with which neoclassical theory deals *plus* phenomena like technological change and dynamic (Schumpeterian) competition about which neoclassical theory is said to be silent. We have seen that Nelson and Winter use their 'realistic' microfoundation, in which the key idea is that firm behaviour is routinized, not only as a cornerstone of their own evolutionary models, but also as an assumption in their formal examination of Friedman's selection argument. Nelson and Winter appear to think that Friedman and Machlup also hold that firm behaviour is rule governed. Both Friedman's 'expert billiard player' and Machlup's 'experienced automobile driver' are discussed by Nelson and Winter as illustrations of their own thesis that individual behaviour often is skilful behaviour rather than the implementation of deliberate choice. Nelson and Winter argue that they only differ from Friedman and Machlup in drawing different theoretical conclusions from this 'stylized fact':

> On the same stylized fact – 'business decision making is the exercise of a skill comparable to other skills, such as driving a car or playing billiards' – Friedman and Machlup built a defense for orthodox theory and we propose to build an alternative to that theory.
>
> (Nelson and Winter 1982: 94)

I have argued in Chapter 2 that whereas Machlup indeed grants that firm behaviour is to a great extent routine behaviour, Friedman prefers to be agnostic about the 'actual determinants' of firm behaviour. But Nelson and Winter are right here in arguing that both Machlup and Friedman hold that what is skilful behaviour from an agent's point of view (that is, how agents perceive of their own behaviour) need not be conceived of as skilful behaviour from a theorist's point of view. Machlup and Friedman seem to concur with the view that skilful behaviour can be modelled as maximizing behaviour.

As we have seen in Chapter 2, Friedman's analogy of the expert billiard player draws from Friedman and Savage (1948). The point of the analogy was that the question of whether people actually pursue the goal and conduct the calculations that are ascribed to them in expected utility theory is irrelevant when it comes to an assessment of that theory. The only relevant question is whether the observed behaviour of people is consistent with the behavioural implications of the ascriptions. As expected utility theory is a 'rational choice' theory *par excellence*, this means that we should not take 'choice' to mean literally that agents are supposed to be engaged in deliberate decision-making processes.

'Orthodox' decision theory thus does not seem to be wedded to the view that decision makers go through the conscious contemplations and deliberations that are ascribed to them. This implies that Nelson and Winter's distinction between routine behaviour, that is the key behavioural assumption in their evolutionary theory, and deliberate, maximizing choice, that would be the key behavioural assumption in 'orthodox' economic theory, collapses.[15] Routine firm behaviour could be equally well accounted for both in rational choice theories as in Nelson and Winter's evolutionary theory. Conversely, deliberate maximizing choice can be accounted for in terms of routine behaviour. Nelson and Winter show that profit maximizing can be translated into an optimal capital utilization rule, for example. Thus viewed, the issue of how to model firm behaviour appears to be a 'red herring'. As long as there is some consistency in behaviour, behaviour can be modelled either way.

Yet it would be wrong to conclude that a 'rational choice' micro-foundation would serve Nelson and Winter's purposes equally well as their own 'realistic' microfoundation. Recall that Nelson and Winter's evolutionary theory ultimately aims at analysing changes in industry behaviour. Their account of firm behaviour is primarily a step towards studying the behaviour of industries. In Chapter 2, we have seen that the same can be said of the neoclassical account of the firm. We have also seen, however, that the neoclassical assumption of 'profit maximization' does not cover just any consistency in firm behaviour. Firm behaviour that is consistent over time may well be *in*consistent with 'profit maximization'. 'Profit maximization' refers to the choice that a maximizing firm would make if it were perfectly informed. The assumption as such does not entail any commitment to the 'real' motives, goals and deliberations of firms. It relates to overt, observable behaviour.

Nelson and Winter's account of firm behaviour as routine behaviour is best contrasted, I think, with 'profit-maximization', and not with deliberate or maximizing choice. Nelson and Winter do not assume a priori that firms display optimal, 'profit-maximizing' behaviour under all conceivable circumstances. In particular, under uncertainty firms are said to be unable to optimize in a consistent way, because firms do not dispose of well-defined and exogenously given choice sets then. Notice that this is reminiscent of Alchian (1950), where it was argued that profit maximization is meaningless under pervasive uncertainty. Nelson and Winter do not take it for granted that firms respond in an instantaneous and optimal way to environmental changes. They do not assume from the outset that all firms in an industry start with optimal behaviour. The main problem Nelson and Winter have with orthodox theory is that it 'premises a standard of performance that is independent of the characteristics of performers' (Nelson and Winter 1982: 94). Neoclassical theory assumes that firms meet the standard of optimal performance at any moment. In contrast, a theoretical focus on skills and routines makes it possible to account for the fact that not all agents are equally skilful and that not all firms do equally well right from the start. In the evolutionary models that Nelson and Winter present in their book, firms are assumed to have different routines initially.

Assuming that firms start with different routines and capabilities does not imply that in the end, after having gone through an evolutionary process, firms cannot wind up displaying optimal behaviour. The behaviour of surviving firms may ultimately be consistent with 'profit maximization'. It is precisely the task of an evolutionary theory to point out when, under what conditions, this result does and does not obtain. The evolutionary process Nelson and Winter have in mind seems to proceed along the following lines. Initially, different firms follow different routines that make for different performances and, thus, for different survival chances. Clearly, their behaviour can be accounted for in 'rational choice' models, but there may be no firm that exhibits behaviour that is consistent with 'profit maximization'. Search for better routines is triggered in firms that have a poor performance. The same holds for firms that initially may have had a good performance but that are confronted with unexpected environmental changes that they are unable to cope with in a satisfactory way. Their search for better routines, and their adaptation to novel circumstances, typically is slower than what would have been the case if they had been perfectly informed profit maximizers. And perhaps the optimal routines will not come about at all. When selection operates on the firms' performances, some routines will spread whereas others will decline in the industry. It is interesting then to analyse what tendencies will result. Will an equilibrium be reached in the long run, and, if so, will it be an 'orthodox' equilibrium?

7. CONCLUSIONS

Nelson and Winter's evolutionary theory is better regarded as a continuation of 'orthodox' appreciative theory than as its 'unorthodox' rival. The basic belief of Alchian, Friedman and Becker that industry behaviour is governed by selection forces takes central stage in Nelson and Winter's theory. Moreover, both the ultimate claim and Friedman's intermediate claim are supported rather than undermined by the models that Nelson and Winter devise to examine the selection argument of Alchian *cum suis*. What remains implicit and at the background of 'orthodox' theory is made explicit and placed 'front stage' by Nelson and Winter. Certainly, Nelson and Winter rightly refer to 'complications and snags' that cast doubts on a universal validity of the claims mentioned. But these 'complications' are not derived from their models. And they do not extend beyond qualifications and warnings that were already observed by Alchian himself (and by early commentators).

What goes beyond the basic beliefs that are implicitly expressed in the selection arguments of Alchian *cum suis* is Nelson and Winter's behavioural assumption that firms display routine behaviour. Initially, this assumption was introduced by Winter as a provisory assumption needed to derive definite results from selection models. In Nelson and Winter's evolutionary theory it gains the status of a fundamental postulate. Indeed, Nelson and Winter seem to treat this assumption as the distinctive feature of an evolutionary economic theory, and not the idea that firm and industry behaviour is governed by selection forces. 'Orthodox' economic theory is said to be committed to the view that firms (and other economic agents) are engaged in deliberate choice. Nelson and Winter argue that routine behaviour and deliberate choice differ from each other in at least two respects. Routine behaviour is said to be quasi-automatic, whereas deliberate choice is said to involve conscious volition and deliberation. And routine behaviour is taken to be rigid or even inert, while deliberate choice is flexible.

I have argued that Nelson and Winter's contention that managers satisfice does not seem to accord with their 'fundamental behavioural postulate'. Satisficing seems to entail conscious deliberation. Yet on the basis of Nelson and Winter's own remarks, a 'mechanical' interpretation of satisficing is given that dovetails with their view that firms quasi-automatically follow persistent routines. The notion of a hierarchy of routines is central to this interpretation. Rigid behaviour is not likely to result from satisficing in any interpretation, however. Satisficing accounts for adaptation, not for inertia. I have introduced several distinctions in order to show that routine behaviour can be flexible behaviour. The real opposite to routine behaviour in a Nelson and Winter type of evolutionary theory, I have argued, is not maximizing or deliberate choice, but 'profit maximization'. Among other things, such a type of theory tries to identify the conditions under which selection brings an industry, that initially consists of firms having different and less than perfect routines (possibly including higher-order search and learning rules), to an 'orthodox' equilibrium in which all surviving firms display behaviour consistent with 'profit maximization'.

What about the new theory of the firm? As Nelson and Winter's systematic examination validates rather than invalidates Friedman's intermediate claim, the new theory seems to be supported also. For the new theory has been seen in Chapter 3 to rely in a general background way on a reinterpretation of Friedman's intermediate claim: firms survive that have efficient organization forms. But there are some caveats here. Nelson and Winter's emphasis on 'the actions really tried' (as opposed to hypothesized perfect actions) suggests that only Simon's and Williamson's *weak* selectionism and not *strong* selectionism *à la* Jensen *cum suis* is warranted. More importantly, Nelson and Winter argue that firms with the most profitable routines are selected. They seem to regard technological decision rules and not contractual organization forms as the factor that decides upon the firms' profitability. Routines and organization forms seem to be two distinct determinants of firm behaviour. They cannot be said to be independent of each other. For example, a firm's organization form seems to set limits on the routines that are feasible. But it seems to be perfectly possible that firms having different organization forms can have the same decision rules and, vice versa, that firms having the same organization form can have different decision rules. This raises several questions. The first question relates to the relative importance of the two determinants. It seems doubtful that any credible a priori assessment can be given. Besides, other determinants may be important as well. A second question concerns the relative durability of determinants. Are organization forms relatively immutable compared with decision rules, or is it just the other way around?

The latter question brings us back to 'organizational genetics'. What, if any, are appropriate economic counterparts of genes? This question cannot be answered before we have a clearer understanding of the role genes play in biological evolution. We have seen that Nelson and Winter take their evolutionary theory to be Lamarckian. What is the difference between Lamarckism and Darwinism? Does this difference bear on the economic issues that are discussed here, and, if so, how? In the next chapter I will turn to these questions.

Part II

FUNCTIONAL EXPLANATION AND EVOLUTIONARY MECHANISMS

5

FUNCTIONAL EXPLANATION

1. INTRODUCTION

In the foregoing chapters, several issues have been touched upon that are raised by economists in overt or covert relation to biological evolutionary theory. First of all, there is of course the clear reference to natural selection in the selection argument. In the discussion of Williamson's transaction cost economics, notions like 'Panglossianism' and 'strong *versus* weak selectionism' have shown up. In this connection, it was also mentioned that Williamson claims that his own explanation of the replacement of the U-form firm by the M-form firm meets the conditions of Elster's 'full functionalism'. We have also seen that Jensen holds that 'survival of the fittest' is a useful tautology. And, finally, there was Nelson and Winter's contention that their evolutionary theory is Lamarckian, not Darwinian.

These issues have not received the attention that they deserve. This chapter is meant to fill up this lacuna. The discussion starts with a brief treatment of functional explanation in biology. In particular, the discussion focuses on Elster's thesis that functional explanation in biology is justified by Darwinian natural selection. Then it is analysed what, exactly, is entailed in 'Darwinian natural selection' in biology. As almost everybody appears to think they have grasped the essence of this notion, this analysis may seem to be superfluous. I shall argue, however, that the popular condensation in the epitomes 'struggle for survival' and 'survival of the fittest' impedes rather than facilitates a profound understanding of Darwinism. Subsequently, attention will shift to allegations of functional explanations in economics.

The purpose of the discussion is not to assess whether the economists who draw the analogies have done their 'homework' properly. If they turn out to come up with explanations that are quite different from functional explanations in biology, they will not be criticized for having failed to develop explanations that are strictly analogous to those advanced in biological evolutionary theory. The purpose rather is to enhance our understanding of the economic arguments, explanations and theories that have been dealt with in the previous chapters.

2. FUNCTIONAL EXPLANATION IN BIOLOGY

Jon Elster holds that functional explanation is a legitimate type of explanation in biology because it has a solid foundation in Darwinian natural selection. In this section, we shall see that Elster's view is controversial. Following the lead of contemporary philosophers of biology, I shall try to arrive at a clear and comprehensive view on the peculiarities of functional analysis in biology.

Probably the best-known type of explanation is *causal* explanation. In a causal explanation, we explain some event or phenomenon by pointing out how it is brought about. Put more precisely, an event or phenomenon is explained causally when it is shown to be the effect of a particular operating cause. We explain the damage done to bridges and buildings in Los Angeles in January 1994, for example, by referring to the major earthquake that took place at that time and place. Or, to give a biological example, we explain blood circulation in vertebrates by showing how their hearts function. To some philosophers causal explanations provide the standard of sound scientific explanation.

Functional explanation in biology is met with scepticism by these philosophers, because it seems to turn matters upside down. A typical example of functional explanation in biology that has often been discussed in the philosophy of science is the explanation of hearts in vertebrates: vertebrates have hearts because they regulate their blood circulation. Apparently, in functional explanation a phenomenon is explained not by citing a cause that has brought about the phenomenon, but by citing the function(s) that the phenomenon serves. As functions are effects, functional explanation seems to reverse the order of cause and effect in causal explanation: a phenomenon is explained by its effects, not by its causes. Functional explanation in biology is sometimes called *teleological* explanation for the reason that it looks as if the phenomenon to be explained is explained by some goal it was intended to serve. It is 'as if' some divine Creator had the *telos* of blood circulation in mind when designing hearts. It may appear that functional explanations, thus conceived, are reminiscent of Creationism, which, of course, is *anathema* to Darwinian natural selection. But the plain fact is that functional explanations abound in present-day evolutionary biology.

Given this interpretation of functional explanation, it does not come as a surprise that Hempel (1965) and Nagel (1961), 'grand old men' in the philosophy of science, dismiss functional explanation. Hempel and Nagel point out that the main problem with the functional explanation of hearts given above is that having hearts may be a *sufficient* condition for performing the function of regulating blood circulation, but that it is not a *necessary* condition for doing so. There may be functional equivalents that could do (or could have done) equally well (see also Salmon 1990: 30). Hence, showing that hearts have this beneficial effect does not warrant the conclusion: that is why vertebrates have hearts. This objection against functional explanation as an explanation of the existence of organs or other features of organisms is still considered to be conclusive. But nowadays most commentators seem to hold that Hempel and Nagel got the *explanandum* of functional explanation in biology wrong. Functional explanation does not and cannot explain the existence of certain features.

Elster (1979, 1983) believes that functional explanation in biology accounts not for the existence, but for the persistence, of features. And he also believes that natural selection ensures the maintenance of features that have beneficial effects for the organisms having the features. Elster holds that natural selection provides the missing feedback loop that links the functions of the features, their beneficial effects, to the survival of the features in subsequent generations. In principle, this feedback loop can be spelled out in detail. If we were to do so, the functional explanation would be converted into a specific type of causal explanation. For we would have shown then that features produce beneficial effects, which in turn are shown to bring about the prolonged existence of the features in the next generation, which in turn produces beneficial effects, etc. Elster argues that such complete causal accounts need not be provided, however. Given the fact that the notion of natural selection is unchallenged in biology, Elster argues, functional explanations are warranted also if no complete causal account is not or cannot be provided.[1]

The idea that natural selection can be regarded as a feedback loop that justifies functional explanation in biology is disputed in Cummins (1975). Cummins argues that functional explanation often is carried on in biology independently of evolutionary considerations. Functional explanations need not be based on natural selection. In Cummins' view, what functional explanations in biology typically account for is not the existence or persistence of traits or features, but the behaviour or the capacities of the containing organism. To say that the function of hearts in vertebrates is to regulate their blood circulation is not meant to be an explanation of hearts as parts of organisms, but is meant to be a contribution to our understanding of the functioning of organisms as comprising wholes. Cummins also argues that it is misleading to call natural selection an instance of negative feedback. Whether organisms have hearts does not depend on natural selection but on the inheritable genetic 'plans' (or 'programs') of organisms. And whether organisms that have hearts are capable of producing offspring depends (among other things) on the 'plans' of existing organisms that do not have hearts (that probably possess other features that are responsible for their blood circulation). Natural selection does not generate genetic 'plans'. Natural selection can only work on the properties or traits of organisms that are determined by existing genetic 'plans'. As Cummins puts it: 'natural selection cannot alter a plan, but it can trim the set' (Cummins 1975: 394). What is at stake here is the relation between natural selection, genetic inheritance and gene mutation in evolutionary biology. A proper insight into this relation requires an understanding of Darwinian natural selection that goes far beyond a dim recognition of the slogans already mentioned: 'struggle for survival' and 'survival of the fittest'.

3. DARWINIAN NATURAL SELECTION IN BIOLOGY

Although the title of Darwin's *magnum opus The Origin of Species* might suggest otherwise, in 'orthodox' Darwinian evolutionary theory it is not species that 'struggle for survival' with each other as elementary units. Darwinian natural selection does not refer to species or group selection, but to *individual* selection. Individual organisms are the units of selection. Darwinian natural selection can account for the extinction of species, but it does not account for this in terms of species competing with other species as inseparable units. Species extinction is the result of selection forces impinging on individual organisms. The *explananda* of Darwinian natural selection typically are located at the level of populations, species and groups. But the 'material' on which selection works is located at the level of individual organisms.

The next thing to notice is that, strictly speaking, 'survival' is not really what Darwinian natural selection is about. What counts in natural selection is not whether an organism lives longer than others, but that it leaves more offspring than others. What really matters is an organism's *relative reproductive success*. 'Reproduction' already indicates that the organism and its offspring must be identical in the relevant respects. The traits or features that are responsible for an organism's reproductive success or failure must be inheritable. They must be encoded in the organism's genotype. The stability assumption of inheritable traits is very important in Darwinian natural selection. 'Natural selection' as an explanatory concept refers not only to the fact that certain organisms in a population succeed in leaving more offspring than others. It refers also, *and crucially*, to the fact that when an individual organism leaves less offspring than others, the frequency of its *genotype* in the 'gene pool' of the entire population will decrease compared with the genotypes of others.

Here, then, we already have the three indispensable ingredients of Darwinian natural selection: variation, inheritance and selection. If there were no variation, that is if all organisms in a population were equally successful in producing offspring, selection would have no bite. Prevailing gene frequencies could not be changed by the force of selection then. Hence, in the case where there is uniformity initially, evolution cannot get started as a result of selection. Inheritance is also presupposed in Darwinian natural selection in that natural selection can only produce changes in the properties of organisms in a population that are passed over from organisms to their descendants. Properties of organisms that are not inheritable cannot evolve in a population under pressure from natural selection.

The *inheritance mechanism* that is presupposed in Darwinian evolutionary theory is analysed in population genetics. Mendelian genetics describes the transmission of genetic material by organisms to their offspring. If organisms produce offspring, the reproduction of their genetic material 'obeys' the laws of Mendelian genetics. The Hardy–Weinberg law in population genetics, for example, can be called a *'counterfactual' zero-force* law. It describes what would have happened with the gene frequencies after sexual reproduction if evolutionary forces like natural selection and mutation had *not* been at work. If selection had not produced differential reproductive success and if mutations had not altered the genetic material (see below), the population would have behaved as stated in the law. The Hardy–Weinberg law can therefore be called a *ceteris paribus* law, or even better, as Sober remarks, a *ceteris absentibus* law. If it is assumed that natural selection has been the only evolutionary force at work, the difference between actual gene frequencies and those that are derived from the Hardy–Weinberg law are due to differences in reproductive success.

The foregoing discussion makes clear that Darwinian natural selection entails two mechanisms rather than one. It entails a selection mechanism that decides upon the relative success or failure of organisms of producing offspring. But it also presupposes the functioning of a replication mechanism that ensures that features that are responsible for reproductive success or failure are transmitted to subsequent generations. The units that the inheritance mechanism works on are genes, or more generally, *replicators*. Selection forces, on the other hand, impinge on *interactors*. The selection mechanism works directly on the organisms' phenotypes, that is their physical constitution and behavioural characteristics. This raises the question of how an organism's genotype, its genetic make-up, is related to its phenotype. This relation seems to be quite complex. Apart from the remark that an organism's phenotype is instructed or programmed by its genotype, it seems that no general remarks can be made about this relation. The instructions that are given by the genotype may or may not be sensitive to environmental circumstances, for example. And the relation between genes and phenotypic traits may be one to one, one to many, or many to one. 'Polygenic effects' relate to the phenomenon that many different genes jointly produce one phenotypic trait. 'Pleiotropy' refers to the opposite phenomenon: one gene (or one cluster of genes) has several effects on the organism's phenotype.

93

'Differential' (in 'differential reproductive success') refers to the variety in genotypes that is needed for natural selection to take place. No selection occurs when all organisms in a population have the same genotype. Natural selection typically works on a *variety* of *individual* organisms that are supposed to have stable, inheritable traits (there is individual *stasis*) and typically brings about *regular* or uniform patterns at the level of *populations*. Sober emphasizes the irreducible population-level character of Darwinian natural selection:

> Population change isn't a consequence of individual change but of individual stasis plus individual selection.
>
> (Sober 1984: 150)

Lamarckism differs from Darwinism in its inheritance mechanism. It is often said that the traits that organisms acquire in their lifetime and that are not inheritable in Darwinism are inheritable in Lamarckism. Although not false, this understanding of the difference between the two is superficial and possibly misleading. It might suggest that traits that are not genetically encoded are inheritable in Lamarckism. This suggestion is false. Hull (1982) argues that Lamarckism entails acceptance of three supplementary theses. The first thesis is that changes in an organism's environment produce changes in its phenotype. The second thesis is that this alteration produces a change in the genotype. And the third thesis is that these altered genes are inherited by the organism's progeny (see Hull 1982: 308). The distinctive causal claim in Lamarckism that is rejected in Darwinism is formulated in the second thesis: phenotypic changes bring about genotypic changes. This means that in Lamarckism there is no individual stasis. Whereas Darwinism accounts for evolutionary change in terms of selection forces working on a variety of *stable* individuals, Lamarckism does so in terms of individual development and change.

It is important to notice that Darwinian natural selection cannot account and does not account for the introduction of new genotypes in the gene pool of a population.[2] The entrance of new genotypes is governed by other evolutionary forces than the two that are entailed in Darwinian natural selection. Natural selection works on a pre-established variety in genotypes; it cannot by itself establish (new) variety. This is exactly what Cummins' remark that natural selection cannot alter plans signifies. Natural selection can only trim the set of already existing plans. An evolutionary theory that deals solely with natural selection working on inheritable traits (and no other evolutionary force) typically explains that the gene frequencies in the gene pool of a population will settle at an *equilibrium*. Sober argues that evolutionary theory that is based on (Darwinian) natural selection often is not able to provide causal explanations. In principle it is possible to give a causal account of selection processes, but in practice the specific forces that have impinged are hard to discover. Most of the time evolutionary theory has to resort to constructing equilibrium explanations. Typically, in an equilibrium explanation some observed persisting configuration of traits in a population is explained by pointing out that it is an equilibrium situation (see Sober 1984: 141 and Sober 1983).

In 'orthodox' Darwinism, evolutionary forces like migration, genetic drift and mutation bring about new genetic material work independently of the selection and inheritance mechanism. For reasons of simplicity, I will henceforth call the mechanism that is responsible for the creation of new genetic material the *mutation mechanism*. In Darwinism, gene mutations are blind. Their occurrence is assumed to be independent of the needs of organisms. Mutations are often likened to sampling errors. Another related characteristic feature is gradualism (as opposed to saltationism): mutation can account for gradual change only. Gradualism is related to equilibrium explanation in the following way. The equilibria that are explained in biology typically are *stable* equilibria. The equilibria are stable in the sense that once a population settles at an equilibrium, it cannot be invaded by 'mutants'. Mutants are 'new' organisms that, as a result of mutations, have a slightly different genetic 'program' than already existing organisms. Saying that mutants cannot invade a population at equilibrium means that they do have less reproductive success than already existing organisms. In other words, the equilibria that typically are explained are *locally* stable.[3] They need not be *globally* stable. 'New' organisms that would have a radically different genetic make-up that could invade a population at a local equilibrium can perhaps be conceived of. But since saltationism is rejected, the probability that they would enter the population is assumed to be nil.

Sober argues that mutation is best thought of as one among several evolutionary forces that can disturb 'pure' Darwinian natural selection. Darwinian natural selection can therefore be said also to be surrounded by *ceteris paribus* clauses. The activity of evolutionary forces that are abstracted from in natural selection, Sober argues, is one of the principal reasons why biological evolution need not be progressive. Another possible reason that is mentioned by Sober is that the environment may be unstable.

4. 'SELECTION FOR' AND 'SELECTION OF'

Now that we have analysed Darwinian natural selection in terms of three mechanisms, the selection, inheritance and mutation mechanism, and their interaction, we are in a position to deal with issues that were raised in previous chapters. The first issue I want to discuss is 'Panglossianism'. Panglossianism relates to an alleged inclination of some biologists to look for anything that exists after a problem that it can be said to solve or after a function that it can be said to perform well.[4] Panglossian biologists would hold that the very existence of something testifies to its optimality. A related doctrine is *panadaptationism*. Panadaptationists hold the view that everything that exists is perfectly or optimally adapted to the prevailing environment.[5] We have seen that Darwinian natural selection does not entail a commitment to either of these doctrines. Natural selection works on existing genetic material and this material need not include the optimal genetic 'program'. If the optimal program is not available, natural selection cannot lead to optimal adaptation. The outcome of natural selection cannot be better than the genetic material that it works on. Introducing the mutation mechanism may appear to offer an escape from this conclusion. If the optimal plan is not available initially it may indeed come about as a result of mutations. But as mutations are assumed to be blind and gradual this is by no means certain. Biologists nowadays seem to concur with the view that Panglossian biology should be avoided. They agree that the slogan 'survival of the fittest' is better replaced by 'survival of the fitter'.

'Fitness' is a somewhat peculiar concept. Many have argued that the statement 'survival of the fittest' is tautological. In Chapter 3 we have seen that Jensen (1983) is one of them. 'Survival of the fittest' is said to have no empirical content. Saying that the fittest survive would be an instance of circular reasoning. 'The fittest' is said to mean that some type of organism is most successful in producing offspring. In other words, 'the fittest' would refer to the type of organism that survives. Hence, they conclude, saying that the fittest survive tells us nothing. Sober (1984) shows, however, that this reasoning is fallacious. In biology, 'fitness' is a *probabilistic* notion. It is perfectly possible that organisms with a relatively high fitness are not reproductively successful *de facto*. Therefore, saying that the fittest survive is not merely empty parlance. A related reasoning that could underpin the charge that 'survival of the fitter' is meaningless is that we have no way of finding out what the fitness of organisms is other than by seeing how successfully they survive and reproduce themselves. But Sober argues that this reasoning is incorrect also: biologists have ways of calculating the fitness of organisms that are independent of the observance of their actual reproductive success.

Sober concedes, however, that the overall fitness of an organism may not be very informative about the causes that make for its chance of having reproductive success. 'Overall fitness' refers to the net force of selection and not to its components. It may be instructive to decompose overall fitness into separate traits that the organism does or does not have. According to Sober, changes in the proportion of traits in a population can be explained by referring to a process of natural selection only if two conditions are met. First, it must be made plausible that having these traits is *selected for*. Some evidence must be given to support the belief that having these traits is causally responsible for relative reproductive success and that lacking these traits is causally responsible for relative reproductive failure. Second, the traits in question must be inheritable. There must be certain genes that are responsible for having the traits. What is selected, then, are these genes.

The distinction that Sober draws between *selection for* and *selection of* is illuminating. 'Selection for' refers to *causes* of natural selection. It refers to phenotypic differences between organisms that determine their relative reproductive success. 'Selection of' refers to *effects* of natural selection. If organisms that do not have the traits that are selected for do not succeed in leaving offspring, then their genes 'die' as well. The *point* of this distinction is expressed concisely in Sober's assertion: ' *"selection of" does not imply "selection for"* (Sober 1984: 100). The mere observance that some traits persist does not warrant the conclusion that these traits are selected for. Their persistence may be a by-product or side-effect of selection for other traits. This testifies to the need for providing a plausible account of the causal relation between having some traits and having reproductive success.

Consider for example a toy in which there are two types of balls: red balls with a (relatively) large size and green balls with a (relatively) small size. In the toy there is a 'filter' halfway with holes of equal size in it that are big enough to let the green balls through and small enough to prevent the red balls from passing through. Now each time the toy is turned only the green balls will reach the bottom of the toy. The toy can be said to be a selection machine. Green balls can be said to be selected, but, of course, 'greenness' is not selected for here. In this simple example, it is evident that the colour of balls is not selected for. The functioning of the selection mechanism, the 'filter', is apparent. In other cases, however, it may be less clear how the selection mechanism (if any) works. Yet to avoid 'non-starters', to identify the traits that are selected for, we must have a prior understanding of the selection mechanism at work.

Let us now return to the question that was raised in section 2, and that bothered prominent philosophers of science like Hempel and Nagel: are functional explanations in biology acceptable? For example, can the fact that vertebrates have hearts be explained by the function of hearts, the regulation of blood circulation? Can Darwinian 'natural selection' warrant or justify such an explanation? It is instructive to follow Sober's account of Darwinian natural selection in order to see exactly what would be implied in an affirmative answer. First, we would have to assume that the alleged function (in our example, the regulation of blood circulation) is *selected for*. The trait that is producing the function (having a heart) must be an adaptation brought about by natural selection. And, second, we would have to assume that the trait is *inheritable*, so that there is *selection of* the trait. Sober's toy example warns us not to take the mere observance of traits as conclusive evidence for the truth of either assumption.

But what exactly would be explained? The answer now seems to be clear: the persistence of hearts in vertebrates. But we should be cautious here. Elster speaks of natural selection as a reproductive link. As we have seen, however, the selection mechanism does not account for the fact that the descendants of vertebrates having hearts have hearts as well. This reproduction is accounted for in the replication mechanism. Whether vertebrates are reproductively successful or not, if they produce offspring, their genetic material will be transmitted to their offspring. Even if they were reproductively unsuccessful, vertebrates have no way to escape this process of reproduction. The replication mechanism takes care of *individual* stasis. What the selection mechanism can be said to reproduce are stable configurations of gene frequencies at the *population* level. If having hearts is selected for and if this is inheritable, the fact that a population continues to consist of vertebrates having hearts can be represented as a stable equilibrium in an evolutionary process.

5. ELSTER'S 'FULL FUNCTIONALISM'

Functional explanations do not figure only in biology. They can be observed also in the social sciences, and especially in sociology.[6] The following example of a functional explanation in sociology of the institution of marriage is derived from Rosenberg (1988). Durkheim, one of the founders of modern sociology, explains the institution of marriage not by citing the motives, intentions and deliberations of the people who get married, but by referring to the function that it fulfils for society as a whole. According to Durkheim, the institution of marriage contributes to a 'healthy' functioning of society. One could say that society is likened by Durkheim to an organism and society's institutions to its organic parts. Marriage is said to enhance social integration, to reduce suicide rates and to repress other 'social ills'. It performs this function without the participants, the individuals in society, being aware of it. For this reason such functions are often called *latent* functions in sociology, in contrast to *manifest* functions, the reasons that individuals have for getting married. Explaining marriage by citing manifest functions would be an instance of *intentional* explanation. In an intentional explanation, human behaviour is explained by reference to some goal or end that the agent(s) involved intend to bring about.

What, exactly, are the phenomena that functional explanation in sociology purports to explain? Rosenberg argues that functional explanation of institutions in sociology accounts for the behaviour, the performance, of the encompassing system: society as a whole. Functional explanation of society's institutions helps us understand why it is that society performs as well or as poor as it does. Recall that this identification of the *explanandum* of functional explanation in sociology is analogous to Cummins' characterization of the *explanandum* of functional explanation in biology. Cummins argued that functional explanation of traits in biology accounts for the behaviour of the containing system: the organism. We have also seen, however, that Elster argues that the *explanandum* of functional explanation in biology is the persistence of traits. Analogous to this identification,

Elster holds that functional explanation in the social sciences accounts for the persistence or maintenance of institutions. The question that functional explanation tries to answer is not 'what is the contribution of the institution of marriage to a smooth functioning of society?', Elster argues, but 'why is the institution of marriage so persistent?'

Elster is very sceptical about the validity of functional explanation in social science. The main problem with most functional explanations given by sociologists, Elster points out, is that it is not made clear why institutions persist when they serve latent functions only. How are they reproduced if not for the reason that individuals recognize their functions? For example, how can the institution of marriage sustain itself without its function being observed by society's members? Why do they keep getting married if it escapes their attention that doing so has beneficial effects? We have seen that Elster believes that biologists do not have to face this problem because they can rely on natural selection. Natural selection is said to provide the feedback loop in biology that would see to it that the best adapted traits are reproduced in subsequent generations. Elster argues that a reproductive causal link of comparable generality and reliability is missing in social science.

Elster specifies five conditions that valid functional explanation in the social sciences has to satisfy:

an institution or a behavioural pattern X is explained by its function Y for group Z if and only if:

(1) *Y* is an *effect* of *X*;
(2) *Y* is *beneficial* for *Z*;
(3) *Y* is *unintended* by the actors producing *X*;
(4) *Y* (or at least the causal relationship between *X* and *Y*) is *unrecognized* by the actors in *Z*;
(5) *Y* maintains *X* by a causal *feedback* loop passing through *Z*.

(Elster 1979: 28)

Let us have a closer look at each of these five conditions. The first condition speaks for itself. To say that *Y* is a function of *X* is to say that *Y* is caused by *X*. The second condition also seems to be implied by saying that *Y* is a function of *X*. Harmful or deleterious effects would not be called functions. Conditions (3) and (4) make clear that *Y* must be a latent function. It is possible that the actors who produce *X* do so because they are striving after some goal. But their goal may not be *Y*. Otherwise, *Y* would be a manifest function. And the explanation would be intentional, not functional. The same holds for recognition. As soon as the actors involved recognize that doing *X* causes *Y*, *Y* ceases to be a latent function. Finally, condition (5) demands that a causal feedback loop, running from *Y* back to *X*, must be demonstrated. It is not enough, Elster argues, that a causal feedback loop is merely postulated or tacitly presupposed. For this would leave the crucial question unanswered: how can a behavioural pattern X be reproduced through its beneficial effects Y if these effects are not even recognized by their beneficiaries? Elster argues that the fatal flaw in almost all (attempts at) functional explanations in sociology he knows of is that this last condition (5) is not satisfied.

Consider again Durkheim's functional explanation of the institution of marriage. If Elster is right that what is accounted for in this explanation is the persistence of this institution (X), then it seems that the first four conditions would be met. A reduction of the suicide rate can be said to be a beneficial effect (Y) for society's members. And this effect can come about without ever being intended and recognized by those who marry. But how then can a reduction of the suicide rate (Y) maintain the institution (X)? No causal mechanism is specified. It is simply assumed, not shown, that such a mechanism exists and that it is producing the alleged result.

6. WILLIAMSON'S 'FULL FUNCTIONALISM'

In Chapter 3 we have seen that Williamson celebrates his own account of the replacement of the U-form firm by the M-form firm as an instance of a functional explanation that satisfies all conditions that are specified by Elster. According to Williamson, the M-form firm was introduced to relieve communication overload. It turned out that the M-form did even better than expected. The reason for this was that the M-form attenuated subgoal pursuit. After a while, Williamson argues, it became clear that the M-form could be used also to support takeovers of firms in which managerial discretion excesses were occurring. In Williamson (1988), Williamson reconstructs his own account as follows: X is said to stand for the M-form innovation, Y for the unexpected and unanticipated beneficial effect of subgoal pursuit attenuation and Z for the spread of multi-divisionalization by takeover.

What Williamson's account shows, I think, is that there are beneficial effects of the M-form firm that were not foreseen at the time of its inception, but that nevertheless help us understand its rapid spread. But it is clearly not a valid functional explanation in Elster's sense. The alleged functions of the M-form firm, the attenuation of subgoal pursuit and the possibility of takeover of inefficient firms, are not latent functions. The functions are manifest. To put it more precisely: the beneficial effects of the M-form firm were not fully grasped in the beginning, but they were recognized later on. The effects may have been latent at the time of the first M-form innovation, but they became manifest after a while. It is only because managers became aware of the full potentialities of the M-form firm that its rapid spread via imitation and takeover can be explained. In other words, at least Elster's condition (4) is not satisfied.

Condition (3) does not seem to be satisfied either. Recall that Williamson follows Knight in arguing that individuals intend to economize on costs in their economic activities. The M-form innovation is explained by Williamson as a conscious attempt to economize on the bounded rationality of top officers. According to Williamson, bounded rationality also explains why there were unexpected and unanticipated effects. The innovators did not foresee all effects of their 'experiment'. But what could the reason for the rapid replacement of the U-form by the M-form be other than that managers wanted to reap all the cost advantages, including the additional, unexpected ones? Managers learned that conversion to the M-form was even more attractive than they thought. Hitherto unexpected and unanticipated beneficial effects were turned into expected and anticipated beneficial effects. The conclusion must be, I think, that the type of explanation that Williamson refers to in his account of the success of the M-form is intentional explanation, not functional explanation. Managers are assumed to strive after beneficial effects. The only peculiarity of the intentional explanation involved seems to be that Simon's notion of bounded rationality is invoked to account for the fact that managers did not know all the effects of the M-form innovation in advance. It took some time before all the effects were clear.

I have argued that Williamson's account of the replacement of the U-form firm by the M-form firm cannot be called an instance of a valid functional explanation in Elster's sense. Conditions (3) and (4) are not satisfied. What about condition (5)? It seems that this condition is met in Williamson's account. A feedback loop can be said to be provided here by learning effects: recognition of the fact that after its introduction, the M-form firm was more efficient (beneficial) than expected, Williamson argues, contributed to its rapid spread over the population. In Chapter 6, I shall argue that what is alluded to here is a mechanism of adaptive learning that, just as natural selection, can be called an evolutionary mechanism.

7. THE SELECTION ARGUMENT AS A VALID FUNCTIONAL EXPLANATION

So far an instance of an invalid functional explanation and an instance of a seemingly valid functional explanation (which appears to be an instance of intentional explanation) have been discussed. This seems to underline Elster's scepticism on functional explanation in the social sciences. Yet in Elster (1979 and 1983) it is argued that there are a few exceptions. Alchian's (1950) and Friedman's (1953) selection argument is said to be the best-known example of a functional explanation that satisfies all conditions:[7]

> I know of only one example where all of the features (1)–(5) are actually present, viz. in the attempt of the Chicago school of economists to explain profit-maximizing as a result of the 'natural selection'

of firms by the market. The anomaly that led to this attempt was the following. On the one hand the observed external behaviour (choice of factor combinations and output level) seemed to indicate that firms in general adopt a profit-maximizing behaviour, by adjusting to market-conditions. On the other hand the internal decision-making process of the firm did not seem to be guided by this objective; rather some rough-and-ready rules of thumb were found to be typical. To bridge this gap between the output of the black box and its internal workings, the economists in question postulated that some firms just happen to use profit-maximizing rules of thumb and others not; that the former survive whereas the latter go extinct; that the profit-maximizing routines tend to spread in the population of firms, either by imitation or by takeovers. If, then, we set X equal to a certain rule of thumb, Y to profit-maximizing and Z to the set of firms, we have a paradigm of functional analysis. The argument clearly is modelled on a biological analogy, and it works (to the extent that it works) only because the notions of fitness, survival, reproduction and inheritance can be transferred without too much modification.

(Elster 1979: 31–2)

Elster praises the 'Chicago economists' especially for having demonstrated a causal feedback loop that he takes to be analogous to natural selection in biology. Their selection argument is said to have the right explanatory structure. But Elster criticizes their claim, which he takes to be: only that rule of thumb (X) survives (is maintained) that yields profit-maximizing results (Y).

Many comments can be made here. I shall confine myself to the most pressing ones. First, what Elster identifies as the claim of the selection argument comes nearest to what I have called Friedman's intermediate claim. Recall that Friedman claims that surviving firms display behaviour that is consistent with the assumption of 'profit maximization'. Presumably, Elster's interpretation of Y in the argument, 'profit maximizing', must be understood as 'maximum profits', the result of 'profit maximization'. On this understanding, Elster's representation would get the spirit of Friedman's claim right: only those firms survive that display behaviour that is optimally adapted to the prevailing circumstances. But Friedman never argued that firms follow rules of thumb. Friedman does not hold any particular view on the actual determinants of firm behaviour. And neither do the other 'Chicago economists' Alchian and Becker. As argued in Chapter 2, what they argued for in their selection arguments is that the actual determinants of firm behaviour are irrelevant.

Elster's representation of the selection argument does no justice to the ultimate claim that is advanced by all 'Chicago economists': regardless of whether firms are rational profit seekers, rule followers or whatever, industry behaviour tends to move in the direction of equilibria (as is predicted by neoclassical theory). I think that the type of explanation that is suggested by the ultimate claim is akin to Sober's notion of equilibrium explanation. As we have seen, Sober argues that biologists often have to revert to equilibrium explanations because they are unable to detect all causal forces that have impinged on the individual organisms in a population. Yet they are able to identify stable equilibria that function as local 'attractors' for a population. Similarly, economists may be unable to identify all actual determinants of the behaviour of individual firms in an industry. But there may be no need to do so, for 'natural selection' forces an industry to move in the direction of equilibria.

Elster seems to have missed the difference between individual firm behaviour and aggregate industry behaviour that, I argued, is so crucial to the selection arguments of Alchian *cum suis*. The 'Chicago economists' developed their arguments precisely to show that 'rational' industry behaviour can come about even if individual firms behave irrationally. It is as if some rational 'superagent' (or 'macrosubject'), who has control over aggregate industry behaviour, punishes irrational individual behaviour so that rational industry behaviour obtains. But in reality this process of 'directing' individual behaviour is due to evolutionary forces. These ideas are captured precisely in Ullmann-Margalit's (1978) *invisible hand explanation of the functional–evolutionary mould*. In this notion, individuals are assumed neither to intend nor to recognize *aggregate* effects of their behaviour. But they may intend to bring about beneficial *individual* effects.[8] Compare this with Elster's condition (3). Elster demands that individual firms may not intend to make maximum profits. This runs counter to Alchian's remark that firms are guided by the profit motive. Ullmann-Margalit's notion of an invisible hand explanation of the functional–evolutionary mould, on the other hand, is compatible with this remark. Firms may be profit seeking. As long as they do not aim at achieving certain results at the aggregate industry level, an explanation of these effects is an invisible hand explanation and not an intentional explanation.

The above elucidation of the explanatory structure of the selection argument in terms of Sober's equilibrium explanation and Ullmann-Margalit's invisible hand explanation more resembles Rosenberg's characterization of functional explanation than Elster's. Like Sober and Ullmann-Margalit, Rosenberg locates the *explanandum* at the level of the comprising system. Functional analysis can help us understand the behaviour of the comprising system. But, unlike Rosenberg, the comprising system (society in Rosenberg's view) is not to be compared with an organism. And the parts of the system (its institutions) are not to be compared with organs. In the selection argument, the comprising system, the industry (or, more generally, the market system), is comparable to a population. And its 'parts', the individual firms, are comparable to individual organisms.

8. 'FULL FUNCTIONALISM' IN NELSON AND WINTER'S EVOLUTIONARY THEORY?

In the foregoing section we have seen that the selection argument is misrepresented in Elster's account. In this section, I argue that Elster's account suits Nelson and Winter's evolutionary models better than original statements of the selection argument. But it is even more appropriate, it will be argued, to conceive of Nelson and Winter's evolutionary theory as an attempt to give a completely causal account of changes in industry behaviour.

Elster's account of the selection argument makes clear that Elster takes the 'Chicago economists' to hold that firms follow rules of thumb (that are also called routines by Elster). In Chapter 4, we have seen that the view that firm behaviour is routine behaviour is one of the cornerstones in Nelson and Winter's evolutionary theory. And we have also seen that this view is ascribed to Alchian and Friedman by Winter in his systematic examination of their selection argument. Indeed, it seems that in his representation of the selection argument, Elster relies completely on Winter's examination. Elster characterizes the position that the 'Chicago economists' are said to take also as 'maximizing-as-satisficing':

> the maximizers are just the satisficers who are selected by the market,
> or more generally by the struggle for survival, because they happen
> to have stumbled across the optimal rules of thumb.
>
> (Elster 1979: 135)

The view that firms are satisficers is held by Winter (and later on also by Nelson and Winter), not by any of the 'Chicago economists'.[9] The fact that Elster mainly refers to Winter's 'cogent objections' to the selection argument in his criticism of the argument's (alleged) claim reinforces the impression that Elster follows Winter's lead here.

A related comment can be made on Elster's remarks about the causal feedback loop in the selection argument. As argued at length in the preceding chapters, Elster is right in identifying 'the 'natural selection' of firms by the market' as the argument's causal feedback loop. Firms that happen to make higher (positive) profits than others have more resources at their disposal to invest, to expand and to support takeovers. But it is strange that Elster takes the 'Chicago economists' to have demonstrated this feedback loop. 'Natural selection' by the market is not modelled either by Alchian, Friedman or Becker. As Elster himself remarks in his represent-ation of their argument quoted above, it is more appropriate to say that Alchian *cum suis* have *postulated* this feedback loop. 'Demonstration' is better reserved for Nelson and Winter's attempt to model 'natural selection' by the market. This suggests that the explanations given in Nelson and Winter's evolutionary theory are better candidates for the predicate 'valid functional explanation' on Elster's conditions than the 'Chicago school' selection argument.

Recall, however, our discussion of functional explanation in biology. It was argued that if a detailed account of the persistence of traits can be given in terms of Darwinian natural selection, functional explanation is converted into a specific type of causal explanation. After having demonstrated the missing causal feedback loop, we would have a 'purely' causal account. It seems that the same can be said of Nelson and Winter's demonstration of the missing causal reproductive link in the selection argument: their evolutionary theory provides a specific type of causal explanation, not functional explanation. What makes their causal explanations specific is the feedback loop that they model. Let us have a closer look at the feedback loop in their evolutionary theory. Can the feedback loop that they model play the same causal role as Darwinian natural selection? If not, what are the main differences?

9. CONCLUSIONS

What insights are gained by the above discussion of functional explanation? Does it help us understand the 'explanatory structure' of the selection argument, of Williamson's account of organization forms and of Nelson and Winter's evolutionary theory better than we did on the basis of the foregoing three chapters? At first sight, the answer seems to be no. Elster's account of valid functional explanation in social science, it was argued, does not fit any of the three theoretical projects well. The explanatory structure that is suggested in the selection argument more resembles Sober's 'equilibrium explanation' and Ullmann-Margalit's 'invisible hand explanation of the functional–evolutionary mould'. Williamson's account of the replacement of the U-form firm by the M-form firm clearly presupposes that the 'function' of the M-form firm does not remain *latent*, but becomes *manifest*. And the explanations that are advanced in Nelson and Winter's theory are better called causal explanations of a specific type.

Yet it would be wrong to conclude, I think, that we have learned nothing at all from Elster's account of valid functional explanation. In his account, Elster rightly concentrates on something that, I argued, is characteristic of all of the three theoretical projects mentioned: the functioning of a feedback loop (that is also called a reproductive link). Change is accounted for in terms of *actual* results, not in terms of results that are intended and expected. In biology, as we have seen, Darwinian natural selection is said to provide the feedback loop. Actual results, the relative reproductive successes or failures of organisms, determine whether there is change at the population level. But we have also seen that we should be careful here. Sober's distinction between 'selection for' and 'selection of' warns us not to treat just any observed trait of surviving organisms as an adaptation produced by natural selection. And saying that natural selection offers 'the missing reproductive link' underlying functional explanations of the persistence of traits in organisms can easily be misunderstood. Darwinian natural selection comprises two mechanisms: a replication and a selection mechanism. The reproduction of genetic material over successive generations is accounted for by the replication mechanism, not by the selection mechanism. What the selection mechanism can account for is that some configuration of gene frequencies is stable, is 'reproduced', at the population level.

It seems that an analogue of natural selection underlies both the selection argument and Nelson and Winter's evolutionary theory. The 'feedback loop' underlying Williamson's account of the rapid spread of the M-form firm, however, seems to be quite *dis*analogous to natural selection. In the chapter to come, I shall discuss the two feedback loops that are involved in more detail.

6

TWO EVOLUTIONARY
MECHANISMS

1. INTRODUCTION

In Chapter 5, three mechanisms have been distinguished in biological evolutionary theory: the selection, replication and mutation mechanism. Another distinction that played a crucial role is that between 'selection for' and 'selection of'. These distinctions will be used in this chapter as an analytical apparatus to dissect the constituent parts and specific characteristics of a Nelson and Winter type of economic evolutionary theory. Again, I want to stress that the notion of 'Darwinian natural selection' in biology is not meant to represent an 'Olympian ideal' for an economic evolutionary theory. Nelson and Winter argue that they do not intend to develop an economic theory that would be strictly analogous to Darwinian natural selection. Their intention is to get at a better economic theory. Likewise, I do not intend to use 'Darwinian natural selection' as an absolute standard to assess the merits and demerits of a Nelson and Winter type of theory. It is my intention to arrive at a better understanding of their theory.

It will be argued that Nelson and Winter's characterization of their own theory as 'unabashedly Lamarckian' does not contribute to our understanding of their theory. The notion of Lamarckism does not clarify the specific types of 'replication' and 'mutation' mechanisms that are involved in Nelson and Winter's evolutionary theory. I shall argue that Nelson and Winter's accounts of these mechanisms can be better understood by distinguishing two evolutionary 'feedback' mechanisms in their theory rather than one: 'natural selection' and adaptive learning. Both mechanisms can produce adaptations via feedback loops working on actual results. But whereas 'natural selection' brings about population dynamics and presupposes individual *stasis*, adaptive learning typically brings about *individual dynamics*. Special attention will be paid to problems that arise if the two mechanisms are assumed to work simultaneously.

2. ECONOMIC 'NATURAL SELECTION'

In Darwinian natural selection, central notions are organisms, populations, fitness, genes and mutations. In Nelson and Winter's evolutionary theory, counterparts of these notions can readily be found. Individual firms are treated as organisms, industries as populations, profitability as fitness, routines as genes and innovations as mutations. Darwinian natural selection entails two mechanisms: a selection mechanism and a replication mechanism. Genetic inheritance is assumed to take care of an accurate reproduction of genetic material and natural selection, working on the organisms' phenotypes, is assumed to produce population dynamics. The selection mechanism that Nelson and Winter have in mind seems to be strictly analogous to natural selection. Initially, there must be some variation in the routines tried by different firms in an industry. And this variation must lead to differences in profitability of the firms that follow the routines. As we have seen in the previous chapters, the key idea then is that firms that make positive profits gain additional resources that they can use for investment. They can expand. Firms that suffer losses, on the other hand, cannot but contract. The causal mechanism that is at work here operates through changes in the material means of firms. At any time, a firm's past results determine its productive opportunities. Firms need money, as a generalized resource, to enlarge their scale of operation in much the same way that organisms need energy, as a generalized resource, to be reproductively successful (see, for example, Ghiselin 1974).

Just as the genes of reproductively successful organisms spread over the gene pool of the population, so do profitable routines spread in an industry at the expense of less profitable routines. Differences in profitability between routines are translated into different growth rates in terms of market shares.[1] Evolution that is produced by this selection mechanism amounts to changes in market shares of extant routines in an industry. This process of evolution may come to rest in an equilibrium. If optimal routines are among the routines that are actually tried in an industry, the industry may in the end settle at an equilibrium in which the market share of the optimal routines equals one. Of course, such an equilibrium would be stable in the sense that no innovation in routines could possibly invade the industry. The best simply cannot be defeated. This equilibrium would correspond to the situation that is circumscribed in Elster's representation of the selection argument: all firms in the industry (Z) follow rules of thumb (X) that are 'profit maximizing' (Y).

This imaginative process of evolution presupposes that routines are replicated by firms over time. Of course, a replication mechanism that is strictly analogous to Mendelian genetics cannot be given here for the simple reason that firms do not leave offspring. But asexual or sexual reproduction may not be the only way to achieve individual *stasis*. Individual stasis requires that the routines of existing firms do not change over time regardless of whether the firms make profits or losses. In Chapter 4 we have seen that Nelson and Winter put much emphasis on the persistence of routines. Routines are said to be self-sustaining and to be followed quasi-automatically by firms. Nelson and Winter argue that one of the things they want to show is that differential growth in an industry can produce change in economic aggregates even if the characteristics of firms are constant:

> This appraisal of organizational functioning as relatively rigid obviously enhances interest in the question of how much aggregate change can be brought about by selection forces alone.
>
> (Nelson and Winter 1982: 10)

The question that Nelson and Winter refer to can be reformulated as follows: what are the effects at the industry level of the combined working of the replication and selection mechanism *ceteris paribus*, that is if the combined working of the two mechanisms is undisturbed by other forces?

So far, I have uncritically followed Nelson and Winter in assuming not only that there is *selection of* routines, but also that there is *selection for* routines. In Nelson and Winter's view, the routines of firms determine their profitability. And differences in profitability in turn determine shifts in the market shares of routines. This means that Nelson and Winter do not distinguish between a firm's 'genotype' and its 'phenotype'.[2] Routines are assumed to be both the plans or programs of firm behaviour and the traits or features that decide upon the firms' survival and growth. It is implausible, however, to assume that the survival and growth of firms depends solely on their routines. As we have seen in our discussion of the new theory of the firm, a firm's organization form is another 'phenotypic' trait that may (co)determine the firm's survival and growth.[3] A firm's profitability is likely to depend on a combination of 'technological' features, including routines as decision rules, contractual and organizational features, and probably other features as well (see also Hirshleifer 1977: 15, Metcalfe 1989 and Saviotti and Metcalfe 1991).[4]

The features mentioned seem to be related to each other in several ways. Routines may or may not fit in well with organization forms. Given some organization form, many routines may simply be infeasible. And within the set of feasible routines, some routines may perform well in combination with the existing organization form while others fare poorly in combination with that form. Vice versa, the same holds: some routine may make a profitable combination with one organization form and an unprofitable combination with another. This means that the impact of either feature, routine and organization form, on profitability can be said to be context dependent. Each of the two features can be said to be part of the other feature's context. If the foregoing is correct, speaking of *the* causal role that either feature would play in determining the profitability of firms does not make sense.[5]

The foregoing would also imply that if some feature is observed in all profitable firms in an industry, this observation does not testify to the feature's adaptedness. Say that a particular organization form is observed to be prevalent in some industry. By itself, this observation does not warrant the conclusion that the organization form alone is causally responsible for the success of the firms in which it features. The success of the firms may be brought about also or even primarily by other features in the organization form's context. Recall Sober's toy example. The balls that are selected all have the same colour. But their colour does not play any causal role in the selection process. It is size that is selected for, and the balls that have the same size just happen to have the same colour also.

One need not assume that organization forms are causally *in*efficacious, just as the colour of the balls, to see that although organization forms are selected, they need not be selected for. In a sense, an observation that some organization form is selected can even be said to be compatible with the organization form's *in*efficiency. To see why, assume that the profitability of a firm depends on two features only: its organization form and its routine. Let us call some organization form (E) more efficient than another form (I), if E leads *on average* to a higher chance of survival than I. In combination with a *particular* routine, however, I may have a higher chance of survival than E has in combination with any routine. Then the combination of I with the particular routine is favoured by 'natural selection' over any other combination and may come to dominate the industry.[6] One can say, then, that the inefficiency of I is compensated for by the particular routine. The conclusion must therefore be, I think, that it cannot be believed a priori that the prevalence of some trait testifies to its efficiency.

As Loasby (1991) rightly points out, the other side of the problem that is at stake here resembles the Duhem–Quine thesis in the philosophy of science: in the 'market test', the test for a firm's profitability, not some single characteristic of the firm is tested, but a collection or package of characteristics. If a firm fails to pass the market test, it may be hard if not impossible to tell on which particular characteristic(s) the blame is to be put. For managers of firms the problem then is to find out which characteristic(s) can and must be changed to get better results. They may have to experiment with new characteristics to get this clear. Or if they think they know, they may try new characteristics to improve their performance. Here we arrive at a problem that I have circumvented so far in this chapter: replication of a firm's characteristics may not be quasi-automatic. It may be optional and deliberate.

3. REPLICATION

In the preceding section, I sketched the outlines of a pure and simple economic selection theory that is strictly analogous to Darwinian natural selection. I drew attention to some difficulties in identifying the relevant entities that can be assumed to be selected for and the entities that, as a result, can be assumed to be selected. Up till now, difficulties in the replication mechanism have not been dwelled upon. Furthermore, mutations have not been discussed so far either. Replication and mutation will be the subjects of this section. I shall argue that the main problem facing an evolutionary economic theory is to give a plausible account of replication and mutation in economics.

A replication mechanism is not required for the selection mechanism to operate. Whether firms change their behavioural patterns or not, their realized profits or losses determine their material means. As Matthews (1984) rightly observes, the selection mechanism can be said to work also when firms are assumed to be engaged in conscious profit seeking:

> although the difference between optimization and competitive selection may reflect a difference in the mental processes of the economic agents, it need not necessarily do so. People may always be trying their best to make the right choices, but their best may not be at all good, either because their powers are so feeble or because the problems are so difficult. Their attempts at optimization may then have no more than random chances of success.
>
> (Matthews 1984: 92)[7]

Recall that the originators of the selection argument did not dispute the behavioural assumption that firms are led by the profit motive either. The only requirement for the selection mechanism to work is that there is variation in the actions that are taken by firms. If all firms in an industry were to display the same behaviour (and if this behaviour were to lead to non-negative profits), selection would not produce any aggregate change. The limiting case would be a situation in which all firms display the same 'profit-maximizing' behaviour.

As long as there is variation in behaviour, selection effects obtain. But in order to be able to predict these selection effects, additional assumptions have to be made. These additional assumptions pertain to consistency in the behaviour of firms over time. As I argued in Chapter 4, from a theoretical point of view firms can be said to follow stable routines if their behaviour exhibits consistency. This holds also for conscious attempts to optimize. In so far as these attempts give way to consistent behaviour, they can be modelled as routine behaviour. As I shall argue, the point to be appreciated is that definite results can only be derived from an economic evolutionary theory if firms continue to exhibit the same consistency in their behaviour. This is just another way of saying that some replication mechanism must be provided. An economic evolutionary theory that is based on the selection mechanism needs some replication mechanism to make qualitative predictions about changes in industry behaviour.

The first thing to notice is that the relevant entities in a Nelson and Winter type of selection theory are routines, not firms. What ultimately counts are market shares of routines, not market shares of firms. Firms are just bearers of routines, just as organisms are no more than carriers of their genes. It does not matter whether routines are followed by a large number of small firms or by a small number of large firms. The 'size' of routines is what such an evolutionary theory is all about. And the 'size' of a routine is the sum of the market shares of all firms in an industry that follow that routine.

Now, consider what would happen if firm behaviour were to cease to exhibit the consistency it had so far. Say that firms change their routines during the selection process. This would be accounted for in Nelson and Winter's evolutionary theory as shifts in market shares of routines. We could say that, strictly speaking, from an evolutionary point of view, a firm that would change its routines ceases to be the same firm. The event would be conceived of as the exit of the 'old firm', having the old routines, and the entry of a 'new firm', having the new routines. As Winter puts it:

> if the organization form associated with a particular institutional identity undergoes a change, this should be regarded as a case of one firm's going out of business and being replaced by another.
>
> (Winter 1964: 249)

If an existing firm were to turn to routines that are unprecedented in the industry, an innovation, as the counterpart of biological mutation, would come about. New 'genetic' material would have entered the industry. In the ordinary meaning of 'exit' and 'entry', changes in firm behaviour have nothing to do with exit and entry. In 'orthodox' economic theory, 'exit' and 'entry' refer to firms (and not to routines) leaving and entering the industry. Notice that, conversely, 'entry' and 'exit' in the ordinary usage need not imply 'entry' and 'exit' in the evolutionary sense. A firm that enters an industry may follow the same routines as firms that already operate in the industry, for example. No new routines enter the industry then; the only thing that happens from an evolutionary point of view is that market shares of already existing routines change.

These differences may appear to reflect a difference in 'accounting system' only. But there is more at stake here than just a terminological issue. For an economic evolutionary theory, the problem with firms changing their routines is that the 'reproductive link' that would take care of 'reproduction' of the same routines in firm behaviour is cut loose. Consequently, the 'feedback loop' no longer works in the way it is assumed to work. From an evolutionary perspective, if a firm changes its routines, realized results no longer determine the material means of the same firm. Realized results, the results that have been obtained by following the old routines, determine the means of another firm, the firm that now follows

112

the new routines. The profits (or losses) obtained by adhering to the old routines enhance (or diminish) the market share of the new routines. The link between past results and present opportunities that is crucial to the selection mechanism is broken. As a result, the selection mechanism is disturbed. Compare this with Darwinian natural selection in biology. Here, genetical inheritance ensures that differential reproductive success of organisms translates directly and automatically into growth or decline of the frequencies of their *own* genes in the gene pool. Individual *stasis*, the stability of genetic material over subsequent generations, is presupposed.

4. 'EQUIVALENCE CLASSES' AND 'LAMARCKISM'

In my opinion, problems with specifying a plausible economic replication mechanism (that can account for stability) in firm behaviour are the main obstacle in the development of an economic evolutionary theory that is modelled after Darwinian natural selection. This is acknowledged even by Hannan and Freeman who advocate an evolutionary theory that is analogous to Darwinian natural selection: 'sociology does not have a simple, well-understood transmission process analogous to Mendelian genetics' (Hannan and Freeman 1989: 20). Winter seems to think that this does not pose a serious problem for an economic evolutionary theory. In Winter (1987a), it is maintained that the inability to complete an analogy of Mendelian genetics is not necessarily a problem for an evolutionary economic theory.[8] Winter argues that what really matters is not that traits are literally inheritable, but that several individuals share the same traits. What matters is that we can form interesting *equivalence classes*, within which the elements (individuals) are close copies of each other in observable respects.

Winter gives the following example to illustrate this point. An evolutionary theorist wants to explain the evolution of a certain undergraduate library by invoking the mechanism of 'natural selection'. The first thing to do then, Winter argues, is to identify 'types' of books, books that are equivalent in certain respects. In principle, there are many ways to classify the library; there are many 'equivalence relations' that can be chosen in order to identify types or equivalence classes. An equivalence relation that suggests itself, Winter argues, is 'same author and title as'. Now suppose that this equivalence relation is indeed chosen. And suppose also that at successive annual inventory times t and $t + 1$ when the academic year is over, no books are on loan. All books that had to be returned are assumed to be returned *de facto* at the inventory times. Then for each title and author the number of elements of each equivalence class that are in the library could be counted both at t and at $t + 1$. According to Winter, the evolutionary theorist is likely to divide the number at $t + 1$ by the number at t, 'and call the result the (observed) "fitness" of that title and author' (Winter 1987a: 614).

The point Winter wants to make is that it is perfectly possible and legitimate to construct evolutionary theories that invoke the mechanism of natural selection when there is *no* sexual (or asexual) reproduction going on. The only thing that is required for the empirical application of the framework of evolutionary analysis is that a system of equivalence relations is developed to which generalized concepts of inheritance, fitness and selection can be applied (see Winter 1987a: 615). I do not agree. Maybe a generalized notion of inheritance can be found that differs from sexual reproduction in biology. But I think that Winter's equivalence classes will not do. Something more is required than just observable traits that individuals share. Many different equivalence classes may be formed. But only one equivalence class yields genuine insights: the equivalence class that denotes the trait(s) that are selected for.

In Sober's toy example, the relevant equivalence class clearly is 'the same size as', and not 'the same colour as'. The fact that green balls are selected does not testify to its adaptedness. In Winter's example, the mere observance that at $t + 1$ there are many more books with a certain title and author in the library than at t, does *not* testify to the 'fitness' of that title and author. We have to know first on what traits or features the books are selected for. Though in this case it is likely that books are selected for their title and author, it is not self-evident or 'obvious' (as Winter calls it). It is possible, for example, that the books in the library are selected for their price. Students may prefer to borrow expensive books from the library. If this indeed was the case, the appropriate equivalence relation would be 'same price as'. Of course, it is probable that books having the same title and author have the same price and that books having different titles and authors have different prices. But, just as in the toy example, if price is what is selected for, the selection of 'same title and author' would be purely coincidental.

A second problem with Winter's equivalence classes concerns the stability of the relevant traits over time. Instability may result from individuals shifting from one equivalence class to another. 'New' books with 'the same title and author' are most of the time copies or reprints of old ones. So the stability requirement seems to be met here. Things may be quite different with routines of firms. Winter's library example seems to be contrived to sidestep problems that haunt Winter's own account of firm behaviour in terms of routines. Nelson and Winter take 'same routine as' to be the appropriate equivalence relation. But unlike books and genes, routines can hardly be said to be copied or reprinted over time. In their models, Nelson and Winter assume that routines are replicated *only* if following the routines has yielded satisfactory profits. Otherwise, firms are assumed to engage in search for better routines. If more profitable routines are found, firms are assumed to change their routines. Replication here is success dependent, as I called it in Chapter 4, and not 'automatically' or success independent.

114

In Darwinian natural selection, reproduction of genetic material over successive generations occurs 'willy-nilly'. If an organism has offspring, it passes its genetic material over to its offspring, regardless of whether there is genetic material around in other organisms that has more reproductive success. This is why realized results (in terms of produced offspring) determine shifts in gene frequencies in the gene pool of a population. Clearly, routines cannot be said to be reproduced in such a deterministic way. Realized results can determine a firm's present material resources. But realized results cannot be said to determine its subsequent behaviour. If Nelson and Winter are right, then dissatisfactory realized results induce firms to search for better routines. This presupposes that firms are assumed to have the option to change their behaviour as long as they have resources at their disposal. Firms may be able to avoid bankruptcy by shifting to other routines. 'Mutations' are not likened to copying (or sampling) errors here, but are assumed to be failure induced.

This feature of 'the timely appearance of variation under the stimulus of adversity' is taken by Nelson and Winter to be unabashedly Lamarckian. Another Lamarckian feature of their theory, Nelson and Winter argue, is that 'acquired characteristics', new routines, are 'inheritable'. Hull (1982) would strongly protest against this use of the term Lamarckian. As we have seen in Chapter 5, section 3, Hull argues that 'Lamarckism' in biology has a precise meaning. Among other things, it entails genetic inheritance. It is clear that Nelson and Winter's 'inheritance of acquired characteristics' is not to be understood literally, as genetic inheritance. Hull argues that, in general, although sociocultural evolution is called Lamarckian by many writers, it is Lamarckian only in the most caricatured sense of this much-abused term:

> The trouble with terming sociocultural evolution 'Lamarckian' is that it obscures the really important difference between biological and sociocultural evolution – the role of intentionality.
>
> (Hull 1982: 312)

But Nelson and Winter appear to relate the role that intentionality plays in their theory to the alleged Lamarckian character of their theory! They argue that they interweave 'blind' Darwinian and 'deliberate' Lamarckian processes. I conclude that coining 'Lamarckian' as a characterization of Nelson and Winter's theory is confusing rather than elucidating. I shall argue in the next section that it is much more clarifying to say that in Nelson and Winter's theory two distinct evolutionary mechanisms are assumed to work simultaneously.

5. ADAPTIVE LEARNING AS AN EVOLUTIONARY MECHANISM

In Nelson and Winter's view, the adoption of H.A. Simon's notion of satsificing introduces an element of intentionality in their evolutionary theory. As we have seen in Chapter 3, Williamson is reluctant to accept this notion of satisficing, primarily because it is said to downplay or even to eliminate the role of intentionality. Williamson takes over Simon's notion of bounded rationality, but rejects 'satisficing' for the reason that it would denote irrational behaviour that would belong to psychology, not to economics. We shall see in this section that Simon himself considers 'satisficing' to be a direct implication of 'bounded rationality'. 'Satisficing' will be seen to entail intentionality by definition. But in Simon's view, intentional behaviour is not to be opposed to behaviour that is governed by rules that have worked fairly well in the past. Satisficing behaviour essentially is backward-looking behaviour, involving adaptive learning that functions via feedback loops. For this reason, satisficing can be said to entail an evolutionary mechanism. I shall argue, however, that there are important differences between the evolutionary mechanism of adaptive learning and that of natural selection that should not be overlooked. Adaptive learning can be said to introduce a good deal of 'psychology' that is completely lacking in natural selection. Maybe this particular character of adaptive learning can explain Williamson's dislike of satisficing.

In Simon (1955), it is argued that the notion of satisficing behaviour follows immediately from the notion of bounded rationality. Simon considers human beings not to be perfectly (or globally, or omnisciently) rational, but *boundedly rational*. Perfectly rational decision makers are assumed to know everything they have to know in order to maximize some well-shaped utility function. By contrast, 'bounded rationality' entails one of the following:

- the decision maker does not (initially) know all possible alternatives for choice (A), or
- the decision maker does not know the consequences (S) of the alternatives considered (or their probability distributions), or
- the decision maker does not possess a general and consistent utility function ($V(S)$).

As a consequence of these limitations, Simon argues, the decision maker will deliberately simplify the situation.[9] According to Simon, this simplification typically involves the use of aspiration levels instead of utility functions by the agent. This means that $V(S)$ takes the discrete value either of 1 or of 0, instead of some value on a continuous scale. The limitations also imply restricted search, Simon argues: the decision maker initially considers only a subset A' of the set of all possible choice alternatives A.

Within this subset A', the decision maker searches for an alternative that is satisfactory (that yields $V(S) = 1$).

If a satisfactory alternative is found, the decision maker will either choose it, or raise the aspiration level. In the former case, search will be terminated. As the satisfactory alternative that is found lies in the 'zone of indifference', the decision maker will not search for better alternatives. In the latter case, further search will be triggered. If the decision maker does not find a satisfactory alternative in A' (or if the decision maker raises the aspiration level after having found one) either search for other alternatives in A will be initiated, or the aspiration level will be adjusted in a downward direction.[10]

Simon does not hold that satisficers always have to engage in time-consuming search to achieve satisfactory results. In handling their everyday affairs, satisficers are assumed to rely on rules of thumb that have yielded satisfactory results so far. According to Simon, experts are disposed of so many practised skills that they can do their work in a routine way. 'Novices' or laypeople, however, do not have a rich repertoire of routines at their disposal. They will have to resort to search in many problem situations. And even experts have to search occasionally; although they are capable of handling most problems in a routine way, they will also be confronted with new unprecedented problems once in a while. But, and this, I think, is the crucial part in Simon's notion, search is not assumed to start from scratch. Simon takes search to be guided also by the past experiences of the problem solver.

It is this idea that underlies Simon's view on learning processes. Throughout his work over the last four decades, Simon has insisted that human learning takes the form of a *selective trial and error search*. If a human agent is trying to solve some problem, the agent's attempts to do so are assumed to be informed 'negatively' by past failures (errors) to solve it (if there have been previous attempts to solve it), and to be informed 'positively' by successful attempts to solve similar problems. The latter give direction to the agent's further attempts at problem solving. The (satisfactory) rules of thumb (or procedures, or routines) that the agent has developed serve as positive *heuristics*; they instruct the agent how to tackle future problems. When a searching agent hits on a satisfactory 'solution' to the problem, the agent will tend to try this solution again when faced with the same (or a similar) problem. According to Simon, learning or *adaptation* refers to the process of: 'gradually and on the basis of experience responding more frequently with the choice that, in the past, has been most frequently rewarded' (Simon 1959: 271).

Simon argues that human learning works essentially via an *adaptive feedback mechanism* (see, for example, Simon 1982: 3).[11] Past results are assumed to determine whether human beings stick to their 'old' rules or experiment with 'new' ones. Simon stresses the analogy of adaptive learning with natural selection in Darwinian evolutionary theory:

The generator-test mechanism is the direct analogue, in the behavioural theory of rationality, of the variation-selection mechanism of the Darwinian theory. Just as in biological evolution we have variation to produce new organisms, so in the behavioural theory of human rationality we have some kind of generation of alternatives – some kind of combinatorial process that can take simple beliefs and put them together in new ways. And similarly, just as in the biological theory of evolution the mechanism of natural selection weeds out poorly adapted variants, so in human thinking the testing process rejects ideas other than those that contribute to solving the problem that is being addressed.

(Simon 1983: 40)

I agree with Simon that in his view, human learning resembles Darwinian natural selection. The 'generator mechanism', the combinatorial process of reassembling rules, can be compared with the replication mechanism when there is sexual reproduction. Variation, new material, results in both cases from recombinations of old material. This reflects Simon's idea that search is governed by already existing rules. The 'testing process' in human thinking can be likened to the selection mechanism in Darwinian natural selection. Past results determine subsequent rates of reproduction of the material selection works on. Poorly adapted variants are weeded out.

Both Darwinian natural selection and Simon's notion of adaptive learning assume reproduction of existing material and both operate via feedback loops. Both can thus be said to have the same mode of operation: they are *backward looking*, not forward looking. It is for this reason that 'adaptive learning' can be called an evolutionary mechanism. I follow van Parijs (1981) here in calling a mechanism *evolutionary* if it works through *actual*, that is *realized, past* consequences (see also Vanberg 1993: 186). As a matter of fact, adaptive learning has much in common with the evolutionary mechanism that van Parijs discusses extensively: *reinforcement*. In its most elementary form, van Parijs argues, reinforcement corresponds to the central notion in behaviourist psychology, *operant conditioning*. Operant conditioning refers to the process of artificially reinforcing (by an experimenter or an owner of a pet animal, for example) a certain way of behaving by rewarding it. As a result, a behavioural pattern may emerge.

The main difference between van Parijs' notion of reinforcement and Simon's notion of adaptive learning is that the latter notion involves intentionality. In Simon's view, individuals learn because they want to solve problems in a satisfactory way. Another difference is that adaptively learning agents are capable of detecting similarities between different problems and of using successful strategies to cope with one problem as positive heuristics for dealing with similar problems. As Simon puts it: 'man . . . is not only a learning animal; he is a pattern-finding and concept-forming animal' (Simon 1959: 272).[12] We should bear in mind, however, that the intentionality and creativity that is involved in Simon's adaptive learning is not opposed to rule-governed behaviour. On the contrary, humans are assumed to have recourse to their 'response repertoire' in their intentional and creative actions. Furthermore, the selection of the rule(s) from this repertoire depends on the results that are actually obtained by following the rule(s). Results are 'binary': either they lie above the individual's aspiration level (the results are perceived as 'rewards'), or they are below the individual's aspiration level (they are perceived as 'penalties'). This is what makes adaptive learning similar to reinforcement.

6. DISSIMILARITIES BETWEEN 'NATURAL SELECTION' AND ADAPTIVE LEARNING

Calling adaptive learning an evolutionary mechanism is not to say that its functioning is identical to that of natural selection. Adaptive learning differs from Darwinian natural selection in at least four important respects.[13]

The first difference is that adaptive learning typically implies changes *within* individuals. Learning individuals typically improve their behaviour in the sense that they learn to behave in ways that lead to satisfactory results. *Beliefs* can be said to be improved in the sense that the agents come to recognize *ex post* what ways of behaving do and what ways of behaving do not yield satisfactory results. The results that are brought about by adaptive learning pertain to another level of analysis than the results that are produced by natural selection. Whereas natural selection produces changes at a *populational* level, adaptive learning generates changes in *individual* organisms. As pointed out in section 2, natural selection as an explanatory concept presupposes individual stasis. It presupposes that there are stable, inheritable traits in a population of individual organisms. In contrast, adaptive learning accounts for *in*stability, for changes within individual organisms. Whereas Darwinian natural selection can only trim the set of (genetic) plans in a population, to use Cummins' phrase again, adaptive learning can change the 'plans' of individuals. Simon's account of satisficing shows that changes within individual agents may not be due only to changes in their beliefs but also to changes in their *goals*. For, as we have seen already, when agents achieve satisfactory results easily, they are likely to raise their aspiration level, and, conversely, when they continually fail to achieve satisfactory results, they are likely to lower their aspiration level.

Second, adaptive learning requires that the learning individual 'registers' in one way or another the causal relation between behaving in a certain way and achieving either satisfactory or dissatisfactory results. As successful attempts at reinforcing animal behaviour show, this 'registering' need not involve awareness of the causal relation. But conscious recognition may be said to be the 'standard' way of 'registering' in adaptive learning. No 'registering' is required in Darwinian natural selection. In Darwinian natural selection, differences in reproductive success are translated 'directly', without any intermediate 'registering', into differences in growth of gene frequencies.

The third difference concerns the 'weeding out' of poorly adapted variants. Eliminations due to natural selection are compulsory. The individuals which are poorly adapted ('unfit') are supposed to have no way of escaping the tough consequences of selection. They simply fail to leave offspring. In the economic realm, individuals who see their opportunity sets shrink to nil can no longer function (at least no longer in their former role as market participants). But ways of behaving that have not yielded satisfactory results for an individual agent can be 'rescued' by lowering the aspiration level. Results that were dissatisfactory can then become satisfactory. This means that the 'weeding out' that is established by adaptive learning is optional.

Even if individuals were not to adjust their aspiration levels, there still remains a fourth difference. The criterion for reproductive success in natural selection is the same for all individuals in the population. The criterion can hence be said to be objective. In the economic domain, this means that having positive material means is a *sine qua non* for persistence; whether firms are profit seeking or not, in order to stay in business they have to acquire material means. Adaptively learning individuals, on the other hand, may all have different aspiration levels. They may have different motives and targets. Hence, there may be a multitude of *subjective* criteria here.

Notice that although adaptive learning can be said to be an evolutionary mechanism, it cannot (as a feedback loop) support a valid functional explanation as specified by Elster. In particular, Elster's conditions (3) and (4), that the beneficial effects of behaviour may be neither intended nor recognized by the agents involved, are not met. Adaptive learning implicates both intentionality and recognition. As the fourth difference between adaptive learning and natural selection indicates, 'beneficial' also acquires another meaning in adaptive learning. In natural selection, 'beneficial' refers to 'objectively useful', whereas in adaptive learning it relates to 'subjectively gratifying or rewarding'.

It can be argued that adaptive learning is the feedback loop that underlies Williamson's 'valid functional explanation' of the replacement of the U-form firm by the M-form firm (which, we have seen, is not a valid functional explanation in Elster's sense at all).[14] Williamson's explanation starts from the assumption that the firms' managers search for efficient organization forms. There is no presumption in Williamson's explanation, however, that the most efficient form is or will be found. It cannot be assumed that managers scan the whole set of organization forms that would be feasible *in principle*. They consider only a subset of this 'complete set'.

Williamson follows Simon in arguing that only 'weak selection' can be defended, not 'strong selection'. Presumably, what Williamson does not like in Simon's 'psychological' notions of satisficing and adaptive learning, however, is that too much room is left for differences between individuals. Individuals may have different aspiration levels, and what is more, their aspiration levels may shift over time. Williamson appears to cling to the 'standard economic' assumption that all individuals have the same goal: economizing on costs. Moreover, Williamson seems to dispense with aspiration levels. He seems to assume that there are no zones of indifference; each individual is assumed to be after efficiency advantages *ad infinitum*. This would explain why Williamson takes the *ex post* recognition of additional efficiency advantages of the M-form firm, that at first were unexpected and unanticipated, to be responsible for the acceleration of its spread over industries.

7. 'SATISFICING' VERSUS 'MAXIMIZING'

Now that we have some idea of the mode of operation of the evolutionary mechanism of adaptive learning, what can be said about the effects that it produces? Can adaptive learning be expected to result in optimal behaviour? Can anything be said in general on this issue? In his earlier writings, Simon argued that we cannot expect a priori that adaptively learning organisms succeed in attaining optimal results: 'evidently, organisms adapt well enough to "satisfice"; they do not, in general, "optimize" ' (Simon 1959: 261). Generally speaking, Simon argues, the outcome of satisficing behaviour will not be identical to the perfect outcome of optimizing behaviour. 'Optimizing' (or 'maximizing') and 'satisficing' were initially taken by Simon to refer to two different mental processes which human beings are supposed to go through when making choices. Each process was said to presuppose different capacities on the part of the decision makers. While 'satisficing' explicitly takes cognizance of the inner constraints of decision makers, 'maximizing' was said to ignore any limitation whatsoever.

In his later writings, Simon argues that the kind of 'maximizing' rationality that is assumed throughout in standard economic theory does not denote a process, but the outcome of a decision-making process. 'Maximizing' is said to be silent on *how* choices are made. It only tells us *what* choices are made.[15] The key contrast is no longer between maximizing and satisficing, but between *substantive* and *procedural* rationality. Procedural rationality focuses on decision-making processes, substantive rationality on outcomes of such processes only. Accordingly, Simon no longer categorically states that satisficing is likely to lead to other results than maximizing. Whether satisfactory results differ from optimal results cannot be assumed a priori, Simon now argues, but has to be investigated empirically. In particular, Simon recommends empirical research on procedures that adaptively learning individuals follow.

Simon suggests that satisficing and maximizing are likely to lead to the same result in relatively simple cases. In Simon (1978), it is argued that a maximizer and a satisficer will often make the same choice when confronted with a small number of discrete alternatives. In explaining the existence of employment contracts, for example, it is not necessary to assume that rational agents equal variables at the margin:

> the rational man who sometimes prefers an employment contract to a sales contract need not be a maximizer. Even a satisficer will exhibit such a preference whenever the difference in rewards between the two arrangements is sufficiently large and evident.
>
> (Simon 1978: 6)

It is interesting to see also that in his more recent writings, Simon acknowledges that neoclassical economists take standard microeconomic theory not to be about individual behaviour, but about aggregate behaviour. He remarks in passing that he has learned that in order to claim the attention of neoclassical economists, it is not enough to present a different account of *individual* human behaviour. A competing account of individual human behaviour is of interest to neoclassical economists only, Simon observes, if it can be shown to lead to different market-level consequences than those predicted by neoclassical economics (Simon 1982: 401). Simon does not seem to contest the neoclassical 'theorems' about tendencies in industry behaviour, however. He seems to accept the standard results that are derived in neoclassical comparative statics. What Simon contests is that these results testify to the 'correctness' of 'maximizing'. The same results are said to follow also from 'satisficing':

> only weak assumptions of rationality (like those implicit in the adaptive feedback mechanism) are essential for most analyses using the methods of comparative statics. Few of the conclusions reached depend on an assumption of optimality or would be altered if optimizing were replaced by satisficing.
>
> (Simon 1982: 3)

In Simon (1979), Becker (1962a) is quoted approvingly by Simon. Becker is said to have shown that the result that demand curves are negatively sloping also holds when individual agents are assumed to follow 'irrational' rules: 'negatively sloping demand curves could result from a wide range of behaviors satisfying the assumptions of bounded rationality rather than those of utility maximization' (Simon 1979: 496).

Simon is right here in arguing that Becker purported to show that downward-sloping demand curves are compatible with several forms of non-maximizing behaviour. But Simon is wrong in claiming that all of these forms (which are *ir*rational in Becker's opinion) satisfy the assumptions of bounded rationality. What is more important, Simon suggests here that Becker would have held that negatively sloping demand curves result from the processes of satisficing and adaptive learning. This is not what Becker wanted to point out, however.[16] As argued in Chapter 2, what Becker wanted to show is that 'natural selection' corrects 'irrational' individual behaviour in such a way that 'rational' industry behaviour results. In other words, the mechanism that Becker takes to be responsible for this adaptation (at the aggregate level) is not Simon's feedback mechanism of adaptive learning, but an altogether different evolutionary feedback mechanism: 'natural selection'. Simon therefore appears to mix up these two mechanisms; a failure, as we shall see, that alas is not all too uncommon.

Even Winter seems to confuse the two evolutionary mechanisms. In Lucas (1987), it is argued that the optimal decision rules that are studied (or assumed) in economics are steady states (or stable end products) of adaptive learning processes. In response, Winter (1987b) argues that Lucas joins Friedman and Machlup in what he calls the 'Classic Defense of the rationality-as-optimization paradigm in economic theory':

> there is a major common theme that is the characteristic feature of the Classic Defense. This is the willingness to concede that the rationality assumptions of economic theory are not descriptive of the process by which decisions are reached and, further, that most decisions actually emerge from response repertoires developed over a period of time by what may broadly be termed 'adaptive' or learning processes.
>
> (Winter 1987b: 244)

It is curious that the man who coined the phrase *selection* argument, and who was the first to examine and criticize Alchian's and Friedman's selection argument in a systematic way, blurs the two distinct mechanisms. In contrast, it is ironic that the person who started all this, Armen Alchian, had already distinguished between *adoption* of behaviour by the market system, 'natural selection', and *adaptation* of individuals to their environment.

8. THE TWO EVOLUTIONARY MECHANISMS WORKING SIMULTANEOUSLY

Nelson and Winter hold that Simon's notion of satisficing can account for persistence of routines in their evolutionary theory. I have argued that rather than providing a replication mechanism, satisficing is better viewed as an evolutionary mechanism in its own right. Both involve the functioning of a feedback loop, and both can (independently of each other) account for adaptations. But whereas natural selection typically produces change at the population level, satisficing produces change at the individual level. In an evolutionary theory that is built on the mechanism of 'natural selection', the problem with allowing individual *dynamics* is, I have argued, that the crucial 'reproductive' link between past, realized results and present opportunities can be broken.

In Nelson and Winter's evolutionary theory, two ways are presented to get around this problem. The first way is to argue that change of routines at the level of the individual is itself rule governed. The idea is that 'natural selection' does not work on first-order routines, but on second-order learning rules. As we have seen in Chapter 4, Nelson and Winter defend this view in their informal discussions on routines. This is not the view of the interaction of natural selection and adaptive learning that is formalized in their models, however. In their models, natural selection and adaptive learning are assumed to have different time scales. Natural selection typically is assumed to work slower than adaptive learning. It is assumed that natural selection comes in only after learning processes have come to an end. In this section, the two views will be discussed in more detail. I shall argue that there are problems with both views.

In Chapter 4, I presented a 'mechanistic' interpretation of satisficing, based on Cyert and March (1963) and Nelson and Winter (1982). The key idea in this interpretation is that firms behave in an 'automatic' routine way also if, after having faced dissatisfactory results, they are looking for better first-order routines. Firms are assumed to avail themselves of a hierarchy of routines. In this chapter, we have seen that this idea can indeed be traced back to Simon's pioneering work. Simon also defends the thesis that search efforts of satisficers are guided by second-order learning rules (that serve as positive heuristics). Now, if indeed changes of first-order (*subordinate*) routines were governed by stable second-order (*superordinate*) learning routines, then we would have the required individual *stasis* that selection forces can work on, not at the first-order but at the second-order level. It could be argued then that there is selection for stable second-order routines.[17]

It should be noticed, however, that such a view on 'organizational learning' implies not only that higher-order routines must be stable, but also that they 'instruct' firms to change in a predictable way. The point is that we can trace selection effects in an industry only if the behaviour of individual firms can be predicted. If only firms were to follow stable and 'deterministic' learning rules, then changes in their first-order routines, the routines on which they act daily, would (continue to) exhibit regular, predictable patterns. Somewhat surprisingly, perhaps, it is argued in Winter (1986) that this condition for predictability is not likely to be met in reality. Winter argues that if we move up the hierarchy of routines, the routines will be less 'deterministic'.[18] The instructions given by higher-order routines are less precise, Winter argues, than those of lower-level routines. For this reason, Winter remarks that: 'the use of terms like *rule* and *routine* involves increasing strain of ordinary usage as we move up the hierarchy' (Winter 1986: 174). Higher-order routines are also said by Winter to be keyed in more complex and more subtle ways than lower-order routines to possible environmental changes. Phrased in the terminology that I introduced in Chapter 4, we could say that in Winter's view higher-order rules often are *conditional* rules. The 'pessimistic conclusion' Winter draws from these considerations is that it may be impossible to predict the outcome of the workings of higher-level routines.

The foregoing may explain why Nelson and Winter revert to another argumentative strategy in their evolutionary models. In their formal treatment of firm and industry responses to changed market conditions, they assume that search and selection processes do not interfere with each other. The effect of changed conditions on industry's output is decomposed by Nelson and Winter into three different (sub)effects: along-the-rule effects, search effects and selection effects. Along-the-rule effects refer to changes in firms' output due to their prevailing (first-order) routines. If a firm follows *conditional* rules, then a shift in factor prices may induce a shift in its output. Search effects refer to changes in the output of firms that are due to their searching for better routines (than their initial ones). Selection effects, finally, refer to changes in the firms' output that are due to ('natural') selection. Unlike the first two effects, selection effects do not refer to changes in the behaviour of individual firms. They refer to changes in the capital share weights of the individual firms in the total amount of capital in the entire industry. Nelson and Winter assume that the three effects come about in a particular temporal sequence: along-the-rule effects are assumed to occur promptly, followed by search effects that, in turn, are followed by selection effects.

What concerns me here is that selection is assumed to work on 'final rules', that is on the rules that firms follow after they have finished their search activities. Search of firms is assumed to be terminated before there is any capital share reweighing among the firms. This means that it is assumed that no capital reweighing effects take place during the time that the firms in the industry are engaged in search activities. Nelson and Winter's assumption is echoed in Elster's (1979) representation of the selection argument. Recall that Elster (wrongly) labels Alchian's and Friedman's position as 'maximizing-as-satisficing': only after satisficing firms have settled on certain rules is selection supposed to become operative (and to pick out the best one).

It is clear that this assumption sidesteps the problem under discussion: how to account for industry *dynamics* if individual firms change their rules during the selection process. In Nelson and Winter's assumption this problem is swept under the carpet. But it is also clear that this assumption is questionable, to say the least. There is no reason to assume a priori that the process of selection is slower than the process of search, let alone that selection forces are waiting patiently in the wings for all firms to terminate their search. As Nelson and Winter concede, it is more realistic to assume that the two processes occur simultaneously (Nelson and Winter 1982: 169; see also Nelson 1986: 458). Whether selection effects will be felt after or before firms have ended their search activities is likely to differ from case to case. Some firms may 'run out of gas' before they have managed to learn how to improve their performance. Or among the firms that may have learned in time how to operate in a profitable way, there may be some that did not have enough time or opportunities to implement their learning effects. After all, Nelson and Winter's informal discussion of the rigidity of routines suggests that it may be very hard for firms to adjust their (first-order) routines in time. Why then do Nelson and Winter not build their model on the assumption that the two processes intermingle with each other? The reason should be clear by now: the problems with building a formal evolutionary model on this realistic assumption may well be insurmountable (see also Faber and Proops 1991: 84).

Nelson and Winter are by no means the only evolutionary theorists who treat adaptive learning as a mechanism that can be studied in complete isolation of 'natural selection'. In Selten (1991), for example, it is argued that the processes of selection ('adaptation of genotype frequencies without mutation') are slower than learning processes. Indeed, Selten argues that the difference in speed between the two is so great that the results of the slower process (selection) can be taken as fixed when studying the faster process (learning). It may be tempting to argue that Selten, just like Nelson and Winter, disentangles the processes of selection and learning in an artificial and unrealistic way.

But it is important to notice that Selten deals neither with 'organizational learning' nor with selection effects at the industry level (as Nelson and Winter do). Selten deals with the learning and selection of individual human beings. In sociobiology, 'human nature' is assumed to have been moulded long ago by the force of natural selection and to have remained about the same ever since. The level of analysis is shifted here from the relation between firms and industries to the relation between individuals and groups. One of the major problems with Nelson and Winter's evolutionary theory is, as we have seen, that notions of inheritance (or replication, or reproduction) and mutation can at best be understood in a metaphorical way if we are concerned with firm behaviour. This problem seems to dissolve if we are concerned with humans as biological organisms. The shift in level of analysis seems to have important repercussions also for the relation between the processes of selection and the processes of learning. These issues will be taken up in the next chapters.

9. CONCLUSIONS

Two main problems with developing an economic evolutionary theory of industry behaviour that is based on 'natural selection' have been discussed. The first problem concerns the difficulties with identifying the traits that are 'selected for'. What properties of firms are causally responsible for their successful or unsuccessful overall performance? A second major problem is, I have argued, that a credible specification of the 'replication' mechanism is hard, if not impossible, to give. It seems that the possibility that firms change their relevant properties in an unprecedented way cannot be ruled out on a priori grounds. The first problem can be said to be a general and intricate problem that any 'selection' theory, either in biology or in economics, has to face. The second problem seems to be peculiar to economic evolutionary theories.

Nelson and Winter seem to downplay the first problem. The second problem can be said to be acknowledged by Nelson and Winter. Their assumption that firms satisfice accounts for the possibility that firms change their behaviour over time. Apparently, Nelson and Winter believe that it is this assumption that makes their theory 'Lamarckian'. I have argued that it is more illuminating to treat 'natural selection' and satisficing as two distinct processes. What the two processes have in common is that both are governed by an evolutionary feedback mechanism. Each of the two mechanisms can in principle, and independently of each other, generate adaptations. But I have also argued that the dissimilarities between 'natural selection' and the mechanism of 'adaptive learning' that, according to its originator, H.A. Simon, is entailed in satisficing, should not be overlooked. An essential difference is that what is presupposed in 'natural selection', individual *stasis*, seems to be denied by adaptive learning. Adaptive learning accounts for individual *dynamics*.

Another difference between the two mechanisms, it was argued, concerns the 'success' criteria that are at stake. In 'natural selection', all firms in an industry are assumed to be confronted with the same objective and 'merciless' criterion: zero profits. Firms that succeed in making positive profits can expand, whereas firms that make negative profits are compelled to contract. In adaptive learning, there may be as many subjective aspiration levels in an industry as there are firms. What is more, if a behavioural rule of a firm yields dissatisfactory results, it can be saved from 'extinction' by a lowering of the aspiration level. Aspiration levels may therefore vary over time.

This may imply that the results that are generated by the mechanism of adaptive learning are indeterminate. Painstaking empirical research may be required to investigate whether individual firms change their behaviour in a regular, 'routine' way. No general statements can be made a priori, it seems, about the probable effects of joint operation of the two evolutionary

127

mechanisms. Nelson and Winter circumvent this problem by making two supplementary assumptions. The first assumption is, as we have seen, that the processes of searching and learning have come to an end before selection comes in. And the second assumption is that firms engage in search activities if their profits fall below zero profits. In other words, Nelson and Winter assume that the subjective aspiration levels of individual firms in the industry *all* coincide with the objective success criterion in 'natural selection'.

The 'benefits' that Nelson and Winter gain by making these assumptions are clear: the assumptions enable Nelson and Winter to model industry behaviour in a relatively simple way. But, judged from their own perspective, they have to pay a 'double price' for doing so. Not only can their model not be said to give a 'realistic' account of industry behaviour, it also cannot but reproduce standard 'orthodox' results. If indeed firms are induced to search for profitable routines (if their existing ones are not profitable), and if indeed they all have ample time to find them before they are subjected to selection, then the mechanisms of adaptive learning and selection mutually reinforce each other. In harmonious interaction the mechanisms will drive the industry in the direction of a new 'orthodox' equilibrium.

Recall the discussion of the 'impotence' of Nelson and Winter's attempt to derive 'perverse' results, results that run counter to 'orthodox' results, from their formal models in Chapter 4. We are now in a position to understand why their endeavour ends in a cul-de-sac. The mechanisms that Nelson and Winter introduce fail to produce neoclassical results only if they are disturbed by other forces and mechanisms. If the mechanisms work *ceteris absentibus*, there seems to be no way in which they could bring about 'perverse' results. And once the industry had settled at an 'orthodox' equilibrium, the mechanisms of 'natural selection' and adaptive learning could only reproduce this situation. To paraphrase Friedman's analogy of the expert billiard player: optimal behaviour simply cannot be surpassed. Firms that are displaying optimal behaviour cannot be outperformed by others, and they cannot improve their own position by shifting to other lines of behaviour.

The processes of selection and adaptive learning that are depicted by Nelson and Winter can be called *frequency independent*: the adaptedness of some routine does not depend on the relative market shares of the routines that are followed in the industry. In particular, in the processes that Nelson and Winter model there is one routine that is optimally adapted regardless of its market share and regardless of the market shares that all other conceivable routines could have. In the chapters that follow, we shall deal with *frequency-dependent* processes. In frequency-dependent selection in biology, what is optimal in one configuration of gene frequencies in a 'gene pool' may be suboptimal in another. As we shall see, the root idea behind the notion of frequency dependency is that the processes of adaptation should take not only the *natural*, but also the *social* environment into account. In fact, this is an idea that Nelson and Winter also refer to in their informal discussion of the selection argument, but that they do not incorporate in their formal models.[19]

Part III

INDIVIDUALS AND GROUPS

7

ALTRUISM AND UNITS OF SELECTION

1. INTRODUCTION

According to Hirshleifer (1977), it is a rather 'odd accident' that biological models entered into economic thought in connection with the theory of the *business firm*. Hirshleifer calls the firm a highly specialized and consciously contrived 'cultural grouping'. If biological models were being explored afresh for possible relevance to economic behaviour, Hirshleifer argues, the first target for consideration would naturally be the *individual* together with the *family*, entities that are of direct biological significance. Whether it is an odd accident or not, we have seen in the previous chapters that Hirshleifer's point seems to be well taken that a plausible analogue of (especially) genetic inheritance is not easily found at the level of the firm. In contrast, nobody doubts that individual human beings *are* organisms that pass (part of) their genetic material over to their children.

In this chapter the focus will be shifted from the firm to the individual as the elementary unit of selection in economics. Two issues will be dealt with in particular: natural selection of inheritable behavioural traits of individuals and units of selection. We shall see that these issues are intertwined. In Chapter 5, it was observed that the unit of selection in Darwinian natural selection is the individual organism. This seems to imply that *altruistic* individuals, individuals who appear to sacrifice (part of) their own fitness for the benefit of other individuals, are supplanted by 'selfish' individuals as a result of natural selection. Yet instances of 'altruistic' behaviour appear to persist in nature. This is one of the central problems with which sociobiologists are preoccupied. One way to get around this problem has been to invoke the notion of *group selection*. As we shall see, this has sparked off a lively debate among (socio)biologists that later on was dubbed the units of selection controversy.

What behavioural traits can be expected to evolve under the sway of natural selection will be seen to depend on the stance that one takes in the units of selection controversy. Proponents of group selection hold that 'cooperative' traits tend to evolve that are optimal to the group taken as a whole. In contrast, individual selectionists argue that behavioural traits can persist that are *sub*optimal to the group. This will be demonstrated with the help of evolutionary game theory. Evolutionary game theory will be seen to show how within-group selection can lead to the decline of 'optimal traits' in groups.

Some (socio)biologists argue that, strictly speaking, the unit of selection is not the individual organism, but the 'selfish gene'. In section 5, this gene-centred view will be discussed. The discussion of altruism and the units of selection controversy in biology prepares the floor for a treatment of two economic analyses that have been inspired by evolutionary biology. Houthakker's analysis of 'division of labour' as the economic analogue of 'speciation' in biology is dealt with in section 6. And Becker's 'Rotten-Kid Theorem', which paved the way for Hirshleifer's and Frank's accounts of passions and commitments (as human behavioural dispositions), will be subjected to a critical analysis in section 7.

2. ALTRUISM IN BIOLOGY

E.O. Wilson, one of the leading figures of sociobiology, declares that 'the central problem of sociobiology [is]: how can altruism, which by definition reduces personal fitness, possibly evolve by natural selection?' (Wilson 1975: 3). Altruism is (implicitly) defined here in terms of consequences of behaviour and not in terms of intentions or dispositions (inclinations) to behave in certain ways. Altruistic behaviour is behaviour that enhances the fitness of the individual helped at the expense of the fitness of the helping ('altruistic') individual.

As pointed out in Chapter 5, in 'orthodox' Darwinian evolutionary theory the mechanism of natural selection works on individual organisms. There seems to be no place for altruism in the ruthless world of 'orthodox' Darwinism. The 'inescapable logic' of natural selection seems to dictate that organisms that are genetically programmed to behave in ways that reduce their fitness will be replaced in due time by those that are programmed in ways that do not reduce their fitness. The problem for 'orthodox' Darwinists is that the animal kingdom appears to be replete with examples of self-sacrificing behaviour of individual organisms. Well-known examples are ant colonies and beehives.

Wynne-Edwards (1962) suggested that the behaviour of animals like ants and bees, though adverse to their individual fitness, is conducive to their reproductive success because it promotes the reproductive success of the groups (colonies and hives) of which they are part. That is, groups consisting of altruistic individuals do better (in terms of reproductive success) than groups consisting of 'selfish' individuals. Therefore the former tend to replace the latter. Wynne-Edwards thus invoked the notion of *group selection*: natural selection works on groups of individuals. Groups compete with each other as units, and as a result the fittest group survives.

Many (socio)biologists have refused to accept this 'retreat' to group selection.[1] Several alternative explanations of altruism have been developed that are consistent with orthodox individual selection. What these explanations have in common is that they reduce apparent altruistic behaviour to selfish organisms. One of them is provided by Hamilton's (1964) notion of *kin selection*. This notion signifies that individuals preferably make efforts to help relatives to a degree that is proportional to their genetic relatedness. Thus parental help can be explained by the fact that (in sexual reproduction) parents on average share half of their genes with their offspring. Biologists often speak of an individual's *inclusive fitness*, which is the individual's personal fitness modified by the weighted fitness of the individual's relatives – weighted by their degree of genetic relatedness. This notion enables biologists to argue that when individuals are engaged in the type of 'altruism' that is accounted for in kin selection, they really are behaving selfishly. For they behave in a way that then maximizes their inclusive fitness.

The notion of *reciprocal altruism* is invoked by Trivers (1971) to show that apparently altruistic behaviour is brought about by selfish organisms. Instances of reciprocal altruism can be observed when individuals act benevolently towards others in the expectation of being rewarded by some reciprocal act of kindness in the future. Mutual grooming and symbiotic relations are paradigmatic examples. Here we see again that what seems to be self-sacrificing behaviour is in fact identified as self-serving behaviour. Reciprocal altruism can only survive, however, if the organisms involved are capable of remembering and recognizing each other. Otherwise, reciprocal altruists would be easy prey for selfish 'cheaters'.

3. THE EVOLUTION OF SUBOPTIMAL BEHAVIOUR

We have seen that opponents of the notion of group selection argue that socially beneficial behaviour, such as altruism, that appears to be explainable only by recourse to group selection, can in fact be explained as the outcome of individual selection. This argument cannot be said to be a decisive ('knock-out') argument against group selection. For what the argument, if watertight, establishes is only that we do not need the notion of group selection to account for the phenomenon of altruism. It does not prove group selection to be non-existent. In this section, I will deal with a more pressing objection against group selection. The objection is based on the observation that in many true-to-life situations *sub*optimal behaviour evolves. Socially beneficial behaviour that would evolve if there were group selection often does not prevail as the result of individual selection within groups (or populations). Maynard Smith's (1982) evolutionary game theory is tailor-made to explicate this objection.

Evolutionary game theory is developed to study particular evolutionary processes. It assumes that evolutionary change is caused by natural selection within populations. In a sense evolutionary game theory can be regarded as a generalization of 'optimization theory' in biology. Optimization theory in biology studies what features of individuals optimize their fitness. Optimization theory is suited to deal with frequency-independent selection: selection processes in which the fitness of individuals depends only on the *natural* environment. Evolutionary game theory is devised to analyse *frequency-dependent* selection. In frequency-dependent selection, the fitness of individuals depends not only on their natural, but also on their *social* environment. That is to say, the fitness of particular phenotypes in a population depends on their frequencies in the population.

In evolutionary game theory, when an individual is said to have a particular phenotype this means that the individual consistently follows some rule of behaviour over time. The rules are assumed to be genetically determined and, as such, they are assumed to be inheritable. Individuals are assumed to be unable to change their behavioural rules, or strategies, during their lifetime. Each individual is assumed to be of a fixed strategic type. Here is the element of *individual stasis* that is typical for all evolutionary theories based on the mechanism of natural selection. Those who hold that game theory is about rational choice of individuals in situations of strategic interdependence will probably wonder what this has to do with game theory. The individuals in evolutionary game theory cannot choose at all! But the situation they are in can be said to have a game-theoretic structure in that their results depend not only on their own behaviour but also on the behaviour of the other individuals in the population. To be more precise, their results depend also on what other rules are followed and on the relative proportions of the individuals that follow the different rules in the population.

Assuming stasis on the individual level does not mean that there is stasis also on the population level. As we have seen in Chapter 5, there is dynamics on the level of the population when the individuals following some rule are more successful in leaving offspring than others. As the rules are assumed to be inheritable, the descendants will be of the same behavioural type as their ancestors. The *replicator dynamics* (or 'Malthusian dynamics') in a population is assumed to be such that the growth rate of some rule depends on its fitness, which in turn depends not only on its fitness in pairwise encounters with other rules followed in the population, but also on their frequencies in the population. Technically speaking, the frequency of some rule increases when its fitness exceeds the population-weighted average, stabilizes when its fitness equals the average, and falls when it lies below the average.[2] The population comes to rest when fitness is equalized in the population; that is, frequencies reach a stationary point (fixed point) when all the rules that are followed have the same fitness.

This notion of a stationary point is not the key notion in Maynard Smith's evolutionary game theory, however. Rather, Maynard Smith's key notion of equilibrium, that of an *evolutionarily stable strategy* (ESS), is a refinement of the notion of a stationary point. The general idea behind this notion is that of resistance to invasion by 'mutant' strategies:

> an ESS is a strategy such that, if all the members of the population adopt it, then no mutant strategy could invade the population under the influence of natural selection.
>
> (Maynard Smith 1982: 10)

A mutant strategy is a strategy in the strategy (or phenotypic) set of the population that differs slightly from the strategies that are already played. The strategy set of the population consists of all pure strategies available to the population and all mixed strategies that can be defined in terms of the pure strategies available. Say there are two pure strategies feasible for a population, A and B. Then the set of possible mixed strategies consists of elements 'play A with probability p and play B with probability $1 - p$', with $0 < p < 1$. What makes the notion of ESS more 'demanding' than that of a stationary point, then, is that an ESS must (and a stationary point need not) be able to resist an invasion of strategies that are now not present in the populations but may show up as mutants in the future. In short, the distinguishing feature of an ESS is its stability in the defined strategy set.

The simplest game that Maynard Smith analyses is the *Hawk–Dove (HD)* game. To avoid misunderstanding, the game is not about a confrontation between individuals of the two species that we know under the names of hawks and doves. The game represents contest situations between individuals of different behavioural types of the same species. It is not about *inter*species but about *intra*species contests. Two animals are imagined to contest some resource with fitness value V. This means that the fitness of the animal that manages to get away with the resource is increased by V. If in contesting the resource it comes to fighting, however, the individual that loses the fight incurs costs C (where $C > V$). It is further assumed that there are two pure strategies available to the species:

Hawk (H): fight for the resource; stop fighting only when injured or when the opponent retreats.

Dove (D): display; retreat as soon as the opponent starts to fight.

Under some additional assumptions, matrix 1 below can be derived. Taking $V = 2$ and $C = 4$, we get matrix 2:

	H	D
H	$\frac{1}{2}(V-C)$	V
D	0	$\frac{1}{2}V$

Matrix 1

	H	D
H	−1	2
D	0	1

Matrix 2

The 'fitness payoffs' in the matrix are the payoffs from the perspective of the Row-'player'.[3] Keep in mind, however, that no 'player' can choose between H and D. Each individual is either of behavioural type H or of type D.

The analysis of this game depends on further assumptions that have to be made. The most elementary analysis proceeds on the assumptions, among others, that the population is of an infinite size (so that H- and D-strategists, and possibly mutant strategists, face the same frequencies in the population), that reproduction is asexual (so that 'like begets like'; the descendants of H-strategists, for example, are also H-strategists), that contests are pairwise (individuals are not 'playing the field'; they do not play against the population as a whole) and that the contests are symmetric (individuals are not assumed to be able to discern differences among their opponents).[4] Another assumption that deserves special attention is that the pairs are randomly assigned. The individuals cannot play selectively against preferred opponents. In particular, when confronted with a H-strategist, neither an H- nor a D-strategist can draw back.

Under these assumptions, the only ESS in the HD-game as represented in matrix 2 is a mixed strategy M, with $p = \frac{1}{2}$. It is easy to check that for any other value of p, $0 \leq p \leq 1$, either H- (if $0 \leq p < \frac{1}{2}$) or D-strategists (if $\frac{1}{2} < p \leq 1$) will grow at the expense of the other type. Only if $p = \frac{1}{2}$ will all individuals in the population have the same fitness. No mutant strategy can invade such a population, for all mutant strategies would have a lower fitness than M. A mixed ESS can be understood in two different ways. Either it means that *genetic polymorphism* exists: the population is split in half then; half of the population consists of pure H- and half of pure D-strategists. Or it means that every individual in the population has the same built-in randomizing device which makes the individual play H one-half and D one-half of the time.

When the population settles at this ESS, each individual will have an average (gain in) fitness of $\frac{1}{2}$. This is far from optimal. For consider a situation in which all individuals were D-players ($p = 0$). Each individual would then have an average (gain in) fitness of 1. If there was group selection going on, we could expect this optimal situation to evolve. In this situation, each individual would behave in a cooperative way. But if there is individual selection, as is assumed here, then this optimal situation, if it could come about at all, crumbles. The optimal situation is extremely

138

vulnerable to an invasion of mutant H-players. For in a population of D-players, a lonely H-player will have a certain (gain in) fitness of 2! Hence the frequency of H-players will increase rapidly at the expense of the frequency of D-players until $p = \frac{1}{2}$ is established. And the larger the proportion of H-players, the lower the average fitness of the group taken as a whole.

This result, that an optimal group performance gives way to a poorer, suboptimal performance, is the paradigmatic example of the deteriorating effects of within-group, between-individuals selection. A peaceful population of cooperating individuals (D-strategists) is undermined by harmful free riders (H-players). Or, to borrow Dawkins' dramatic terminology, the flourishing group suffers from 'treachery from within'.

4. RESTORING OPTIMALITY BY EXTENDING THE STRATEGY SET

Is a population of individual organisms that are 'playing' the HD-game bound to get stuck in the suboptimal mixed ESS M? Not necessarily. It all depends on the strategy set. If the mutant strategies that enter the population all lie within the specified strategy set, then there is no way in which natural selection can produce a more optimal outcome. But if mutant strategies enter that lie outside the strategy set, then the situation may change radically. The intrusion of such mutant strategies leads in effect to an extension of the original strategy set. Strictly speaking, then, a different game emerges. This is illustrated by Maynard Smith by introducing the pure strategy *Bourgeois* (B) in the original HD-game:

Bourgeois (B): if owner, play Hawk; if intruder, play Dove.

It is important to notice that B is not a mixed strategy that can be defined in terms of the pure strategies H and D. The new element that is introduced here is that of individuals having different roles: owner or intruder. If the individuals are able to discern what roles they and their opponents have in particular encounters, the game is *asymmetric*. Under several assumptions,[5] we can derive matrix 3 from matrix 2:

	H	D	B
H	−1	2	½
D	0	1	½
B	−½	¾	1

Matrix 3. The HDB-game

139

In the game represented in matrix 3, the only ESS is B. When the population settles at this ESS, all individuals have a (gain in) fitness of 1. This is exactly equal to the optimal (gain in) fitness of individuals in a population consisting only of D-strategists. The important difference between these two 'population states' is, however, that whereas 'all individuals play B' is stable in the asymmetric HDB-game, 'all individuals play D' is highly unstable both in the original symmetric HD-game and in the asymmetric HDB-game.

According to Maynard Smith (1982: 23), what this shows is that even without altering the payoffs, the convention of the asymmetry of ownership is sufficient to settle the contests in a peaceful and optimal way. If all individuals in a population are B-strategists, then owners of resources are never attacked by intruders. Ownership can thus be said to be 'respected' *de facto* by all individuals in such a population.

It is important to notice that Maynard Smith's account of the evolution of the 'convention of the asymmetry of ownership' presupposes an extension of the original strategy set of the HD-game. Within the strategy set of the original HD-game, no strategy can beat the ESS M. Only within the enlarged strategy set of the HDB-game can M be invaded (by B). But if the original HD-strategy set can be enlarged by adding B, there seem to be many other strategies that could be added as well. As I want to point out now, it is this open-endedness or indeterminacy of possible extensions of the strategy set that makes Maynard Smith's account vulnerable to several objections.

B-strategists can only appear in a population playing the HD-game as a result of gene mutations. Recall from our discussion in Chapter 5 that gene mutations are assumed to produce *gradual* change. It seems that it takes quite a leap to arrive at a relatively sophisticated B-strategist if we start with simple H- and D-players. Let us ignore this complication, however. Let us concentrate on another aspect of gene mutations: mutations are assumed to be blind. Assume that a mutation causes a lonely B-strategist to appear in a population of M-strategists playing the original HD-game. It can be calculated from matrix 3 that the (gain in) fitness of the lonely B-strategist does not exceed that of the rest of the population. M-strategists and the B-strategist will all have a (gain in) fitness of ½. This implies that the lonely B-strategist cannot invade a population of M-strategists in the same straightforward way that a lonely H-player can invade a population of D-players.

Things are different as soon as more B-strategists are introduced in the population of M-strategists. For then the (gain in) fitness of the B-strategists would exceed that of the M-strategists. The more B-strategists, the faster the B-strategy will spread over the population. But as mutations are assumed to be blind, why would we expect new mutations to produce exactly the same B-strategists? It seems that we cannot rule out the possibility that an X-strategist would be produced that attaches the converse behavioural consequences to the same asymmetry of ownership that is perceived by B-strategists:

strategy X: if owner, play D; if intruder, play H.[6]

It is easy to check that if repeated mutations were to cause X-strategists and B-strategists to be introduced in equal numbers in a population of M-strategists, then the 'mutant mix' would again have the same fitness as M-strategists. Only if one of the mutant strategies is produced more often than the other will that strategy eventually prevail in the population. Whether X or B will ultimately dominate the population is determined by the 'blind' mutation mechanism.

It is also possible that a mutant strategy shows up that is based on another asymmetry than ownership. As Maynard Smith himself argues, a strategy 'Assessor' may be introduced that is based on the perception of differences in body size:

Assessor (A): if larger, play H; if smaller, play D.

If we add strategy A to the HDB-strategy set (and if we assume that if it comes to fighting, the larger individual will always get away with the resource), we can derive matrix 4 below from matrix 3:[7]

	H	D	B	A
H	−1	2	½	−1
D	0	1	½	½
B	−½	³⁄₂	1	−½
A	−½	³⁄₂	⁵⁄₄	1

Matrix 4. The HDBA-game

As an A-strategist can be observed to do better against a B-strategist than a B-strategist against another B-strategist ($\frac{5}{4} > 1$), a lonely A-strategist can invade a population of B-strategists playing the HDB-game. A is the only ESS in the extended HDBA-game. The results of a population consisting of A-strategists are as socially beneficial as the optimal results of a population consisting of B-strategists (and of a population consisting of D-players).

It can be pointed out, however, that if we make the HDBA-game more realistic, a population of A-strategists would no longer yield optimal results, even if A was still the only ESS.[8] In other words, in this more realistic HDBA-game A could still invade a population of B-strategists. But by outperforming B-strategists, the A-strategists would turn optimal into sub-optimal results (in the same way as the invasion of H-players in a population of D-players is deleterious for the individuals).

141

The lesson to be learned from this is, I think, that whether individual selection leads to suboptimal social outcomes or not depends crucially on the correct identification of the strategy set. This sensitivity of the results of evolutionary game theory to specifications of the strategy set has incited many critical remarks. A prominent example is Gould (1980). Gould's main objection against the sociobiologist's approach is that sociobiologists typically invent speculative adaptive *'just-so stories'* for each and every bit of behaviour. That is, the 'trick' to be done is to present a story in which the behaviour that is to be explained features as an optimal solution (or adaptation) in some stipulated problem situation. Sociobiologists rest content when they have shown that natural selection favours the behaviour in the problem situation:

> virtuosity in invention replaces testability and mere consistency with evolutionary theory becomes the primary criterion of acceptance.
>
> (Gould 1980: 267)

Gould's objection here is that a lot of detailed and painstaking empirical research would have to be carried out to substantiate the sociobiologist's claim that some bit of behaviour is an adaptation produced by natural selection. Empirical research could show, for example, that some particular behaviour is not an adaptation at all, that it is produced by some other evolutionary force than natural selection, or that it is a by-product of natural selection working on other features.

Maynard Smith's (1982) and Dawkins' (1980) rejoinder to Gould's general criticism of the adaptationist's programme is that Gould misidentifies the purpose of evolutionary game theory. The Hawk–Dove game, for example, is not meant to be a representation of any specific animal example. Evolutionary game theoretic analyses of this game do not yield (and are not intended to yield) testable hypotheses. As Maynard Smith puts it, they rather 'reveal the logical possibilities (for example, the likelihood of mixed strategies) inherent in all contest situations' (Maynard Smith 1982: 6). But, Maynard Smith hastens to add, the 'practical force' of Gould's criticism is that when particular cases are analysed, much more attention must be paid to a correct specification of the strategy set.[9] Dawkins seems to believe that 'biological common sense' can be relied on here (see Dawkins 1980: 359). Maynard Smith remarks more cautiously:

> ideally, the phenotypic set could be discovered by studying the range of intraspecific variability under intense selection over a long time-scale; in practice, we will often have to rely on a mixture of common sense and a study of intra- and inter-specific variability.
>
> (Maynard Smith 1982: 175)

At any rate, Maynard Smith is right in arguing that individual selection does not necessarily lead either to optimal or to suboptimal social outcomes. If the persistent behaviour of individuals in a population is correctly identified as individuals playing B in an HDB-game, then the evolutionary game-theoretic analysis is similar in kind to the individual selectionist accounts of altruism. In both cases a phenomenon that has the appearance of being the result of group selection is shown to be the result of individual selection.

5. THE 'SELFISH GENE' AS THE UNIT OF SELECTION

Evolutionary game theory is consonant with 'orthodox' Darwinism, or, to be more precise, evolutionary game theory takes the correctness of 'orthodox' Darwinism for granted. That is, the individual organism is the unit of selection. Dawkins (1976) draws heavily on Maynard Smith's work on evolutionary game theory. Yet he holds that the unit of selection is not the individual organism, but the 'selfish' gene.[10] This calls for clarification.

Dawkins (1976) argues that the individual organism cannot be regarded as the unit of selection mainly, it seems, because the individual organism is not stable enough in evolutionary time. As argued in Chapter 3, natural selection needs stable material to work on. According to Dawkins, an entity must possess the properties of longevity, fecundity and accuracy to qualify as the unit of selection. Individual organisms do not qualify, especially when reproduction is sexual (and not asexual). In genetically hetero-geneous populations, the *meiosis* (genetic recombination) that is involved in sexual reproduction constantly leads to recombinations of genetic material. In contrast, the genes themselves are long lived and do qualify as units of selection also in the other respects (fecundity and accuracy). Genes are paradigmatic examples of *replicators*, entities that make fairly exact copies of themselves.[11]

Hamilton's (1964) attempt to give an 'orthodox' Darwinian individualistic account of altruism in terms of inclusive fitness is seen by Dawkins as an important step in the direction of gene selection. For, after all, what is decisive in this account is whether different organisms have a fair chance of sharing genetic material with each other. Only when this chance is high enough may the decrease in the fitness of the helping individual be compensated by the increase in the fitness of the helped individual so that the helper's inclusive fitness is increased. As Dawkins argues, this can readily be reformulated in terms of genes that serve their own interests only by helping copies. Only then can the benefits of helping outweigh the costs.

The rejoinder of 'orthodox' Darwinians is straightforward. They stress that it is organisms and not genes on which selection pressures work directly. It is organisms that may or may not suffer from hunger (or, more generally, from lack of resources), that may or may not arrive at repro-ductive age, that may or may not leave more descendants than others. Selection pressures act upon genes only indirectly. Only if an organism succeeds in being reproductively successful can its genes spread in the gene pool. If an organism does not leave offspring, its genes get lost to the gene pool as well.

Part of this controversy can be resolved, I think, by bringing in some of the distinctions that I discussed in Chapter 5. Sober's (1984) distinction between 'selection for' and 'selection of' and Hull's (1988) related distinction between 'interactors' and 'replicators' are illuminating here. No participant in the controversy seems to deny that there is 'selection of' genes, or, more generally, of replicators. That is, 'orthodox' Darwinians agree with Dawkins that the *effects* of natural selection pertain to gene frequencies in the gene pools of populations. And nobody seems to deny that it is phenotypic traits of organisms that are 'selected for'. Natural selection works on interactors. Dawkins concedes to 'orthodox' Darwinians that the immediate manifestation of natural selection is nearly always at the individual level.

But there is more to the controversy. The camps differ in their view on the relation between genes and organisms. In particular, they seem to hold different views on how genes instruct organisms to interact with their environments. Dawkins seems to deny that organisms have an independent role to play in the selection process. He prefers to speak of organisms in terms of *vehicles*, of 'survival machines' used by genes to serve their ends. For, as Dawkins argues, it is genes that instruct or program the vehicles to interact in certain ways with their environment. Therefore, the picture that emerges is one in which differential changes in replicators are not only effects of selection processes, but also the *causes* of the differential extinction and proliferation of organisms. Or, to be more precise, the picture is one of sequences of causal processes in which genes play the pivotal, if not the only, role. Given certain environmental circumstances, the gene frequencies in the gene pool of a population determine the relative reproductive successes or failures of the organisms in the population. In turn, differential replication of genes is caused so that gene frequencies may change. The new frequencies determine new differential successes of organisms, and so on. This is what makes Dawkins say that gene survival is 'the currency that really matters, the "gold-standard" of evolution' (Dawkins 1976: 133).

Those who hold that the individual organism is *the* unit of selection, or, more moderately, that the organism is a unit of selection, reply that the relation between an organism and its genes is much more complex than Dawkins suggests. They do not deny that organisms are programmed by their genes. But, for one thing, they do deny that genes are in full control of the functioning of organisms. Genes do not dictate the behaviour of organisms, at least not the behaviour of organisms of the 'higher' species. Curiously enough, we will see later on in this chapter that Dawkins himself subscribes to the idea that humans can and hopefully will liberate themselves from the dictates of their selfish genes!

Even if genes were fully to determine the phenotypic characteristics of organisms, Sober (1984) argues, they may not do so on a one-to-one basis. Sometimes the relation is many to one: some phenotypic trait is not the result of one single gene, but of the interaction among an ensemble of genes. This phenomenon of *polygenic effects* is well known among biologists. According to Sober, this phenomenon implies that the contribution that some single gene makes to the reproductive success of organisms is context dependent. The conclusion that Sober draws is that:

> if a gene raises the probability of a given phenotype in one context and lowers it in another, there is no such thing as the causal role that the gene has in general.

> (Sober 1984: 313)

It may be noted in passing that in Chapter 6 a similar phenomenon of context dependency was referred to in the discussion of the complex interaction of routines and organization forms in producing a firm's overall performance.

Dawkins (1976) does not ignore the phenomenon of polygenic effects. Genes are said to collaborate and interact in inextricably complex ways, both with each other and with their external environment. Dawkins calls the 'manufacture' of a leg a multi-gene cooperative enterprise. Building an organism is teamwork. Nor does Dawkins deny that the effect of some gene on its organism's phenotype depends on the gene's context, that is on the other genes in the organism. But he denies that this is incompatible with his gene-centred view. Dawkins argues that although it is in each particular instance *teams* of genes that are selected for, the selection process is such that the best *single* genes will *on average* be reproductively most successful. For as sexual reproduction continually leads to a reshuffling of genes, single genes will permanently find themselves in other teams, that is to say in the company of other genes. It may be the case that occasionally a 'bad' gene is lucky in that the poor performance of a 'bad' gene is compensated by the good performances of its superior team members. But on other occasions its team will lose. 'Bad' genes will therefore be consistently on the losing side and the best genes consistently on the winning side.

Dawkins' conclusion seems to be that only those individual genes are selected that *on average* have the best phenotypic consequences. This conclusion is contested by Sober. Sober's main objection is based on the reverse phenomenon of polygenic effects: the phenomenon of *pleiotropy*. 'Pleiotropy' refers to a one-to-many relation between a cluster of genes and several phenotypic traits. For example, the same cluster of genes that is responsible for the human jaw is shown to be responsible also for the human chin. Sober argues that if two (or more) phenotypic traits are perfectly correlated because of pleiotropy, it is possible that a phenotypic trait survives that *on average* is deleterious to the fitness of the organisms possessing the trait. The correlated traits that are produced by the same cluster of genes may be so advantageous that the organisms that are programmed by the cluster are fitter than the organisms that are programmed by another cluster.

There is another aspect to Dawkins' defence of his gene-centred view that deserves special attention. As genes have to work together with other genes in teams, what is relevant is not what they would produce in isolation. What is relevant is what they are able to produce in combination with the other genes that are co-members of the teams they find themselves in. As Dawkins argues:

> a good gene must be compatible with, and complementary to, the other genes with whom it has to share a long succession of bodies.
>
> (Dawkins 1976: 91)

The result of this is that well-integrated organisms evolve. Dawkins argues that this result could easily give one the impression that compatible combinations of genes are selected together as units, where in fact there has been selection going on purely at the level of the independent gene.

The careful reader may have noticed that Dawkins uses the same line of argument here as individual selectionists do when criticizing the notion of group selection. Recall that they argue that, for example, the persistence of altruistic behaviour in a group may seem to be the result of groups that would act as wholes and would outcompete others, where in fact it is the result of the selection of individual organisms. As a matter of fact, Dawkins believes that Maynard Smith's evolutionary game theory (and its central concept ESS), which was meant to apply to the behaviour of individual organisms in populations, can be applied 'one level below' to analyse 'gene behaviour' in organisms. Dawkins illustrates this by the following rowing analogy:

> suppose an ideally balanced crew would consist of four right-handers and four left-handers. Once again assume that the coach, unaware of this fact, selects blindly on 'merit'. Now, if the pool of candidates happens to be dominated by right-handers, any individual left-hander will tend to be at an advantage: he is likely to cause any boat in which he finds himself to win, and he will therefore appear to be a good oarsman. Conversely, in a pool dominated by left-handers, a right-hander would have an advantage. This is similar to the case of a hawk doing well in a population of doves, and a dove doing well in a population of hawks. The difference is that there we were talking about interactions between individual bodies – selfish machines – whereas here we are talking, by analogy, about interactions between genes within bodies.
>
> (Dawkins 1976: 92)

I think that this analogy is seriously misleading. To see why, let us elaborate on the analogy. If individual left-handers in a pool dominated by right-handers will tend to be at an advantage in precisely the same way as individual Hawk-players will be at an advantage in a population of players dominated by Dove-players, then the crew that results is not ideally balanced at all. Consider once again the numerical example of the HD-game represented in matrix 2. This example accords with Dawkins' example in that in both cases an evolutionarily stable polymorphism will result in 50 per cent right-handers (D-players) and 50 per cent left-handers (H-players). This polymorphism, however, is far from 'ideally balanced' from the perspective of the crew (the population). The crew (population) would achieve better results if it consisted only of right-handers (D-players).

The problem with Dawkins' analogy is, I think, that it mixes up two levels of organization: the level of (the gene pool of) the population and the level of the organism. The analogy with the HD-game applies (if it applies at all) to the level of the population. To be more precise, a population of organisms playing the HD-game will settle on stable gene frequencies in the gene pool. If Dawkins is right that organisms ('vehicles') have no independent causal role to play in the selection process, we are talking here about the interaction of genes (or clusters of genes) in the *gene pool*.

The interaction of genes in *organisms* is of an entirely different kind. As Dawkins himself has asserted repeatedly, the interaction of genes in organisms is of a cooperative kind. The element of conflict that characterizes the HD-game is absent here. Genes within organisms are selected for their compatibility and complementarity. Genes and their alleles can only be called 'deadly rivals', as they are by Dawkins at one point (Dawkins 1976: 40), in the gene pool of the entire population. They are not rivals in one and the same organism. For an organism simply either has a certain gene or has one of its alleles. It cannot have both at one and the same time. Furthermore, genes can be said to be specialized. They cannot be 'seated' in any place in the boat. Hence, the only rivals of genes for some seat in the boat can be their alleles in the gene pool.

According to Maynard Smith (1987), this is the main reason why organisms can and groups (populations) cannot evolve adaptations by natural selection.[12] Whereas individual organisms in groups can outcompete and replace others, genes in organisms cannot. As Maynard Smith puts it, 'genes do not multiply horizontally' (Maynard Smith 1987: 130). In organisms, 'the replicators, or genes, that are responsible for heredity behave in a way that, typically, does not permit within-individual, between-replicator selection' (Maynard Smith 1987: 121). Typically, then, 'only those genes survive that ensure the survival of the individuals in which they find themselves' (Maynard Smith 1987: 130). In contrast, in groups the interests of organisms conflict (to some degree) so that there is within-group,

147

between-organism selection. Organisms can 'free ride', can survive at the cost of others, even if that leads to a poorer performance of the group.

The picture of the interaction between genes within organisms that emerges from this discussion is one in which the genes are viewed as complementary. The genes are supposed to be involved in team production, with each gene playing its own indispensable part. To an economist, this sounds like a joint venture of specialized genes. As a matter of fact, we will see in the next section that there are economists and biologists who have speculated about the division of labour both within and between organisms.

6. 'THE DIVISION OF LABOUR IS LIMITED BY THE EXTENT OF THE MARKET'

Here is another example of the transfer of ideas from biology to economics and vice versa. The economist Houthakker argues that economists may derive some useful insight from observation of the non-human world. In particular, Houthakker argues that specialization in economics is closely connected with what biologists call speciation, or the formation of species. Conversely, the biologist Ghiselin (1974) argues that biologists might profit from viewing biological phenomena from a classical economic point of view. As in Houthakker's paper, the division of labour is one of the key issues that is addressed in Ghiselin's book. We shall see that in Ghiselin's criticism of Houthakker's paper, a similar issue pops up that is central to the units of selection controversy. Ghiselin argues that the type of specialization that Houthakker analyses has its biological counterpart in the *cooperative* division of labour between organs *within* organisms and not, as Houthakker presumes, in the *competitive* division of labour *between* organisms or species.

Houthakker elaborates on Adam Smith's famous but also somewhat puzzling statement that 'the division of labour is limited by the extent of the market'. Houthakker argues that:

> it is in fact from indivisibilities that the division of labour takes its start, and the basic indivisibility is that of the individual, whether human or animal. [. . .] The indivisibility of the individual consists in the fact that, although it may be capable of a great many different activities, it can perform only few activities simultaneously because most activities utilize the same resources and more particularly that coordinating resource that is known as the brain.
>
> (Houthakker 1956: 182)

Consequently, an individual person is faced with what Houthakker calls *internal* (or individual) coordination costs when that individual conducts many different activities. As Houthakker shows, it may then be advantageous for individuals to specialize on one (or a few) activities. Whether this is advantageous depends not only on the internal coordination costs saved but also on the *external* coordination costs to be made. For example, individuals have to incur transportation costs when they exchange their products or services.

In Houthakker's analysis, individuals are assumed to make a trade-off between internal and external coordination costs: 'the optimum amount of specialization therefore depends on the balance between internal and external coordination costs' (Houthakker 1956: 188). Adam Smith's 'extent of the market' is taken here quite literally in spatial terms. The greater the number of specialized market participants and the larger the distances that they have to bridge, the higher the transportation costs, and, hence, the higher the external coordination costs. Houthakker takes his analysis to be applicable also to the issue of spatial competition between firms. If several firms produce a good for a population of customers which is distributed along a road, then the area served by each firm will depend critically on its transportation costs. Thus the balancing between internal and external coordination costs as described above determines the number of firms in the market here. Likewise, Houthakker holds that the same analysis may be used in the biological realm to determine the optimum range and optimum amount of members of species:

> We may, for instance, consider each species as adapted to one particular range of foods (though this is by no means the whole story). The wider the range of foods, the more complicated the anatomical and physiological arrangements necessary to obtain and digest each type of food efficiently; or in the above terminology, the higher the internal coordination cost. On the other hand, a wider range of foods makes possible a larger number of members of the species, because the danger of starvation is smaller.
>
> (Houthakker 1956: 186)

What we see here is that *speciation*, that is compared by Houthakker with specialization, does not refer to the division of the animal kingdom (or a part of it) in species (or to 'the formation of species', as Houthakker calls it), but to the division of a species in members. And what we see here also is that Houthakker's contention that his analysis shows that economists can learn something from biologists is misleading. It is rather the other way around: Houthakker analyses 'speciation' *as if* individual organisms economize on costs.[13]

It is ironic to see that the biologist Ghiselin (1974, 1978), who says that he is promoting the analytical transfer of ideas from economics to biology, criticizes both Smith's original account of the division of labour and Houthakker's elaboration of Smith's account. Ghiselin praises Smith for drawing attention to limitations to the division of labour. In Ghiselin's interpretation, 'the extent of the market' basically refers to three function-ally related variables: space, energy (which stands for resources in general) and time. But Ghiselin argues that Smith failed to distinguish between two different types of division of labour. On the one hand there is *competitive* division of labour which occurs between independent firms, and on the other hand there is *cooperative* division of labour which occurs between members of the same firm (see Ghiselin 1974: 235 and 1978: 234). The first thing to notice is that the two types operate on different levels of organiz-ation: the competitive type operates on the level of the market or the industry (and generates separate firms) and the cooperative type operates on the lower level of the firm (and generates new types of firm members).

What is more important, Ghiselin argues that the two types reflect different relations between the wholes and parts that are involved. As the term competitive division of labour already indicates, the interests of the entities that emerge conflict with each other. Consider Houthakker's ex-ample of spatial competition again. The larger the area that a firm manages to serve exclusively, the less is left for its competitors. One can generalize this by thinking in terms of market shares of firms. According to Ghiselin the proper biological analogue here is the subdivision of ecological niches. Ghiselin argues that in the biological realm cooperative division of labour refers to the differentiation of organ systems in organisms. Here the entities that emerge, the organ systems, work together in order to produce the best possible outcome for the comprising whole, the organism. Organ systems in organisms do not compete with each other. They typically are complementary.

Ghiselin criticizes Houthakker for making the same failure as Adam Smith: that of conflating the two types of division of labour. As we have seen, Houthakker argues that the same principle of balancing internal and external coordination costs can be invoked to explain the spatial com-petition between firms and to explain 'speciation'. Ghiselin holds that there are two different types of division of labour at stake here. Whereas spatial competition is an example of competitive division of labour, 'speciation' is an example of cooperative division of labour. Ghiselin argues that the principle that Houthakker invokes can be used only to explain the latter type.

In his account of 'speciation', Houthakker argues that internal coordi-nation costs are higher when the anatomical and physiological arrange-ments that are necessary to obtain and digest food are more complicated. Houthakker seems to conclude from this that the range of foods available will be divided among the members of a species in the same way as an area is divided among competing firms in spatial competition. To Ghiselin this conclusion is misguided. What can be explained by the principle that Houthakker invokes is not how many members a species has, but the organic structure ('how many organs') members of a species have. Ghiselin demonstrates how Houthakker's principle of balancing internal and external coordination costs explains 'the definitive trend toward the specialization and effective spatial organization of organ systems in evolutionary series' (Ghiselin 1978: 235). That is, Ghiselin explains that labour is divided among the organs within an organism to prevent mutually incompatible activities from interfering with each other. As a result of this division of labour, new species may emerge.

As noted above, Ghiselin appears to regard the division of labour within firms between their members as the economic counterpart of the division of labour within organisms between their organs. However, this should not be taken literally. He compares the functioning of organs in organisms with that of members within firms to bring out the point that 'organisms should be compared to factories, not battleships' (Ghiselin 1978: 237). Just like firms, organisms are cooperative productive ventures. What counts in natural selection is the reproductive output of organisms and not, or at least not only, their combat power. But Ghiselin leaves no doubt that human beings and not firms are the proper analogues of organisms: 'in economics firms are analogous to species, employees to organisms' (Ghiselin 1978: 237).

What we have in economics then are not two but three different levels of organization (or integration): individuals, firms (and households) and industries. At each of these three levels, there is a different relation between the whole and its parts. At the highest level of the industry, the parts, firms, compete for market shares. Their interests conflict. At one level below, the level of the firm, the parts, the individual firm members, can be said to be involved in mixed-motive games (or cooperative games) of the HD type. There are opportunities for shirking, for 'free riding', for 'moral hazard'.[14] The interests of the parts conflict to some degree here too. But what is more important, suboptimal firm ('group') outcomes may result. At the lowest level, that of the individual, the parts, the organs, cannot be said to have interests other than that of the whole, the organism. Combinations of activities in one organ or divisions of activities in separate organs are not prolonged unless they add to the differential reproductive success of their comprising organisms.

What makes the level of the organism different from higher levels of organization is that the interests of organisms can be said to coincide with the interests of their parts. At higher levels of integration, this identity of interests between the encompassing whole and its parts is lacking. In so far as genes or organs, or any inheritable biological determinants of the constitution and behaviour of organisms, can be said to have interests at all, they have no other way of serving their own interests than by serving the interest of the organism of which they are part, that is by serving the organism's inclusive fitness.

151

7. ALTRUISM IN ECONOMICS

The true economic counterparts of organisms in biology, Ghiselin argues, are individual human agents, not firms. If we conceive of a human being as an organism that is subject to the same merciless force of natural selection as other organisms, then it seems that the classical image of *Homo oeconomicus* is reinforced. It seems that individuals who would not have been led by the desire to improve their own material welfare would have been replaced by individuals who are driven by selfish motives. Yet there are economists who argue that altruistic individuals can survive in such a harsh material world. Becker is one of them.[15] In Becker (1976) it is argued that altruistic behaviour can be selected as a consequence of individual rationality. As we shall see, in Becker's argument 'orthodox' economic reasoning and 'orthodox' (socio)biological reasoning are combined in a special way.

Becker adopts the conventional economic conception of individual rationality. Rational actors are assumed to maximize utility functions subject to limited resources. But both 'utility function' and 'limited resources' are given an unconventional meaning in Becker's analysis. The utility of an altruist b who is altruistic towards an egoist i is assumed to be a function not only of b's own consumption, but also of i's consumption. And, likewise, b's limited resources, the 'basic' budget constraint, which is also called b's *social income* by Becker (see Becker 1974), is composed not only of b's own income but also of the value to b of i's income. In this setup, if b is able to transfer money to i without any monetary loss, then an equilibrium is reached (b maximizes utility) when b transfers just enough money to i so that a small change in b's own consumption has exactly the same marginal utility as a small change in i's consumption.

The analytical apparatus that Becker applies here is that of standard indifference curve analysis. But now the indifference curves do not represent the preferences of some individual over pairs of goods, but the preferences of an altruist b over pairs of incomes, consisting of b's own income and that of i. The theoretical result that Becker is able to infer from this analysis is the famous *Rotten-Kid Theorem*. The theorem says in effect that the egoistic 'Rotten Kid' i may be induced by 'Big Daddy's' (b's) altruism to behave *as if i* too is altruistic. For it may be in i's own (selfish) interest to anticipate what b is likely to transfer (given b's altruism) in such a way that b is made better off as well. Not only is b's 'subjective' utility enhanced, but b's 'objective' income is improved also by i's behaviour.

The Rotten-Kid Theorem can therefore be said to entail two related results. The first result concerns the cooperative behaviour that Rotten Kid (i) displays in anticipation of Daddy's (b's) altruistic behaviour. As a consequence of the rational behaviour of both, both maximize their own utility function. This first result is not really surprising. As we shall see, it is the outcome of 'standard' economic analysis of a specific instance of interaction. It is the second result that is counterintuitive. The second result relates to the 'objective' benefits that are gained by altruistic Daddy. On the basis of this result, Becker concludes that altruistic inclinations can be advantageous for the fitness of the individuals having the inclinations, even if other individuals with whom they interact have selfish inclinations. Altruism can have survival value in groups that are populated with egoists. This is the (socio)biological part of Becker's argument. I shall discuss the two results in turn.

In his comment on Becker (1976), Hirshleifer (1976) emphasizes that Becker's theorem is valid only when 'Big Daddy' h has the last word. That is, only when Rotten Kid i has to decide what to do *before* Big Daddy h decides how to divide the 'family' income, can Rotten Kid be induced to behave in a cooperative way. Otherwise, if Rotten Kid can decide *afterwards*, it will simply use its money regardless of whether Daddy is pleased by it or not and regardless also of whether Daddy's income is enhanced by it or not. Becker's analysis can be said to exhibit an implicit game-theoretic structure in that the effects of the actions taken by both Kid and Daddy depend not only on their own actions but also on the actions taken by the other.[16] Hirshleifer's comment makes clear that the game-theoretic structure is of a 'peculiar' type. Kid and Daddy, the players, are assumed to play a single game but they are not assumed to make their decisions simultaneously (or at least they are assumed to have no information about the other's decision). Kid and Daddy are assumed to make their decisions in turn, first Kid then Daddy.

In this setup of sequential decision making, if Kid takes Daddy's reaction into account when making its decision, selfish Kid behaves *as if* it were altruistic also. This means that cooperative behaviour does not testify to altruistic dispositions. According to Hirshleifer, this reflects a valuable insight that economic analysis brings in: 'actual behaviour always represents the *interaction* of two determining factors – on the one side preferences, on the other side opportunities (constraints)' (Hirshleifer 1977: 21). Hirshleifer argues that in many analyses the latter factor is often ignored so that preferences are wrongly inferred *linea recta* from behaviour and vice versa. In the Rotten-Kid example it is the shape of the joint productive opportunity boundary that, given Daddy's degree of altruism (and his having the last word), makes it profitable for Kid to behave in a cooperative way. To avoid confusion, Hirshleifer proposes to drop the term altruism altogether and to speak instead of cooperative behaviour.

Hirshleifer surely is right in stressing that actual behaviour is determined not only by preferences but also by opportunities. But he omits to mention a crucial third codetermining factor: *beliefs*. In order to derive Becker's Rotten-Kid Theorem, Kid must not only make the first move. It must also correctly anticipate Daddy's reaction. If Kid underestimates Daddy's true degree of altruism, for example, it may make a non-cooperative decision so that both are worse off than they could have been had Kid found out Daddy's true degree of altruism. What this brings out is that both Becker and Hirshleifer tacitly assume that Kid's belief about Daddy's degree of altruism (or its expectation of how Daddy is to react) is correct. Kid and Daddy are clearly assumed to be perfectly informed utility maximizers. The 'mechanism' of interaction that is explicitly analysed by Becker and Hirshleifer is the standard economic one. In my own interpretation of 'evolutionary theory', then, this makes their analyses non-evolutionary.[17]

This does not mean, however, that evolutionary mechanisms do not play any role in Becker's and Hirshleifer's analyses. On the contrary, the evolutionary mechanism of natural selection is assumed to determine whether altruistic inclinations can survive. But this mechanism is presupposed, and not explicitly analysed by Becker and Hirshleifer. Without due consideration, they take over the (socio)biological notion that behavioural traits that are maladapted are replaced by fitter traits. As Becker's second result shows, the (socio)biological notion of fitness is translated into 'objective' income, or, more generally, material payoffs. This result, that Kid's cooperative behaviour confers material benefits to Daddy, is taken by Becker to demonstrate that altruism has survival value.

Apparently, Becker and Hirshleifer believe that their economic analysis may help (socio)biologists to arrive at a better understanding of cooperative human behaviour. But, conversely, they are convinced that economists may also learn something from biology. Becker remarks that:

> the preferences taken as given by economists and vaguely attributed to 'human nature' or something similar – the emphasis on self-interest, altruism toward kin, social distinction, and other enduring aspects of preferences – may be largely explained by the selection over time of traits having greater genetic fitness and survival value.
>
> (Becker 1976: 826)

This accords perfectly with Hirshleifer's 'programmatic contention': 'preference patterns, despite seemingly arbitrary elements, have survived because they are mainly adaptive to environmental conditions' (Hirshleifer 1977: 18).[18]

Hirshleifer's attempt to substantiate this programmatic contention has resulted in a number of papers. In these papers, Hirshleifer applies Becker's modified indifference curve analysis in combination with a game-theoretic format. The latter analytical technique is employed in Hirshleifer (1987b) to explicate the 'adaptive' function of emotions such as benevolence, malevolence, anger and gratitude in enforcing threats and promises. Consider the following Prisoners' Dilemma (PD) game:

	C	D
C	(3,3)	(0,5)
D	(5,0)	(1,1)

Matrix 5. The PD-game

The payoff pairs (.,.) in the matrix refer to the material results of the Row-player and the Column-player respectively. In the standard analysis of this game, it is assumed that, as D is the dominant strategy for both players, the suboptimal situation will obtain in which both players choose D.[19] If they both take each other to be rational, then a promise of either player to play C is not credible to the other player. As Hirshleifer points out, the situation changes to the material advantage of both players if there is a player who has the last move (say 'Column') and who is known to be benevolent by the player having the first move (say 'Row'). Then Column's promise 'I do C, if you do so' may induce Row to do C. Row's belief that Column is so 'irrational' as to respond to Row's C with C (instead of the 'rational' D) may thus result in cooperative behaviour by both. If it does so, both players will be better off in material terms than they would have been if they knew each other to be rational.

A similar type of argument can be found in Frank (1988). Frank also argues that 'irrational' commitments of persons may be rewarding in terms of material payoffs. Commitments can be said to be 'strategic devices' in the sense of Schelling (1960). But Frank's commitments can entice cooperation from others only if they cannot be manipulated at will; they are best conceived of as behavioural (pre)dispositions that eliminate potentially attractive options (such as the option of doing D in the PD, if the other does C). Frank shows that mutual cooperation may result even if the players choose simultaneously. As is observed by Frank himself, however, this result obtains only if commitments are (almost) perfectly correlated with observable signals. The players must be able to detect commitments. Otherwise, the door would be opened to impostors: rational opportunists who can fake the observable symptoms of committed persons.

Just as animals in evolutionary game theory are assumed to be programmed to follow a fixed strategy, so are committed persons in Frank's view individuals of a certain behavioural type. Some options of behaviour are foreclosed to committed persons. But that does not mean that Frank takes committed persons to be engaged in mindless, repetitive behaviour. Unlike the animals in evolutionary game theory, committed persons can choose, for example, whether to pair randomly with others, or to incur costs to 'get sensitized', after which the true identity of others is revealed so that they can pair selectively. What is not questioned by Frank, however, is that changes of behavioural types in populations are governed by the replicator dynamics of evolutionary game theory. Replicator dynamics is implicitly assumed by Frank. It is not explicitly argued for. I think that this is a serious omission, for he does not hold that commitments are fully determined by genetic material. Frank emphasizes the influence of cultural training in cultivating some behavioural dispositions and suppressing others. This implies that the presupposition of 'like begets like' that underlies evolutionary game theory cannot be maintained without further argument.

Frank follows Becker and Hirshleifer in assuming that the material results that are obtained are the means of existence that determine how many descendants can be sustained. This assumption may have been realistic in days long gone when 'human nature' was moulded. More problematic is their implicit assumption that behavioural dispositions are carried over from parents to their children. If altruistic parents fail to transmit their altruism to their children for whatever reason, then their beneficiaries can be non-altruistic individuals! It is curious that Becker, Hirshleifer and Frank do not address this issue. After all, they cannot be said to have failed to notice that an altruistic Daddy can produce a selfish Rotten Kid.

8. BIOLOGISTS ON CULTURAL EVOLUTION

Biologist S.J. Gould objects to the sociobiologists' inclination to regard natural selection as the only force that brings about evolution. Sociobiologists are said to commit the fallacy 'if adaptive, then genetic' in their attempts to explain human behaviour. According to Gould, the problem is not that, in general, human behaviour is not adaptive. He believes that much of human behaviour is adaptive. The problem is, Gould argues, that the primary *transmission* mechanism along which adaptive human behaviour spreads over populations is not genetic inheritance. Evolution in human societies is of a different, *cultural* type:

> an adaptive behavior does not require genetic input and Darwinian selection for its origin and maintenance in humans; it may arise by trial and error in a few individuals that do not differ genetically from their groupmates, spread by learning and imitation, and stabilize across generations by value, custom and tradition.
>
> (Gould 1980: 264)

Gould mentions three major areas in which cultural and Darwinian evolution differ profoundly: rate, modifiability and diffusibility. Cultural evolution can go on much more rapidly than natural selection, can have sudden disruptive changes in its 'inputs' (instead of gradual change in genetic material produced by mutations in Darwinian evolution) and its results can simultaneously spread over several populations at one and the same time (instead of the restriction of the effects of natural selection to the transmission of genetic material from ancestors to descendants). Gould argues that the profound differences especially in rate and diffusibility warrant the conclusion that cultural evolution operates in the 'Lamarckian' mode.

Dawkins seems to agree with Gould. That is, Dawkins agrees that there are other mechanisms at work in evolutionary processes in the human realm than natural selection and genetic inheritance. Dawkins (1976) argues that natural selection has endowed humans with brain capacities of conscious foresight and rapid *imitation*. The latter capacity enabled humans to develop a new sort of replicator: *memes*.[20] Memes, cultural ideas and habits ('ways of doing things'), can be transmitted culturally over populations through imitation just like scientific ideas can spread over scientific communities via acceptance. 'Cultural mutations' occur when mistakes are being made in imitations. In Dawkins (1980) it is suggested that this type of 'mimetical evolution' can be analysed in terms of *culturally stable strategies* (*CSSs*). The rule of the road (of whether to drive on the left or on the right) is taken by Dawkins to be a good example of a CSS. Besides the concepts of ESS and CSS, Dawkins introduces a third concept, that of a *developmentally stable strategy* (*DSS*). The concept of DSS is applicable when humans or animals *learn* certain patterns of behaviour via trial and error.[21]

The root idea behind Dawkins' introduction of the concepts of CSS and DSS seems to be that evolutionary game theory, with its central notion of an ESS, is applicable also in analyses of evolutionary processes different from Darwinian selection. The only difference Dawkins seems to acknowledge between the three types of evolution is what Gould calls the difference in *rate*: 'all we have to do is adapt the ESS idea to a different time scale' (Dawkins 1980: 355). Darwinian natural selection, with its associated notion of an ESS, works in evolutionary time, cultural evolution, with its associated notion of a CSS, in historical time, and individual trial and error learning, with its associated notion of a DSS, in developmental time.

Maynard Smith (1982), who adopts Dawkins' notions, acknowledges also the differences in diffusibility between the evolutionary processes. In natural selection only those properties are passed over from one generation to the next that children inherit genetically from their parents. In contrast, in cultural evolution children can take over non-genetically determined properties not only from their parents, but also from, say, mentors. And, of course, adults may also have their own 'cultural heroes'. The interesting observation Maynard Smith adds to this is that there is one common 'currency' in natural selection, (inclusive) fitness, but that a similar currency may be lacking in cultural evolution. The criteria of 'success' in cultural evolution are themselves to some degree culturally determined.

Neither Dawkins nor Maynard Smith acknowledges the differences in modifiability between the evolutionary processes. Humans appear to have a fairly large repertoire of sophisticated strategies between which they can switch. Moreover, they seem to be able to experiment with new rules of behaviour which differ radically from their former ones. If individual learning and cultural evolution can be couched in terms of evolutionary game theory at all, this would imply that large strategy sets must be fully represented. And it would imply also that among the strategies available there must be rather complex, conditional ones and *meta*strategies that would represent the way individuals switch between existing strategies and experiment with new ones. In the next chapter, these issues will be explored in more depth.

9. CONCLUSIONS

In this chapter several levels have been distinguished on which selection might operate: that of the group, of the individual organism and of the genes. We have seen that there is persistent disagreement as to what are the units of selection. We have also seen that what can be expected to evolve may depend crucially on the stance that one takes in this controversy. Those who believe that there is group selection tend to argue that groups evolve that display optimal group behaviour. Individual selectionists argue that optimal group behaviour can, but need not, result from selection working on individual organisms. It all depends on the specific conditions under which the selection mechanism is operating. Under some conditions, cooperative 'altruistic' behaviour is the fittest strategy; under other conditions, 'free riding' may be a fitter strategy than 'cooperate' in a population of cooperators. We have seen that evolutionary game theory is developed to analyse selection processes under the latter type of conditions. Evolutionary game theory shows how suboptimal behaviour can be evolutionarily stable if there is frequency-dependent selection in contest situations.

Contest situations typically entail an element of conflict. Elements of conflict, I have argued, are likely to be current at higher levels of organization, such as the group or species. For this reason, within-group, between-individuals selection cannot be ignored. But conflict seems to be absent at the level of the individual organism. There is no within-individual selection between genes or organs. This is what makes the individual organism fundamentally different from higher levels of organization. It also makes clear what is wrong with Dawkins' gene-centred view on selection: unlike animals that are involved in contests, genes do not compete with each other. They cooperate with each other in building and instructing organisms. In so far as genes can be said to have interests at all, genes within individual organisms all have the same interest: promoting the (inclusive) fitness of the organisms they are in.

Single genes can be said to be 'specialized'. The discussion between

Houthakker and Ghiselin shows that we can speak of 'specialization' (or 'differentiation') and 'coordination' (or 'integration') at each level of analysis. In the biological realm, 'specialization' ranges from 'speciation', the division of living nature into species, at the highest level, to the division of labour of organs in organisms. In the economic realm, we can also say that genes and organs are specialized within individual persons at the lowest level. At higher levels, persons can be specialized within firms and firms within industries. But, again, we should distinguish between competitive and cooperative 'division of labour'. Fully cooperative division of labour can be assumed only at the lowest level of integration.

Saying that elements of conflict can be present at higher levels of integration does not imply that suboptimal behaviour evolves. As we have seen in section 4, in contest situations optimal behaviour can evolve if more sophisticated mutant strategies show up in the population. It all depends on the specification of the strategy set. We have seen that it is conceded by the founder of evolutionary game theory, Maynard Smith, that much more effort should be put into defining the strategy set.

In 'replicator dynamics', the dynamics that underlies the notion of an evolutionarily stable strategy (ESS) in evolutionary game theory, it is assumed that 'like begets like'. We have seen that the same replicator dynamics is implicitly assumed in Becker's, Hirshleifer's and Frank's claim that altruistic behaviour can be adaptively functional. Becker, Hirshleifer and Frank do not provide any justification for making this assumption. Yet a justification is badly needed, for Becker's original result related to an altruistic Daddy who enticed cooperation from his selfish Rotten Kid. It seems that we have to account for this phenomenon of 'like begets unlike' in terms of (a lack of) cultural training. In the last section, we have seen that the importance of learning and cultural transmission in social behaviour is stressed also by sociobiologists. This does not imply, however, that they take the notion of an ESS to be inapplicable in analysing processes of learning and of cultural evolution.

Maynard Smith treats both individual learning and cultural imitation as analogues of genetic inheritance (see Maynard Smith 1982: 54 and 170–2). In Chapter 6, I have argued that it is more appropriate to regard individual learning (or reinforcement) as a *selection* mechanism, distinct from but comparable with natural selection. In the next chapter, I shall address the question of whether cultural imitation can be properly called a *replication* mechanism, comparable with genetic inheritance. And I shall also discuss whether there is a proper or credible analogue of the *mutation* mechanism to be found in cultural evolution.

8

THE CULTURAL EVOLUTION
OF BEHAVIOURAL
DISPOSITIONS

1. INTRODUCTION

In Chapter 7, the natural selection of behavioural traits in biology has been discussed in combination with the units of selection controversy. The discussion in this chapter will also focus on group *versus* individual selection and the evolution of optimal *versus* suboptimal rules of behaviour. But now the evolutionary processes that will be analysed are of a *cultural* type. I shall consider the views of leading *social* theoreticians on learning individuals and on cultural evolution. In particular, I will concentrate on the 'Popper–Hayek connection'. The following issues concerning cultural evolution take centre stage. What is the *selection* mechanism; what is the decisive standard that determines which behavioural rules spread over society? What is the *replication* mechanism; how are rules passed over from some individuals to others? What is the *mutation* mechanism; where do new rules come from? And what behavioural rules evolve through the joint operation of the three mechanisms? Are they efficient or inefficient?

Section 2 deals with K.R. Popper's contention that individual trial and error learning resembles natural selection in important respects. I shall compare Popper's ideas about individual learning with Simon's. Simon and Popper primarily discuss practical and theoretical search activities of single individuals. The discovery processes of interdependent individuals in groups are extensively analysed by F.A. Hayek. Here attention shifts from action to interaction. Hayek's view on the spontaneous cultural evolution of social order is discussed in sections 3 to 6. We will see that Hayek emphasizes that cultural evolution is quite different from biological evolution. But he also claims that both lead to a similar end result: only the best adapted rules survive. The best adapted rules are taken by Hayek to be the rules that are efficient for the group involved.

In sections 7 to 9 I deal with interesting attempts to give a game-theoretic account of Hayek's notion of cultural evolution. I shall argue that Lewis' notion of a convention comes close to Hayek's idea of self-sustaining rules in a social order. Hayek's thesis of the spontaneous evolution of *efficient* conventions seems to be plausible only in coordination games, however, in which the interests of the players do not conflict. Special attention will therefore be paid to analyses in which it is claimed that efficient conventions may evolve spontaneously also in so-called cooperation problems.

2. BLIND VERSUS SELECTIVE SEARCH?

In Chapter 6 I have discussed H.A. Simon's concept of procedural rationality. I argued that the notion of adaptive learning that is entailed in Simon's concept of procedural rationality can be called an evolutionary mechanism. Like natural selection, adaptive learning can be said to operate via feedback loops and to work on existing stable material. The stable material adaptive learning is assumed to work on is the repertoire of rules individuals are assumed to have at their disposal. The rules in this repertoire are assumed to govern not only the individual's everyday behaviour in standard situations. The repertoire is assumed to consist also of search rules, rules that guide the search activities of the individual when standard response rules do not yield satisfactory results. In Simon's view, search is selective. As we shall see, K.R. Popper also likens human learning to natural selection. But Popper holds a view on search that seems to contradict Simon's: search is blind. I shall argue that this impression of a contradiction is illusory. Simon's and Popper's views on learning can be reconciled with each other.

Popper's critical rationalism, with its insistence on the falsifiability of scientific theories (and on the rejection of theories that are falsified), is well known. What is perhaps less known is his lifelong contention that his view on the growth of (scientific) knowledge is consistent with Darwinian natural selection. Popper (1934) already contains a comparison of the succession of theories in science with Darwinian natural selection. In Popper (1963), it is argued that 'the method of trial and error is applied not only by Einstein but, in a more dogmatic fashion, by the amoeba also' (Popper 1963: 52). This argument is elaborated upon in Popper (1972). Here it is maintained that the claim that natural selection refers to 'the elimination of unfit hypotheses' is not meant metaphorically (Popper 1972: 261). I want to point out, first, that on Popper's own understanding of human learning, 'hypotheses' *must* be understood metaphorically when used in connection with natural selection. And, second, what is meant literally to apply both to learning and selection in Popper's view is captured in the phrase 'elimination of the unfit'.

Popper does not hold that amoebas and other 'simple' organisms really deliberately put forward conjectures that are to be subjected to severe tests, just as scientists are supposed to do. The selected 'hypotheses' of amoebas are taken to be genetically programmed ways of responding to environmental stimuli. One of the crucial features that makes Einstein differ from a amoeba is that the former was able to express hypotheses explicitly. Owing to 'the tremendous biological advantage of the invention of a *"descriptive and argumentative language"'* (Popper 1972: 70), human beings can expose their linguistically formulated hypotheses to criticism.

Here we enter Popper's *world 3* which is populated by *objective contents of thought*. Objective contents of thought are not to be confused with *beliefs* as mental states of human beings. The latter belong to *world 2*. World 2 consists also of behavioural dispositions. *World 1*, finally, is inhabited by *physical objects and states*. I do not want to discuss the merits and problems of Popper's distinction between these three worlds here. I will concentrate on what may be called the 'evolutionary function' that Popper attributes to world 3. With the emergence of world 3, which is open to human beings only, human beings are able to engage in scientific activities. They can subject their publicly expressed hypotheses to severe criticism. If their hypotheses do not survive scientific scrunity, human beings can eliminate their hypotheses instead of being eliminated themselves. In contrast, amoebas and other simple organisms do not have this attractive option:

> while animal knowledge and pre-scientific knowledge grow mainly through the elimination of those holding the unfit hypothesis, scientific criticism often makes our theories perish in our stead, eliminating our mistaken beliefs before such beliefs lead to our elimination.
>
> (Popper 1972: 261)

The foregoing suggests that Popper believes that scientific progress helps to solve pressing *practical* problems of humans, pertaining to their survival. In Popper's opinion, however, the help offered by scientific progress is not direct, but indirect. Science addresses *theoretical* problems. The 'fittest' hypothesis best solves the theoretical problem it was designed to solve. It need not be the hypothesis that best promotes our own survival. Yet Popper holds that there are significant feedback effects from the developments in world 3 upon the entities in world 2, the entities that seem to be decisive for our own survival: 'the repercussions, or the feed-back effects, of the evolution of the world upon ourselves – our brains, our traditions [. . .], our dispositions to act (that is, our beliefs), and our actions, can hardly be overrated' (Popper 1972: 122). These feedback effects are responsible also for the continuous generation, as 'unintended by-products' of scientific development,[1] of new problems. Thus scientific progress accords with the basic evolutionary scheme

$$P_1 \rightarrow TT \rightarrow EE \rightarrow P_2 \rightarrow \ldots ,$$

where P_1 stands for an initial problem, TT for a tentative theory, EE for evaluative error elimination and P_2 for a new problem that has arisen (as an unintended by-product).

Popper argues that natural selection of animals and plants conforms to the same scheme: 'just like theories, organs and their functions are tentative adaptations to the world we live in' (Popper 1972: 145). Here we get to the similarity that Popper sees between human learning processes and processes of natural selection. The similarity relates to the way in which adaptations are supposed to come about. Processes of human learning and of natural selection are both supposed to be governed by the same mechanisms of the elimination of errors and the generation of new trials. Learning processes and processes of natural selection are said not to work in a 'Lamarckian' way. That is, there is no cumulative process, no instruction by repetition involved in these processes. In both areas progress is not founded on past successes. Past successes do not provide a solid base that instructs organisms how to go on. Progress is founded only on past failures. Errors are eliminated, but that does not give the organisms any clue as to how to proceed other than that making the same mistakes again is better avoided. New trials are *blind* in so far as they are reliably informed only by past errors.

Popper's view on human problem solving does not seem to match Simon's on this point. Whereas Simon holds that the processes of trial and error in problem solving are *selective*, Popper believes that they are *blind*. It may be tempting to argue that this disagreement is due to the fact that Simon is writing primarily about 'routine' practical problem solving and Popper about 'creative' theoretical problem solving. But in Simon (1992) it is maintained that scientific discovery, far from being determined by 'inexplicable creativity', can be explained in terms of sets of 'selective heuristics'. Indeed, Simon protests against a tradition in the philosophy of science that is dominated by Popper's conviction that it is impossible to develop a general theory (a 'logic') of discovery. Once again, Simon contrasts selective search with undirected trial and error search. In selective search previous positive experience typically is taken as a guide for future behaviour.[2] Rules of thumb that have done reasonably well in certain problem situations are applied again in comparable new situations. In a limiting case, Simon argues, experts dispose of so many well-practised, domain-specific skills that they can do their work without engaging in any search at all.

Simon believes that even creative and innovative behaviour is rule governed. He also seems to believe that this idea of selective search runs counter to Popper's idea of blind search. I do not agree. Popper (1987) quite rightly argues that selective search, search that is directed by some positive heuristics, is opposite to *random* search, not to blind search. Blind search is compatible with selective search. Saying that individuals are engaged in selective search can be taken to mean, I think, that the range of options that the individuals take into consideration is limited. Skilful routine behaviour is a limiting case in which we could say that the range of options that is 'considered' reduces to one. To say that individuals are searching blindly is to say nothing about the range of options considered, except that the options that proved to be a failure are excluded. It is to say that whatever the outcome their search may have, it is and cannot be more than just a conjecture, an informed guess. It is reliably informed only by past failures, not by past successes. An individual may feel pretty confident about behavioural rules that were successful in the past. This may explain why the individual sticks to these rules. But it is no guarantee for further success. Each new move has to prove itself in a 'context of justification'. Or, as Popper puts it, each 'trial' is a foray into the unknown.

I think that Simon cannot but subscribe to this reconciliation of selective and blind search. Simon does not rule out the possibility that rules of thumb that have done fairly well in the past at some time cease to work satisfactorily. When individuals face simple, recurrent problems, there need not be any trouble in relying on specific skills and routines.[3] But when individuals are confronted with novel, unprecedented problem situations, or when they wrongly judge new problem situations to be similar to ones they have already been in, difficulties may arise. Generally speaking, we can say with Popper that each time a rule is applied, it is subjected to a test. If the rule fails the test, search for a better one is started. Popper's blind search says that search is narrowed down only by past failures. Simon's selective search in effect says *in addition* that the range of options that is considered in search is narrowed down *de facto* also by higher-order rules.[4]

After due consideration, Popper appears to agree with Simon that it is quite reasonable for individuals to follow 'positive heuristics' that have so far been fruitful. And, conversely, Simon appears to concur with Popper in that no matter how successful some rules of thumb have been in the past, there is always the possibility that they may break down in new situations. There is always the possibility that expectations are frustrated. This need not be due only to unusual changes in the 'natural' environment of individuals. If the results of their own behaviour partly depend on the behaviour of others, unexpected results may show up also because of changes in their 'social' environment, because of unforeseen changes in the behaviour of others. As I shall argue in the next sections, this is the main issue in Hayek's work on the spontaneous evolution of social order.

3. HAYEK ON CULTURAL EVOLUTION

Hayek is well known for his view that social order can evolve spontaneously. In this section, I shall try to elaborate on his view. What does 'social order' signify? And what is the conception of spontaneous evolution that is involved? In particular, what is the selection mechanism that generates processes of spontaneous evolution?[5]

In Hayek's view, *order* refers to some regular pattern(s) on an aggregate level. When Hayek speaks of '*social* order', he is talking about some regular pattern of the actions of a *group* of individuals. To be more precise, 'social order' refers to situations, or to sequences of events, in which the actions of the individual members of the group are compatible with each other. Situations of social order contrast with situations in which the actions of the individuals clash or conflict with each other. Hayek suggests that the actions of the individual group members are compatible when their plans come true. That is, a situation of social order emerges when the expectations of the individuals are mutually consistent. If such a social order comes about, the individuals involved will not have any reason to revise their expectations, plans and actions.

Hayek gives several examples of social order. In some of his publications (Hayek 1968, for example) he stresses the order produced by the market. In the market, under the pressure of competition some order will form itself. Economists are able to predict only the abstract character of such order, and not its precise, detailed structure, in so-called *pattern predictions*. What Hayek seems to have in mind here are exactly the qualitative laws of tendencies that I discussed in Chapter 2. Recall that the paradigmatic example there was: if (real) wages in an industry rise, the labour–capital ratio in that industry will tend to fall. Such a law precisely captures Hayek's idea of order, of a regular, recurrent pattern of behaviour at an aggregate, industry level: the same tendency is forthcoming in situations that are similar in the relevant aspect(s).

Hayek holds not only that the market produces order, but also that the functioning of a market presupposes some pre-existing institutional order. 'The market' does not refer to some state of nature. In Hayek's view markets do not function in an institutional vacuum, but rather imply some institutional framework. This framework defines the rules of the game, or the *constitutional rules* as Vanberg and Buchanan (1988) put it. Hayek argues that the institutional framework of the market is itself properly to be viewed as the order within which the market transactions take place. Thus the notion of order applies not only to market behaviour exhibited within the institutional framework of the market but also to the framework itself. Indeed, we shall see that followers of Hayek have applied his idea of the spontaneous evolution of order mainly to the latter, to institutions that facilitate, complement or prevent the efficient working of the market.[6]

Hayek argues that 'we are all tempted to assume that wherever we find an order it must be directed by a central organ' (Hayek 1967: 73). We tend to believe that any order we encounter is the result of *deliberate design*. We are likely to attribute social order to the conscious planning of some authoritative organ, notably of course the government, or, in case such agency is absent, to the concerted collective action of a group of individuals.[7] In both cases the account of social order runs via the intentions of those who we hold responsible for the emergence of the order. Hayek does not deny that instances of such intended social orders can be found in reality. What Hayek has emphasized over and over again, however, is that social order may have come about, and often does really come about, *spontaneously*, that is, that it is the *unintended* result of individual actions. Social order may be the result of human action but not of human design, to use Ferguson's famous words. Individuals may be totally absorbed with their own affairs without being concerned about the affairs of others and indeed without any awareness of the impact of their actions on the well-being of others. And yet there may result a situation in which the well-being of all is optimal.

We clearly hear the echoes here of Adam Smith's *invisible hand*. Indeed, the views voiced by the well-known representatives of the Scottish Enlightenment, Hume, Smith and Ferguson, are acknowledged by Hayek to be an important and perhaps the most important source of his own ideas. In turn, the moral philosophers were indebted to Bernard Mandeville. According to Hayek (1978), Mandeville was the first to escape from the Greek dichotomy between that which is natural (*physei*) and that which is artificial or conventional (*thesei*). For centuries this dichotomy prevented social theorists from thinking of order other than in either of the following two ways. Either it was an order of nature, and then it was considered to be independent of the intentions and actions of humans, or it was some other kind of order, and then it was thought to be the result of the deliberate arrangements of humans. The major breakthrough in social thinking that Mandeville achieved consisted in conceiving of a third type of order, an order that is 'natural' and 'artificial' at one and the same time. This third type of order is 'artificial' in that it is the result of human action and 'natural' in that it is not designed by any of the agents.

Hayek sometimes calls the Scottish philosophers (and along with them Burke, Herder and Savigny) 'Darwinians before Darwin'. This expression is coined by Hayek to stress that the idea of *evolution* was commonplace in the social sciences in the nineteenth century long before Darwin. Indeed, recent investigations in the history of science have pointed out the great influence the thinking of Hume and Smith exerted on Darwin's inception of the idea of natural selection (see, for example, Schweber 1968). Hayek urges social scientists to go behind Darwin, back to the Scottish moral philosophers for a proper understanding of *cultural* (or social) as opposed to biological evolution. What then does Hayek think the moral philosophers have to tell us about cultural evolution?

I think that an outline of the answer to this question is to be found in Hayek's conception of *competition*. Hayek (1948) argues that competition typically entails a dynamic process of adjustments.[8] The 'market's method' is said to be one of trial and error. Individual participants gradually learn the relevant circumstances in which they operate: 'competition is essentially a process of the formation of opinion . . . . It creates the views people have about what is best and cheapest' (Hayek 1948: 106). Or, as the title of a later paper (1968) of Hayek aptly puts it, competition is basically a discovery procedure. So what is adjusted in competition are the plans of action of the participants, or, to be more precise, the opinions of the participants about how to proceed in order to realize their goals. Their views are adjusted to 'the relevant circumstances' that include not only the outside 'natural' world, but also the outside 'social' world, that is the actions of the other participants. Thus we can speak of *mutual* adjustments of the views of participants, or of the *coordination* of their plans, against the background of a common outside 'natural' world. The process of mutual adjustments comes to an end when no participant, given his or her ends and given the results he or she obtains, has an incentive to change his or her opinions. This situation, in which the market, the social system, has come to rest is called an equilibrium by Hayek.

The *selection mechanism* that, according to Hayek, is operating in cultural evolution is clearly some kind of trial and error learning, and not some sort of Darwinian natural selection. 'Competition' here refers to processes in which the opinions of individuals are revised due to past performances and not to processes in which scarce resources are (re)distributed among competitors according to their relative past performances. So much is clear. But there is a problem here. The individuals, the market participants, are assumed to be engaged in forward-looking, goal-directed actions. Hayek argues that no individual intends to bring about social order, but that does not mean that individuals are assumed not to act intentionally. On the contrary, in Hayek's account all individuals intend to achieve their own individual ends. But at the same time, Hayek appears to hold that individual behaviour is rule governed. He seems to argue that in cultural evolution behavioural rules are both what are selected for and what are selected. It is rules that are taken to be decisive for the success or failure of individuals and groups. And it is argued by Hayek that in the course of evolution successful rules supplant unsuccessful ones. Indeed, the preservation of social order is said to depend on whether the individuals at stake follow and keep following the same rule. How then does the view of individuals all consciously pursuing their own ends link up with the view of individuals all following the same rule?

4. GOAL-DIRECTED ACTION VERSUS RULE-GOVERNED BEHAVIOUR?

As argued in Chapters 2 and 4, one way of reconciling goal-directed action with rule-governed behaviour is to consider rules from a theorist's (or observer's) point of view. Any consistent goal-directed behaviour can be described in terms of rule-following behaviour. Hayek holds, however, that the assertion 'individuals follow rules' is not only true from a theorist's point of view but also from the individuals' own (agents') point of view. Can individuals follow rules and deliberately pursue ends at one and the same time? In Chapter 4 we have seen that Nelson and Winter (1982) hold that this is impossible. They argue that individuals either choose consciously and deliberately, or behave in an unconscious, automatic way. Goal-directed action and rule-governed behaviour are treated as mutually exclusive modes of behaviour. I shall argue that although Hayek's interpretation of rule-governed behaviour is strikingly similar to that of Nelson and Winter, Hayek sees the two as compatible modes of behaviour. To be more precise, I shall argue that Hayek believes that goal-directed action can be said to *presuppose* rule-governed behaviour in at least three ways.

As is rightly emphasized in several studies, the starting point of Hayek's account of rule-governed behaviour is the *ignorance* of the individuals involved. No one knows exactly what the future will bring, nor what actions others will take, for example. No one will ever be able to give a perfectly reliable detailed prediction of the future. Just as economists cannot hope to achieve more than 'pattern predictions', Hayek believes that economic agents can at most trace general tendencies. Rule-following behaviour is regarded by Hayek as a response of individuals to this 'brute fact of life'.

Some hold that the rule-following behaviour of individuals is a rational response to their ignorance. They take this to mean that individuals conceive of two options available, rational choice and rule following, acknowledge their ignorance, and therefore consciously (and rightly) choose the latter option. The standard neoclassical reaction to Simon's idea of satisficing reflects such a view: following rules of thumb can be perfectly rational once maximizers take information costs into account. In Elster's terms, this is the position of 'satisficing-as-maximizing'. This is not Hayek's position, however.

There are others who explicitly reject the notion of 'perfect (or omniscient) rationality' that underlies this reaction and who opt for Simon's 'bounded rationality', but who nevertheless argue the same thing: rule-governed behaviour is a rational way for individuals to cope with their ignorance. They argue in effect that for all the individuals know (given their limitations related with 'bounded rationality'), the individuals believe they would do better to follow some rule than to try to find out what is the best action. As we have seen in Chapter 4, this is an argument that can be found also in Nelson and Winter (1982).[9] Nelson and Winter assume that boundedly rational individuals consciously choose between two options: rigid, but reliable, rule following and flexible, but time-consuming and fallible, optimizing.

There is no doubt that in 'true-to-life' situations choices are made between engaging in costly search or resorting to established rules of thumb. But, again, this does not seem to be Hayek's view on the relation between deliberate action and rule following. Hayek does not seem to believe that individuals consciously choose between these two alternatives. What he believes is that individuals try to optimize, that they do their best, and that in their attempts to do so rule following is involved in at least the following two senses. First, individuals must master some rules in the sense of having the skills that are required for successful performances. And, second, rules, now understood as behavioural dispositions, delineate the options for action that the individuals take into consideration. I shall discuss these two points in turn.

The first sense in which goal-directed action presupposes rule-governed behaviour resembles Nelson and Winter's informal discussion of routines. Hayek speaks of 'tacit knowledge' and of 'know how' as opposed to 'know that'. Rules as skills relate to a 'capacity to act according to rules which we may be able to discover but which we need not be able to state in order to obey them' (Hayek 1962: 322). Hayek refers to Friedman and Savage's discussion of the skills of the expert billiard player. Possessing certain skills can be said to be a *conditio sine qua non* not only for routine behaviour but also for successful deliberate action. Skills are required not only in finding a satisfactory choice, but also in implementing it. The skills that someone masters determine his or her competence. They are part of that person's resources, of his or her 'human capital'.

Rules can be said to facilitate goal-directed action also in a second sense: rules as behavioural dispositions delimit the range of alternatives that are taken into consideration. Hayek stresses that rule following usually leaves room for conscious choices between several alternatives:

> The rules of which we are speaking [. . .] will often merely determine or limit the range of possibilities within which the choice is made consciously. By eliminating certain kinds of action altogether and providing certain routine ways of achieving the object, they merely restrict the alternatives on which a conscious choice is required. The moral rules, for example, which have become part of a man's nature will mean that certain conceivable choices will not appear at all among the possibilities between which he chooses. Thus even decisions which have been carefully considered will in part be determined by rules of which the acting person is not aware.
>
> (Hayek 1962: 335)

The rules that are at stake here are also called negative rules by Hayek, as they eliminate certain possibilities. Only in limiting cases is the range of possibilities narrowed down to just one option. Routines can be said to do exactly that. Rules then take the form of imperatives or norms of the type 'if A, do B', the form that is associated with more deterministic accounts of rule following.

Hayek also makes clear here that although, 'objectively speaking', the ignorance of individuals stands in the way of true optimizing, 'subjectively speaking', the individuals may be convinced that they are optimizing. Whether the individuals do notice it or not, any attempt to optimize takes place within some 'choice space' which is determined by their rules. Again, we can say that in limiting cases the 'choice space' may be reduced to one option or strategy. We would then have individuals of a fixed behavioural type such as are analysed in evolutionary game theory. As we shall see, however, it is emphasized by Hayek that individuals in principle can experiment with new rules.

Hayek's remarks on rules as behavioural dispositions are similar to Simon's notion of selective search. Recall that in this notion rules are also assumed to direct the attention of individuals to a subset of the complete set of alternatives. Moreover, the views of Hayek and Simon seem to resemble each other also in the idea that there may be a hierarchy of rules. Hayek (1962) writes of 'dispositions to change dispositions'. This indicates not only that individuals are not supposed to be 'chained' to certain dispositions, but also that changes in their dispositions may show some regularity.

The foregoing account of Hayek's views on rule following does not tell us whether individuals are assumed to follow the same rules. It is compatible with the view that individuals in groups follow different rules. It may even be said to suggest such a view, for, after all, individuals have different skills and dispositions. But this does not seem to be Hayek's view. Hayek concentrates on the rules that the individuals in a group have in common. His emphasis is on custom and shared tradition. This raises the question as to how rules of custom and of shared tradition come about; that is, how do the individuals in a group come to adhere to the same rules? According to Hayek, this is primarily due to *imitation*. Imitation is the *replication mechanism* along which rules are transmitted from one member of a group to another. Imitation is said to be the typical way in which individuals acquire the skills of other group members.[10]

Hayek suggests that imitation covers a wide domain of behaviour ranging from more or less deliberate forms such as mimicry and learning skills, to thoughtless aping, like that of a 'man induced to yawn or stretch by seeing others doing the same' (Hayek 1967: 47). What this heterogeneous list makes clear is that Hayek holds that imitation need not be intentional or even conscious. The point that is emphasized by Hayek is that in imitation some observed pattern of movements typically is translated *directly* into the corresponding behaviour by the imitator. The imitator often is not aware of the elements of which the pattern consists.

Although Hayek acknowledges that the mechanisms of imitation are only dimly understood,[11] he seems to be pretty confident about its consequences: by and large the individuals in a group will come to follow the same rules. These alleged consequences hint at a third way in which rule following may assist individuals in achieving their goals. If individuals can count on other group members adhering to the same rules, in the sense of behavioural dispositions, this makes their future behaviour more pre-dictable. And if the results of their own actions partly depend on the actions taken by others, as Hayek assumes, then this offers valuable information. Here is another sense in which rule following can be said to be *functional* for individuals. Shared rules alleviate their ignorance.

Of course, not all conceivable rules assist the individuals equally well in achieving their goals. This holds for any of the three ways in which rules have been said to be helpful. Successful action often requires specific skills. Some dispositions may be more conducive in certain cases than others. And although all shared rules enhance the predictability of each other's behaviour, some may have better consequences for all than others. In the next sections we will see that this is exactly what underlies Hayek's views on the cultural evolution of rules. Rules as behavioural dispositions evolve because mutually dependent individuals can discover what rules suit their interests best. But before we come to that, I have to deal with Vanberg's (1986) penetrating criticism that Hayek is wedded to some notion of group selection.

5. GROUP SELECTION IN HAYEK'S WRITINGS?

I have argued that in Hayek's view of cultural evolution the replication mechanism is provided by imitation and the selection mechanism by trial and error (adaptive) learning. So far I have assumed that Hayek's selection mechanism works on individuals. It cannot be denied, however, that there are statements in Hayek's work that suggest his affiliation to some kind of group selection. Vanberg criticizes Hayek for being inconsistent. Hayek would both advocate methodological individualism and endorse some controversial holistic concept of group selection. Many of his remarks that suggest such a concept of group selection, I shall argue, can be interpreted in a way that is consistent with 'individual selection'.

Vanberg makes a laudable attempt to give a clear account of Hayek's ideas about cultural evolution. His careful analysis clarifies a lot that remains somewhat obscure in Hayek's own writings. But in the end Vanberg winds up detecting an inconsistency in Hayek's writings that he is unable to resolve:

> there is a tacit shift in Hayek's argument from the notion that behavioural regularities emerge and prevail because they benefit the individual practicing them, to the quite different notions that rules come to be observed because they are advantageous to the group.
>
> (Vanberg 1986: 83)

According to Vanberg, the latter notions suggest a collectivist account of the evolution of rules in terms of *group selection.* Hayek states, for example, that 'rules of conduct . . . have evolved because the groups who practised them were more successful and displaced others' (Hayek 1973: 18), and that group selection is a frequent phenomenon in cultural evolution (Hayek 1988: 25). It seems that Hayek believes that groups compete with each other as unitary agents, and that group performance determines which groups do and which groups do not survive as wholes.

Yet I think that we are not obliged to take Hayek's statement so literally. I think that a clue to an understanding that is more in line with Hayek's overall view is given in the following remark:

> we shall occasionally use the pairs of concepts 'order and its elements' and 'groups and individuals' interchangeably.
>
> (Hayek 1967: 66, footnote 1)

If we change 'order' to 'group', Hayek's statements becomes less puzzling. The replacement of one group by another can then be read as the replacement of one order by another. The point of this reinterpretation is that a replacement of groups is not the only way in which changes in orders may be brought about. One order can be replaced by another in various ways, many of which are in accordance with the individualistic notion that individuals, and not groups of individuals, are responsible for the emergence, maintenance and alteration of rules.

Vanberg suggests an interpretation that points in the same direction. He observes that Hayek argues that groups practising more successful rules will expand by attracting outsiders, or that more successful orders will tend to prevail by being imitated by 'outsiders' (Vanberg 1986: 85, footnote 12). That is, individuals will try to join successful groups ('between-group migration'), or will stay in their own group and imitate rules practised by more successful groups ('between-group imitation'). Vanberg argues correctly that there is no problem in giving an individualistic account of the replacement of groups by other groups with more successful rules based on the process of between-group migration. For less successful groups may simply disappear when their members migrate to more successful groups.

But Vanberg fails to see that if we change 'order' to 'group', we can also give an individualistic account of the replacement of groups based on the process of between-group imitation. If all individuals in one group perfectly imitate the rule(s) that are followed by all individuals in another group, then we can say that the former 'group' is replaced by the latter, for the (new) order that is produced in the former group will be identical to the order in the latter group. This is just a roundabout way of saying that when individuals in a group start to imitate individuals of another group they will change their rules of conduct. As a consequence, the imitating individuals may produce a new order, an order that may be the same as the order already produced in the other, imitated group.

A new order may emerge also when individuals within the same group begin to imitate each other. At least some rules that are followed in the group will then change. Such a process of *within*-group imitation may also result in the creation of a new social order. This means that there is a third 'individualistic' way besides the two already mentioned by Vanberg in which a 'group' may be replaced by another.

The replacement of the pair of terms 'group' and 'individuals' by the pair of 'order' and 'rules' brings out clearly, I think, that what is accounted for in Hayek's notion of cultural evolution is the evolution of rules. What counts is the 'differential reproductive success' of rules, not of individuals. In this respect, Hayek's notion of cultural evolution resembles Nelson and Winter's notion of an evolutionary economic theory. Recall that in Nelson and Winter's evolutionary theory the evolution of market shares of routines in industries is accounted for. In Hayek's view, it is the growth and decline of rules in groups that is to be accounted for.

In a 'free society', Hayek argues, individuals typically have the opportunity to change their rules. Changes in the rules of individuals may lead to a change in the resulting social order. And a change in the social order may in turn induce other individuals to change their rules too. As Hayek argues:

> the individual with a particular structure and behaviour owes its existence in this form to a society of a particular structure, because only within such a society has it been advantageous to develop some of its peculiar characteristics.
>
> (Hayek 1967: 76)

This quote brings out clearly that what is endangered when the order ('of a particular structure') changes need not be so much the physical existence of individuals as their 'particular structure and behaviour'. When their prevailing rules do not work out well any more as a result of changes in their environment, they may be enticed to search for better ones. When they find better rules, what has 'gone extinct' is their previous rules. As Popper argues, the possibility of trial and error learning allows human beings to eliminate their beliefs instead of being eliminated themselves. Similarly, the same possibility allows human beings to change their rules of conduct. The entities that do or do not 'survive' in Hayek's notion of cultural evolution are the rules that individuals follow and not the individuals themselves.

We can conclude, I think, that the selection mechanism that is assumed in Hayek's notion of cultural evolution need not work on groups treated as indivisible units. Hayek's statements that suggest group selection can be reinterpreted in a way that is inspired by the remarks of Hayek himself and that is consistent with Hayek's professed methodological individualism. I think we should distinguish sharply between the *mechanism* that is involved in group selection and the *claim* that is associated with it. The *claim* that Hayek argues for seems to be that only those rules can survive that make for an order that is optimal for the group taken as a whole. This is precisely the claim that group selectionists would defend. But in Hayek's case, I venture, the claim is not based on a problematic group selectionist *mechanism*, but on a problematic view of the interdependency of individuals in groups. This view can be called *organicism*. 'Organicism' refers to the view that the parts (here: the individuals) relate to the whole (here: the group) as organs relate to an organism. What is problematic in this view is not the level or unit of selection that is implied in it. Organicism is compatible with individual selection. What is problematic is that the relation between individuals in a group can be quite different from that between organs in an organism. Elaborating on an argument in Chapter 7, I shall argue in the following section that Hayek's organicistic point of view is unwarranted.

6. ORGANICISM AND INTERDEPENDENCY

Hayek's 'organicistic' view can be traced back, I think, to Menger's (1985) [1883] idea of the 'organic origin' of institutions. Menger argues that to say that an institution has an organic origin is to say first of all that its emergence is an unintended result of individual human actions. But there is more to it. It is also to say that the institution is part of an encompassing *social organism*. In Menger's opinion society or the whole economy can be regarded as a social organism, as the proper counterpart of a natural or biological organism in the social realm. Like organisms, societies are said to exhibit an organic unity. To be more precise, Menger seems to hold that this entails two things. First, an institution that works well in some institutional setting may do badly in another. The welfare effects of some institution thus cannot be judged in isolation. The effects depend crucially on the other institutions that exist in society. The second thing that seems to be implied in Menger's saying that societies exhibit organic unity is that institutions relate to society as organs relate to organisms. Institutions (like organs) cannot 'survive' other than via the 'survival' of the society (like the organism), the whole of which they are part. Or, to put it more exactly, institutions are maintained only if their welfare effects for society are optimal.

Menger calls his own approach 'anatomical–physiological'. In an anatomical–physiological approach, the parts (organs) of an encompassing whole (organism) are analysed in terms of their contribution (function) to the functioning of the whole. It may be remarked here that in Menger's anatomical–physiological approach the explanations are of a (holist) functionalist type. In contrast, in an exact–atomic approach, the way is analysed in which atoms and forces (parts) 'build up' observable objects (wholes). Menger argued that, given the fact that the scientific knowledge of social 'atoms' and 'forces' is in its infancy (at the time of writing), an anatomical–physiological approach is indispensable. But his hope is clearly that with the growth of scientific knowledge, an exact–atomic approach would come within reach. To Menger, this exact–atomic approach would have to take individual persons as atoms and their efforts, in particular their efforts to come to learn what is in their interests, as forces.

Hayek can be said to offer a rough outline of such an exact–atomic approach. Learning individual persons take central stage in his view on cultural evolution. In this he differs from Menger. But he seems to take over Menger's idea of the organic unity of institutions *in toto*. Hayek seems to accept both implications of Menger's notion of organic unity. The first implication, that the welfare effects of society's institutions are interdependent, does not stand in the way of developing an exact–atomic approach. It rather seems to be a sensible starting point for such an approach. After all, all individuals in a society learn against the background of some institutional setting. And what they learn may be dependent on this setting and may lead to a change in this setting, both for themselves and for others.

The *interdependency* of the welfare effects of rules can indeed be said to be a recurrent theme in Hayek's work. Whether the following of some rule is advantageous to an individual depends on the rules that are followed by others in the group. As Hayek puts it:

> a new rule of individual conduct which in one position [read: institutional setting, JJV] may prove detrimental, may in another prove beneficial.
>
> (Hayek 1967: 71)

This holds for any individual in the group. And if individuals find new rules that happen to be beneficial, and if they stick to the new rules, the consequence may be that the institutional setting of the group is changed. One can express the same point by saying that the adaptedness of rules depends not only on the 'natural' environment of the individuals, but also on their 'social' environment, the rules adopted by others. Changes in rules may lead to a different social environment for all individuals that, in turn, may have (*feedback*) repercussions for the attractiveness of the rules being followed.

In the following sections I shall argue that Hayek's theme of interdependency is captured to some extent in evolutionary game-theoretic treatments of frequency-dependent selection. But Hayek's acceptance of Menger's view that a society and its institutions relate to each other as an organism relates to its organs, the second thing that is entailed in 'organic unity', amounts to an unduly and arbitrary restriction of the set of possible situations of interdependency.[12] As we shall see, it presupposes that the situations of interdependency in which the individuals find themselves are always of the pure coordination game type. Hayek ignores the possibility that individuals may be involved in other types of situations, for example in situations of the Hawk–Dove (Chicken) game type. As we shall see in the next section, in situations like these rules may survive in 'Hayekian' processes of cultural evolution that are not optimal for the group taken as a whole.

7. CONVENTIONS, NORMS AND INSTITUTIONS

As game theory is developed to study situations of interaction, it seems to be well suited to deal with Hayek's theme of interdependency. Indeed, game theory is used also in Vanberg (1986) to point out that the validity of Hayek's thesis that rules that evolve in groups are efficient is limited to some well-defined situations of interdependency. Vanberg argues that efficient rules can be expected to evolve spontaneously only in (pure) coordination games, and not, for example, in cooperation games. I will discuss this argument in detail here. I argue that pioneering attempts by Ullmann-Margalit (1977) and Schotter (1981) to show that in cooperation games efficient rules must be externally enforced are not successful, because they fail to address the right question.

Several commentators presume that game theory is well suited to analyse Hayek's thesis that rules evolve in groups that are efficient for groups taken as wholes (see, for example, Bianchi 1993). And, indeed, Hayek's theme of interdependency, saying roughly that the success of certain lines of action depends on the behaviour exhibited by others, appears to be grist for the mill of game theorists. The notion of equilibrium that Hayek suggests to elucidate his notion of social order closely resembles the notion of equilibrium that has taken centre stage in game theory: that of a Nash equilibrium. Hayek states that:

> the orderliness of the system of actions will in general show itself in the fact that actions of the different individuals will be so co-ordinated or mutually adjusted to each other, that the result of their actions will remove the initial stimulus or make inoperative the drive which has been the cause of activity.
>
> (Hayek 1976: 69)

I take this statement not to mean that when there is social order, the individuals cease to act. Presumably, Hayek means that when there is social order individuals have no incentive to change their existing patterns of behaviour. The same idea seems to underlie the notion of Nash equilibrium. Informally stated, a set of actions is in Nash equilibrium if no individual can improve his or her situation by deviating from playing his or her part in the equilibrium, given that the other individuals play their part in the equilibrium.

This implies that if all individuals expect the others to play their part in the Nash equilibrium, they are all better off when they play their part in it.

If the notion of Nash equilibrium really captures the kernel of Hayek's ideas on social order, the criticism of commentators such as Vanberg seems to be to the point. For it is a well-known result in game theory that Nash equilibria in games need not be Pareto efficient. Nash equilibria are Pareto efficient only in some well-defined problem situations. The following matrix represents a simple example of a so-called pure *coordination game*:

	L	R
L	(1,1)	(0,0)
R	(0,0)	(1,1)

Matrix 6

The payoff pairs (.,.) in the matrix here do not denote material results. They denote the results of the several possible pairs of actions in terms of the utility, or psychic satisfaction, of the Row- and the Column-player respectively. This reflects the fact that we are dealing here with learning and not with natural selection.[13] It will be assumed throughout here that players prefer the option(s) with the highest utility. In coordination games there may be several Nash equilibria. In matrix 6, the pairs of actions of the Row- and Column-player that are Nash equilibria are (L,L) and (R,R). It is immediately clear that both equilibria are Pareto efficient. If both individuals choose the same option, their actions are coordinated or mutually adjusted to each other in an optimal way.

Things are different, however, when we analyse other types of games. In impure coordination games, for example, the players may get stuck in a self-enforcing Nash equilibrium that is not Pareto efficient. This is illustrated in matrix 7 below.

	L	R
L	(2,2)	(0,0)
R	(0,0)	(1,1)

Matrix 7

	L	R
L	(1,2)	(0,0)
R	(0,0)	(2,1)

Matrix 8

Here, too, the pair of actions (R,R) is a Nash equilibrium. But it is not Pareto efficient. It is the other Nash equilibrium (L,L) that is Pareto efficient. Nevertheless, once the individuals both follow rule R, it is self-enforcing.[14] It is characteristic of coordination games that there is no conflict of interests between the individuals. The individuals can be said to have the same interest: to coordinate on a Pareto-efficient Nash equilibrium. There is a host of games in which the individuals' interests conflict to some degree. Matrix 8 represents a game of the 'Battle of the Sexes' type. As in matrix 1, (L,L) and (R,R) are both Pareto-efficient Nash equilibria here. But now the Row-player prefers to coordinate on (L,L), while the Column-player prefers the (R,R)-equilibrium.

Games in which the interests of the players do not coincide completely are often classified in mixed-motive games and pure conflict games. The most-discussed mixed-motive game is the Prisoners' Dilemma (henceforth PD). Its generic form is presented in matrix 9. The numerical example that was already given in Chapter 7 is repeated here. (Keep in mind, however, that we are dealing here with 'subjective' valuations, and not with 'objective' material results.)

	C	D			C	D
C	(a,a)	(b,c)		C	(3,3)	(0,5)
D	(c,b)	(d,d)		D	(5,0)	(1,1)

Matrix 9
(where $c > a > d > b$)

Matrix 5

The degree of conflict in the PD-game is considerably greater than in the Battle of the Sexes. In the one-shot version of PD, (D,D) is the only Nash equilibrium. Yet (D,D) is Pareto inferior to (C,C). Both players would be better off if they were to cooperate. (This is why PD is sometimes called a cooperation problem.) The point is, however, that each player is better off by defecting if the other were to cooperate. D strictly dominates C for both players; whatever the other player does, D is always the best choice.

So far, I have discussed several different types of games under the standard assumptions that there are two players involved and that they play games only once. It is clear from the discussion in section 4 that Hayek assumes that there are more players involved and that they face recurrent problem situations. Thus it seems that, as a first approximation, we have to look for game-theoretic treatments of repeated play in which a possibly large group of individuals is involved. References that suggest themselves here are Lewis (1969), Ullmann-Margalit (1977) and Schotter (1981).

Lewis (1969) argues that in situations such as the one depicted in matrix 6, *conventions* may evolve. Lewis defines a 'convention' as follows:[15]

A regularity *R* in the behavior of members of a population *P* when they are agents in a recurrent situation *S* is a *convention* if and only if it is true that, and it is common knowledge in *P* that, in any instance of *S* among members of *P*,

(1) everyone conforms to R;
(2) everyone expects everyone else to conform to R;
(3) everyone prefers to conform to R on condition that the others do, since S is a coordination problem and uniform conformity to R is a coordination equilibrium in S.

(Lewis 1969: 58)

In matrix 6, either 'do L' or 'do R' can emerge as a convention. This seems similar to Hayek's idea of social order: once a convention is established in a group, all individuals are better off by following the convention. Unilateral deviations do not pay. Furthermore, Lewis's second point in the definition fits Hayek's conviction that the coordination of actions of individuals in social order is achieved via the coordination of their expectations. When all individuals expect others to adhere to the convention, they all will adhere to the convention themselves, thereby reinforcing each other's expectations that all keep following the routine, and so on. In short, a convention denotes a system of mutually consistent, self-confirming expectations.

In pure coordination games, 'Hayekian' optimal conventions can emerge that, once existing, sustain themselves. But by the very same argument, suboptimal self-sustaining 'conventions' may evolve in impure coordination games and cooperation games. In matrix 7, for example, the inefficient 'do R' can sustain itself. And in PD, the inefficient 'always D' is similarly self-enforcing. Ullmann-Margalit (1977) argues, however, that in PD-like situations so-called 'PD-norms' may emerge that resolve the cooperation problems at stake in an optimal way. Likewise, Schotter (1981) maintains that optimal institutions may evolve in recurrent PD-games. What arguments are offered by Ullmann-Margalit and Schotter to support their claim that an efficient norm or institution evolves spontaneously in a repeated PD-game?

Ullmann-Margalit (1977) associates PD-like situations with a Hobbesian 'state of nature' of a war of all against all. This situation is said to correspond to a situation in which all individuals play 'always D' in recurrent PD-games. Sooner or later the individuals are assumed to settle on a covenant, a tacit agreement of 'cease fire'. If sustainable, this agreement would lift the situation up to a situation in which all individuals would play the optimal 'always C'. By itself, however, the agreement falls short of achieving this. As Hobbes argues, 'the bonds of words are too weak to bridle man's ambition, avarice, anger, and other passions without the fear of some coercive power' (Ullmann-Margalit 1977: 89). The fear of sanctions installed by Leviathan, an authoritative sovereign, is needed to prevent individuals from breaking the agreement. In effect, then, PD-norms are sustained because the payoffs are changed by the coercive power. Taking matrix 5, a sanction larger than 3 (in utility units) on defecting will do the job. But the game ceases to be a PD then. It is turned into a pure coordination game.

The same line of argument underlies Schotter's conception of a social institution. Schotter argues that in contradistinction to 'conventions', which Schotter takes over from Lewis, 'institutions' may not be self-policing. Although it is necessary for an institution to be agreed to by all members of the group, it may not be sufficient:

> for instance, it is common knowledge that the famous prisoners' dilemma game can be solved through the use of a binding contract that is enforceable by an external authority.
>
> (Schotter 1981: 11)

Here, again, the crux is that threats of punishments by an external authority are necessary to prevent players from defecting.[16]

Although both Ullmann-Margalit and Schotter state that they work in the tradition of Hayek, their analyses contrast with the spirit of Hayek's views on spontaneous cultural evolution in at least two respects. First, PD-norms and PD-institutions are not self-sustaining. And second, their emergence seems to require deliberate and concerted collective action by individuals. I will discuss both points in turn. PD-norms and PD-institutions must be policed by some external authority. Otherwise they cannot be sustained. They are not stable Nash equilibria in the original PD-game; they can be stable Nash equilibria only in some other, modified game. An external authority is needed to execute this transition in the problem situation of the individuals.

Ullmann-Margalit and Schotter argue that the external authority can only enforce an already existing tacit agreement among the individuals. How is this tacit agreement assumed to come about? Ullmann-Margalit explicitly announces that she is not going into this question. She does not analyse the mechanisms and processes that are responsible for the generation of the tacit agreement. Likewise, Schotter states that the most that a game-theoretic account can do is to show that some institution is stable. Schotter does suggest, however, that the mechanism that produces the emergence of institutions is learning. Individuals are assumed to learn not only to restrict themselves, but also so that they can rely on the self-restriction of the others. How do they do this? The problem is that long before the new rule of self-restriction establishes itself as the rule that is followed by all individuals, the first pioneers or innovators must have found their way in a hostile environment. If everyone expects the others to adhere to the rule and if everyone is willing to adhere to the rule on the condition that the others do, the rule may be sustained. But what if no one expects the others to do so, and someone converts to the new rule? Can the latter get a foothold? It seems inevitable that in recurrent PD-games in which initially all play the dominant D-strategy, the first one to deviate is even worse off than the rest. Of course, this individual will not be encouraged to continue such deviant behaviour then.

It seems that Ullmann-Margalit's and Schotter's claim that norms or institutions can evolve out of a 'state of nature' PD-like situation is warranted only if the individuals involved all instantly agree on a collective 'cease fire'. There is no other reason to think that they would be able to arrive at such a situation than that they are engaged in deliberate, concerted, collective action. Of course this does not conform with what Hayek meant by spontaneous cultural evolution.

Ullmann-Margalit and Schotter analyse norms and institutions as (parts of) solutions to recurrent problems. They do not attempt to model the evolutionary processes in which the 'solutions' are generated. In Ullmann-Margalit's own terms, they try to bring out the rationale, or *raison d'être* of norms. This is a typical instance of an invisible hand explanation of the functional–evolutionary mould as discussed in Chapter 5. The real problem facing social theorists who want to analyse the spontaneous cultural evolution of a social institution is not, as Schotter argues, 'to infer the evolutionary problem that must have existed for the institution as we see it to have developed' (Schotter 1981: 2). It is rather the other way around. Starting with some well-defined problem situation, the theorist is to analyse where evolutionary processes of trial and error learning and imitation will lead to. In the next section, we shall see that some progress has been made in this respect by Axelrod.

8. CAN TIT FOR TATTERS INVADE A POPULATION OF DEFECTORS?

Axelrod (1990) can already be called a classic. It has attracted many comments and a lively debate that is still going on. What is perhaps best known is the success of a relatively simple strategy, 'tit for tat', in computer tournaments organized by Axelrod. Axelrod invited people to send in strategies (computer programs) that they thought would have the best overall results in randomly assigned pairwise confrontations in a sequence (of unknown length) of PD-games. Of the strategies that were sent in, tit for tat performed best. After this first round, and after its results were publicly announced, Axelrod organized a second round with an open invitation to any solicitors to beat tit for tat. But, again, tit for tat outperformed the rest.

Tit for tat is called a 'nice' strategy by Axelrod. A 'tit for tatter' starts to cooperate and continues to do so until the opponent defects. But it cannot be easily exploited by 'mean' adversaries. If an opponent defects, a tit for tatter hits back once by defecting too in the next confrontation with the opponent. This presupposes that the strategists are able to recognize each other. Axelrod assumes that each individual has a short but accurate memory: each individual is assumed to remember the last move of any opponent it has encountered. Axelrod ventures that since tit for tat has the best overall performance it may in the end, after some process of evolution, be the only strategy that survives. In a population consisting only of tit for tatters all individuals cooperate with each other all the time. Tit for tat can therefore be called a rule that is as efficient as Ullmann-Margalit's PD-norms and Schotter's PD-social institutions. The major difference with the accounts of Ullmann-Margalit and Schotter is that Axelrod argues that tit for tat does not require the help of an external authority for its maintenance. Axelrod attempts to point out that tit for tat is a stable, self-sustaining strategy. What is more, Axelrod does not leave it at that. He tries to show also that tit for tat can emerge in a population consisting of D-strategists.

The idea of computer tournaments suggests that Axelrod is dealing with sophisticated players who are trying to outsmart each other. This impression is reinforced by the fact that Axelrod assumes that the players are able to recognize each other. It seems to be further vindicated by the fact that he assumes that the players have a stake in their future payoffs. Axelrod introduces a discount parameter representing the degree to which the payoff of each move is discounted relative to the previous move. Axelrod's result that tit for tat is an evolutionary stable strategy hinges crucially on these assumptions.[17] Yet Axelrod stresses that foresight on the side of the players is not necessary to derive this result:

> There is no need to assume that the players are rational. They need not be trying to maximize their rewards. Their strategies may simply reflect standard operating procedures, rules of thumb, instincts, habits or imitation. [. . .] The actions that players take are not necessarily even conscious choices. [. . .] There is no need to assume deliberate choice at all.
>
> The framework is broad enough to encompass not only people but also nations and bacteria.
>
> (Axelrod 1990: 18)

Indeed, chapter 5 in the book, which is written together with the distinguished biologist W.D. Hamilton,[18] is about 'the evolution of cooperation in biological systems'. Here, the discount parameter is reinterpreted as the probability that after the current interaction the two individuals will meet again. And several substitute mechanisms or functional equivalents for the human capability to recognize are discussed. In this chapter, Axelrod deals with the question of under what conditions Darwinian natural selection can favour cooperative behaviour. Later on in the book, Axelrod argues that the evolutionary approach that he advocates is compatible with various mechanisms. He mentions trial and error learning and imitation as another possible evolutionary mechanism.

Axelrod expresses his indebtedness to Maynard Smith's evolutionary game theory for developing his own evolutionary approach. Axelrod's notion of *stability* is based on Maynard Smith's notion of an evolutionarily stable strategy (ESS), just as 'ESS' is Axelrod's notion of a collectively stable strategy defined in terms of uninvadibility: 'a strategy is *collectively stable* if no strategy can invade it' (Axelrod 1990: 56). Axelrod's definition of invasion is more strict than Maynard Smith's. In Maynard Smith's definition mutants can invade a population of 'native' players if a mutant does equally as well as a native when playing against a native but does better when playing against a mutant.[19] In Axelrod's definition, such mutants cannot invade. In his definition, mutants can only invade when they do better than natives when playing against natives. Axelrod adopts this slightly different definition because he wants to distinguish the possibilities for invasion by a single mutant and the possibilities for invasion by a small group of mutants.

Axelrod uses his notion of collective stability both in his 'genetic approach' of biological evolution and in his 'strategic approach' of socio-cultural evolution. This indicates that he assumes that the different types of evolutionary mechanisms involved in these two different processes of evolution generate the same dynamics. In combination with imitation, trial and error learning is apparently supposed to produce the same 'replicator dynamics' that is produced by natural selection in combination with genetic inheritance and that lets a population converge on a collectively stable strategy. There is no argument in Axelrod (1990) to substantiate this assumption. The assumption is not even explicitly stated.

Axelrod argues that tit for tat is a collectively stable strategy. Once tit for tat is established as the strategy that is followed by all individuals in the population, it cannot be invaded by any single mutant strategy. In this sense, universal adherence to tit for tat, and hence efficient cooperative behaviour, can persist without being enforced by an external coercive power. But there are some caveats here. Axelrod claims that tit for tat is not only stable, but also robust and initially viable. Axelrod apparently believes that it has shown its robustness by being the winner not only in the first tournament round, but also in the second one. Several commentators have pointed out, however, that it is relatively easy to devise strategies that can invade a population of tit for tat players.[20] The stability of tit for tat crucially hinges on the strategy set (or space) that is specified. But of course not every extension of the strategy set is credible. It seems to make sense not to allow strategies that on the face of it are infeasible.[21]

Axelrod's demonstration that tit for tat is initially viable is not straight-forward either. Can tit for tat invade a population of players who 'always play D'? In Axelrod's own definition of invadibility it cannot. For a single tit for tatter does worse than a defector when playing against a defector. Even the introduction of a small group of tit for tatters cannot get a foothold. It is true that the performance of the tit for tatters improves if several tit for tat mutants enter at the same time. But the problem is that the defectors profit even more. Only if the proportion of tit for tat mutants in the population has risen above some critical threshold value, which is quite high,[22] can they invade the population. If the standard assumption is accepted that the group of tit for tat mutants is small, some additional mechanism must be assumed to let the proportion of tit for tatters grow.

This problem is acknowledged by Axelrod. His way out of this trap is to assume that the tit for tatters can play selectively with each other in clusters. Cooperation can get started only when tit for tatters initially (after one encounter that they need to identify defectors) refuse to play with defectors, thereby leaving defectors no other choice than to play with other defectors. Although this assumption of selective play is essential in arguing for the initial viability of tit for tat, it is something of a *Fremdkörper* in Axelrod's analysis. It amounts to a change in the original rules of the game that state that individuals are paired at random in each sequence of the game.

9. LEARNING TO PLAY EFFICIENT STRATEGIES IN COOPERATION GAMES

Is the conclusion inevitable, then, that in recurrent cooperation games cooperation cannot get off the ground if we stick to the assumption that pairing is random? Sugden (1986) refuses to accept this. He sets out to argue that efficient conventions may evolve spontaneously in such games. What is more, Sugden claims to show this even under the weak assumption that individuals are not able to recognize each other in subsequent rounds. Sugden's analyses are about anonymous individuals. Or, to put it in game-theoretic terms, he deals with evolutionary game theory proper, not with supergame theory, as Axelrod does.

Sugden takes over Maynard Smith's notion of an ESS (without any modification) as the pivotal notion of his evolutionary approach. But he emphasizes that he is concerned with cultural (or socio-economic) evolution and not with biological evolution. In particular, he states that the mechanism that is operative is *learning by experience*, not natural selection. Sugden assumes that individuals are able to learn from their own experience and that of others what strategy yields the best results. The strategy that yields the best results is here taken to be the strategy that has the highest average payoff in terms of utilities. The payoffs that figure in the matrices in Sugden's book represent utilities, not material payoffs (in terms of monetary rewards, for example). Contra Axelrod, it is assumed that individuals do not discount future payoffs. Sugden's equation of the best strategy together with the strategy that has the highest average payoff imply that individuals value the results obtained in any meeting equally, no matter whether the meeting is now or in the remote future.

Sugden discusses several types of recurrent games. I will concentrate here on the game of 'Chicken', a game that has the same features as the Hawk–Dove game discussed in Chapter 7. I have two reasons for doing so. The first reason is to counterbalance the misplaced impression that PD is *the* archetypical type of cooperation problem. To some, PD is supposed to cover almost any cooperation problem, ranging from ecological problems pertaining to overgrazing, overfishing, overhunting and the like, through political problems pertaining to the necessity of the existence of a strong coercive power, to economic problems pertaining to the provision of public goods or to the problem of shirking in joint ventures. According to Sugden, however, 'Chicken' is more appropriate for analysing for example the Hobbesian 'state of nature', 'free riding' problems and (simple) bargaining situations. The generic form of Chicken or the Hawk–Dove game (henceforth referred to as HD) is given in matrix 10, and the numerical example of chapter 7 is again provided in matrix 2:

	D	H
D	(a,a)	(b,c)
H	(c,b)	(d,d)

Matrix 10
(where $c > a > b > d$)

	D	H
D	$(1,1)$	$(0,2)$
H	$(2,0)$	$(-1,-1)$

Matrix 2

In HD, there is no dominant option. There are two Nash equilibria in the one-shot HD-game: the 'pure' pairs of action (H,D) and (D,H). In recurrent HD-games a pair of mixed strategies (M,M) is to be added as a third Nash equilibrium, where M is 'do D half of the time and H half of the time'. In symmetric games, the first two equilibria cannot be ESSs for the simple reason that individuals do not distinguish between two different roles. If the population is homogeneous, individuals are not identifiable as occupying roles that relate to being a Column- or Row-player respectively. The only ESS then is M. Just as 'always play D' is Pareto inferior to 'always play C' in the PD-game, 'always play M' is clearly Pareto inferior to 'always play D' in the HD-game.

In Chapter 7 it was pointed out why 'always play D' is not evolutionarily stable. It is nevertheless instructive to see how learning individuals undermine this cooperative and efficient strategy. Here I come to my second reason for focusing on the HD-game. The HD-game nicely brings out the phenomenon of frequency-dependent selection. This phenomenon can be said to capture the element in Hayek's theme of interdependency that a rule may do well in one institutional setting but badly in another. This is exactly what we see happening in the HD-game. If all individuals in a population follow the strategy 'always do D', a single 'mutant' who experiments with playing H experiences an increase in utility of one unit. This mutant will therefore keep playing H. Others who happen to witness the success of the mutant will imitate the behaviour. They will also shift to playing H. Consequently, the proportion of H-players in the population will increase. This continues up to the point when more than half the population play H. For then the average payoff of D-players will exceed that of the H-players. And then the proportion of D-players in the population will grow.

Sugden does not claim that the population necessarily settles at the ESS M. The population may keep oscillating around it for ever without ever reaching it. But he does claim that once M is established, it will be self-enforcing. For if individuals deviate from it, they will find out that this does not pay. Hence, they will revert to playing M. This does not mean, however, that Sugden holds that the population is bound to stay at this inefficient state for ever. He argues that *de facto* property rights may evolve, as conventions in the sense of Lewis (1969), that lift the population to a Pareto-superior situation. *De facto* property rights are established when all individuals follow the same strategy P, based on a perceived labelling asymmetry between role U and role V:

strategy P: if U, play H with probability p; if V, play D with probability q, where $(p,q) = (1,0)$ or $(p,q) = (0,1)$.[23]

An example that Sugden discusses is one in which U stands for 'possessor' and V for 'intruder'. If $(p,q) = (1,0)$, we get the strategy B(ourgeois), and if $(p,q) = (0,1)$, we get the paradoxical strategy X as discussed in Chapter 7. But the definition that Sugden gives of *de facto* property rights leaves open the possibility that U and V may stand for 'larger' and 'smaller' respectively. So if $(p,q) = (1,0)$, we get the strategy A(ssessor). This means that Sugden holds that if all individuals in the population follow A, *de facto* property rights are established. Apparently, Sugden thinks that whatever the roles may be that are signified by U and V, as long as every individual on average occupies role U and role V half of the time and adheres to the same strategy P, there will be no hostile meetings. 'Property rights' that go either to the individuals occupying role U or to the ones occupying role V (depending on whether $p = 1$ or $q = 1$) will then not be challenged in any meeting by those occupying the other role.

Sugden shows that strategy P is the only ESS when it is added to the strategy set of the original HD-game. For any specific pair of roles and for any specific pair of values for (p,q), P indeed cannot be invaded by any strategy within the newly specified strategy set. In this sense, any specified P is stable. But is it also robust? Recall the discussion in Chapter 7 where it was pointed out that B can be invaded by A when the costs of assessment are low and the chance for the larger animal of winning the contest is high. Just like Axelrod's tit for tat, the stability of any specified system of *de facto* property rights depends on the kinds of 'mutant' strategies that might enter the population. It is dependent on the strategy set that is taken into consideration.

What about the initial viability of a strategy P in a population playing the mixed ESS M? According to Sugden, 'the vital stage in the evolution of a convention is the initial one' (Sugden 1986: 47). The first thing to note is that individuals cannot learn to play P from their experience when playing the original HD-game. As Sugden puts it, it takes an 'imaginative leap' of the pioneering 'mutants' to spot an asymmetry in a sequence of games that was formerly believed to be symmetrical. It is a creative jump which cannot be based on the experiences of playing the symmetrical game. This seems to be more in line with modifiable human behaviour, as Gould calls it, than with gradual change induced by gene mutations. As argued in Chapter 7, a single individual experimenting with some strategy P in a population of M-strategists does equally as well as the other individuals. In this situation of 'drift' it is unclear what will happen next. Only when a small group of individuals experiments with the same strategy P will the individuals within the group experience a higher payoff than they had formerly when playing M. Only then will they learn that it pays to keep playing P. The situation here is different from that of a small group of tit for tatters entering a population of D-players playing the PD-supergame. Whereas a small group of tit for tatters cannot invade the 'all D' population, a small group of P-strategists can get a foothold in an 'all M' population.

There is a snag here, however. Why would the several individuals experiment with the same strategy P? It seems to be perfectly possible that they can spot different asymmetries or attach different behavioural consequences to the same asymmetry. There is nothing in the original HD-game that suggests one asymmetry rather than another, or one behavioural consequence rather than another. In Chapter 7, we have seen for example that when a group of individuals spots the same asymmetry, and when there are as many individuals who attach the one behavioural consequence to it as there are those who attach the opposite consequences to it (as in B and X), the advantages of spotting the asymmetry are annihilated. A situation of drift results again then.

Yet, Sugden argues, there may be something outside the game that could give the individuals the same cue. He refers to notions such as salience or prominence that are introduced by Schelling (1960) and Lewis (1969). Some asymmetry (and behavioural consequence) may stand out for several individuals, because of their shared cultural background. Although its uniqueness is not based on experience acquired by playing the symmetrical game, it can be said to be based on their previous common experience. 'Salience' and 'prominence', thus understood, seem to fit perfectly with the ideas of Popper and Simon discussed earlier: that although trials are blind, they are not random but directed. The idea that it is some shared cultural background that gives the trials direction is compatible also with Hayek's views.

Assume for the sake of argument that all the individuals who experiment in an 'all M' population try exactly the same P. What follows from this? Sugden seems to believe that the rest of the evolutionary story is straightforward. The 'dumb' players, who initially do not spot any asymmetry, are supposed to learn by experience that it is better for them too to follow the same strategy P. Sooner or later they are said to recognize patterns in their experience too that will lead them to play P also. I believe, however, that there are complications here that are downplayed by Sugden. The complications relate to specific problems of learning and imitation in the type of evolutionary games that Sugden analyses.

It is clear that the individuals belonging to the pioneering group will continue to play P. It is also clear that the 'dumb' M-players would profit from shifting to P. But how are the 'dumb' players to know this? Sugden states that 'success breeds success'. In his own account of cultural evolution this would mean that the 'dumb' players are to learn by experience that changing to P is profitable. The problem is, however, that the 'dumb' players will not witness any change in their experience when playing the game. The persistence of a group of P-strategists in the population does not alter their average payoff. The average payoff of the M-strategists will remain ½. It does not change the frequencies of meeting individuals playing H or D either.[24] Nor will they observe any change in the payoffs that their opponents receive.

The point is that the 'dumb' players have no way of identifying a new strategy P in the population. This is due to the fact that they are assumed to play an anonymous game. They cannot recognize individuals they have met before. Hence they cannot keep track of the behaviour that other individuals exhibit in several meetings, which is necessary for spotting new patterns of behaviour. Therefore, imitation cannot have a 'bite' here. All the 'dumb' players perceive is pairs of individuals meeting each other playing the familiar H or D and receiving the payoffs as represented in the original HD-game. This means that their expectations are not frustrated and that they are likely to stick to strategy M.

The 'dumb' players need quite a lot of information in order to identify P, more than they can get by playing the anonymous evolutionary games they are supposed to be playing. We can think of several possible ways that they could get the required information. There may be a central office, for example, that registers and publicly announces both the behaviour of the individuals in their meetings with others and their payoffs. Or, as Sugden suggests, the P-strategists may tell the 'dumb' players about their new successful strategy. The pioneers have an interest in doing so, for the larger the group of P-players, the higher are their average payoffs. In contrast to the PD-game, communication may be sufficient here to establish a Pareto-superior situation. But then we are leaving the domain of evolutionary game theory. What is more important, we are resorting to types of explanation then that do not fit with Hayek's ideas on 'spontaneous evolution'.

In conclusion, we may say that just like Axelrod's analysis, Sugden's approach is strong in arguing for the stability of efficient conventions in recurrent cooperation games. Conventions here refer to systems of expectations that, were they to become established, would be self-confirming.[25] Even this is subject to all kinds of qualification, as we have seen. But the really weak point is that neither of them analyses how such a system of expectations can come about in processes of cultural evolution. They both simply assume that the dynamics in cultural evolution, produced by trial and error learning and imitation, is the same as the replicator dynamics in biological evolution. This should not be taken for granted, but must be argued for. The processes of trial and error learning and imitation should be studied in different types of games and situations. Appropriate notions of equilibrium, fixed points, steady states and the like should be based on such studies, and not the other way around (see also Friedman 1991).

10. CONCLUSIONS

On the basis of the foregoing discussion we can identify the mechanisms that are at work in cultural evolution. Individual trial and error learning is the *selection* mechanism. Ways of doing things are maintained by individuals as long as they bring them satisfactory results. Otherwise, they will try out something else. Here we come to the *mutation* mechanism. New trials are experiments, which are performed either intentionally, as attempts to innovate for example, or unintentionally, as mistakes in following existing rules. Although they may be directed or guided by some heuristics, they are blind in Popper's sense of being 'forays into the unknown'. Imitation provides the *transmission* (or replication) mechanism.

We could say that blind trial and error learning is at the core of this view on cultural evolution. For wherever new trials may come from, and no matter how confident individuals may be that they will be successful, 'the proof of the pudding is in the eating'. In particular, imitation of the successful behaviour of others is not a way to get around the troubles of trial and error learning. It rather yields new inputs to this process. Whether imitation occurs more or less unconsciously, as Hayek seems to believe, or deliberately, it leads to new trials that may turn out to be not as successful as was hoped for.

At first sight, what is selected in trial and error learning is beliefs (or hypotheses). This, indeed, is Popper's view. But Hayek appears to believe that behavioural rules are selected in cultural evolution. Trained economists who are used to distinguishing between preferences and beliefs (and resources) would perhaps view rules as substitutes for preferences and not for beliefs. So it seems we have a disagreement here between Popper and

Hayek. But this disagreement is only a superficial one. Popper's hypotheses, when transferred to world 2, function in exactly the same way as Hayek's rules: as behavioural dispositions. They give direction to (or channel) the behaviour of individuals by eliminating certain possible options for action. It seems that Hirshleifer's notion of passions and Frank's notion of commitments, that were discussed in the previous chapter, can be shared under the same rubric. They too refer to an (unconscious) exclusion of options that individuals in principle could have taken into consideration and that could have been advantageous to them.

Behavioural dispositions can thus be said to be constraining. But they can also be seen to facilitate action once we view individuals not as isolated and independent agents but as interdependent agents. This shift in perspective is Hayek's most important contribution. If rules are truly social rules, that is if they are followed by several individuals, the strategic uncertainty about each other's behaviour is reduced. The prevailing rules may be such, however, that some may be enticed to try new ones. Whether the new rules are successful or unsuccessful may depend on the rules followed by others. Eventually, this process of cultural evolution may come to rest in a social order in which the expectations of all individuals are mutually consistent and self-confirming. Evolutionary game theory, with its emphasis on frequency-dependent selection, and Lewis' notion of a convention seem to be suited for analysing these essentials of the Hayekian picture of cultural evolution.

The clarification that is gained by bringing in evolutionary game-theoretic analysis comes at the cost of several simplifications, however. I will confine myself to what I take to be the most obvious simplifications. A 'strategy' in an evolutionary game-theoretic analysis seems to leave no room for conscious choice at all. It seems to coincide with a limiting case of a behavioural disposition in Hayek's understanding; a limiting case in which all options are excluded but one. Furthermore, in Hayek's view sets of rules evolve. This does not mean, as we have seen, that they evolve in indivisible units, but as part of each other's environment. In contrast, rules are analysed in evolutionary game theory in an institutional *vacuum*.[26] Next, the stability of some strategy may be restricted to a given, specified strategy set. It may be destroyed by the invasion of a genuinely novel strategy.

Another simplification in the evolutionary game-theoretic analysis of cultural evolution is that there is some 'common currency' in cultural evolution, similar to material rewards (or resources) in natural selection. All individuals are assumed to be after the highest ('undiscounted') sum of utilities that they can get. And, last but not least, the dynamics in cultural evolution is taken to be the same as in natural selection. Strategies with an expected utility that is higher than the population-weighted average are supposed to grow, and those with a lower expected utility are supposed to decline in the population. It is not investigated systematically whether individuals are all interested in relative utility (instead of in absolute utility) nor whether they have the opportunity to learn which strategy has the highest expected utility.

9

A REALIST RECONSTRUCTION OF ECONOMIC EVOLUTIONARY THEORY

1. INTRODUCTION

In this final chapter I want to bring together some of the results of the present enquiry. Yet this chapter is intended to be more than just a summary or a recapitulation. It is meant to deepen our understanding of what is essentially at stake in evolutionary arguments and approaches in economics. To be more precise, I want to present both a stylized history of the evolution of evolutionary theorizing in economics and a philosophical reconstruction of the characteristic explanatory structure of economic evolutionary theory. In order to do this, I shall first develop a philosophical framework that is based on J.S. Mill's methodology of economics and on more recent work on the issue of realism. I then demonstrate the fruitfulness of the framework for providing both the stylized history and the philosophical reconstruction. The framework will also be used to unravel points of agreement and of disagreement between current trends in economic evolutionary modelling. And, finally, the framework will be employed to formulate an agenda for further research in the field of evolutionary theorizing in economics.

2. MILL'S METHODOLOGY OF ECONOMICS REVISITED

Lately, we have witnessed a revival of J.S. Mill's methodology of economics. Cartwright (1983 and 1989) argues that something like Mill's concept of a tendency is needed to make sense of the modelling efforts of economists and econometricians. Hausman (1992) claims that modern microeconomics can best be understood in a Millian vein as expressing inexact laws with implicit *ceteris paribus* clauses. And, finally, Mäki (1994) draws on Mill in developing his own account of isolations and abstractions in economics. In order to give an admittedly speculative, but as I hope also illuminating, philosophical reconstruction of the material presented in the previous chapters, I shall develop my own Millian concepts in discussion with these authors. Although I believe that the view on Mill's methodology that will be expounded can be defended on textual grounds, I shall not be concerned with exegesis. What I try to do here is to lay out a conceptual scheme that enables us to deepen our understanding of the evolutionary arguments and approaches in economics discussed in this book. In line with the inside and historical point of view I have adopted throughout the book (and that I circumscribed in Chapter 1), the conceptual scheme is meant to make sense of the ways the arguments and approaches are understood by their proponents. It is not my purpose to evaluate their self-understanding from some philosophical metalevel of analysis.

Mill held that the subject matter of 'pure economic theory' is the production and use of wealth. In studying this, Mill argued, economists focus on the human desire to pursue material advantage. Mill believed that the presence of this desire in every human creature is undeniable. He considered it to be part and parcel of human nature; in his eyes it was a psychological law which all human beings obey. This is not to say, however, that Mill took this human desire to be the only force behind activities that bear on the production and use of wealth. Other desires, causes and forces can (and often do) also affect the production and use of wealth. They can counteract and modify the workings of the human desire to maximize wealth and thus lead to results other than those predicted by 'pure economic theory'.

Mill entertained the paradoxical position that although the laws expressed in 'pure economic theory' are true, their implications for the production and use of wealth need not be true. The paradox can be resolved by distinguishing, as Mill did himself, between truth in the abstract (*in abstracto*) and truth in the concrete (*in concreto*). Mill held that the laws of 'pure economic theory' are true in the abstract, but not that they are (always) true in the concrete. To Mill the laws of 'pure economic theory' may be and often are false in the concrete.

This is not to say that the laws are to be regarded merely as statements denoting empirical regularities that hold for the most part. If in an attempt to verify the laws (that is, to show that they are true in the concrete) it turns out that the laws are false (in the concrete), then this is not to be taken to be an exception to the rule, Mill argued. It rather signifies that disturbing causes have been at work. A thorough understanding of what happened would reveal, Mill held, that the desire for material wealth has been counteracted by other causes. For this reason, Cartwright convincingly argues that Mill's laws are not 'tendency laws', which would state what happens in *most* cases, but 'laws of tendencies', which assert what tends to happen in *all* cases (even if the tendency is counteracted by other forces).

Mill was very sceptical about the possibilities for economists to conduct controlled experiments. According to Mill, physicists (and other exponents of the natural sciences) are able to improve their understanding of nature precisely because they can avail themselves of controlled experiments. But experiments, let alone controlled experiments, are rare in economics. This means that unlike physicists, economists cannot materially isolate some cause under study by artificially suppressing other influences. But it does not imply, as Mäki stresses, that economists are unable to isolate one cause theoretically. Economists can in a thought experiment (a *Gedankenexperiment*) subtract all potentially counteracting causes in order to examine what happens if one cause were to act alone.[1] By doing so, some economic system under consideration that may be subject to a multitude of interacting causes is analysed as if it were under the influence of one cause only. What is thus achieved is theoretical closure; an open system is conceived of as a closed system.

Mill is often said to have argued in this connection that economic laws hold only *ceteris paribus*. But Mill has not used this phrase frequently to clarify his methodological position. Indeed, it can be questioned that saying that Mill held that economic laws hold *ceteris paribus* accurately represents his position. The literal translation of *ceteris paribus* is 'other things being equal (or constant)'. But Mill's main point seems to have been not that the influences of other forces are 'frozen' in pure economic theory, but that other forces are assumed to exert no influence at all. Thus, in Mill's conception of economic laws other forces and causes are assumed to be inoperative or absent. It would therefore be more appropriate to say that in Mill's view economic laws are surrounded by *ceteris absentibus* clauses.

A *ceteris paribus* clause does not say that causes which are external to the system under consideration have no impact on the system. It says only that their influence on the system is assumed not to change. Paradigm examples in standard neoclassical economics are tastes and technology. In neoclassical theory tastes and technology are assumed to set the parameters of the system under study. *Ceteris paribus* clauses involve stabilizing idealizations, as Mäki rightly argues, for the values of the parameters are assumed not to change. But Mäki is wrong, I think, in arguing that *ceteris absentibus* clauses involve nullifying idealizations. I think that Cartwright (1989) is right in maintaining that Mill's notion of abstraction (or idealization) does not entail an idealization at all.

In a nullifying idealization the value of a parameter is assumed to be zero. The paradigm example of a nullifying idealization is the assumption of frictionless planes in physics. Mäki follows Williamson in suggesting that the analogue of this in economics is the assumption of zero transaction costs. No doubt the existence of positive transaction costs in the real world may account for other observed economic behaviour than the predicted behaviour in the idealizing model, just as the existence of friction leads to other physical behaviour than the predicted behaviour in a frictionless world. But the existence of transaction costs should be distinguished sharply, I think, from the operation of other forces and causes than the desire to gain material advantage. Transaction costs are one more type of costs that a rational wealth maximizer would take into account. But this is quite something else than when, say, the desire to do (morally) good interferes with the desire to maximize wealth. In Mill's view, Cartwright convincingly argues, the laws of tendencies in pure economic theory subtract (in a thought experiment) all causes but one: the desire to maximize wealth.

Cartwright conceives of tendencies as properties or qualities of an object that are at least partly responsible for its behaviour. Capacities, in the Aristotelian sense of causal powers, are treated by Cartwright as a subset of tendencies. In contrast, Hausman seems to take the laws of tendencies, or inexact laws as he prefers to call them, not as statements about causal powers themselves, but as their implications. Hausman deals in particular with laws in equilibrium theory. On Hausman's interpretation, then, inexact laws do not apply to the behaviour of individuals, but to market or industry behaviour that can be deduced from individual behaviour (plus information concerning prevailing conditions). If we take Hausman's interpretation of the laws of tendencies, then the laws can be seen to involve both *ceteris paribus* and *ceteris absentibus* clauses. The laws are based both on the assumption that the desire to seek material wealth is the only cause in action and on the assumption that relevant parameters are stable.

In economic reality, Mill held, the desire to maximize wealth seldom if ever is the only operating force in economic affairs. This means that Mill expected observable behaviour not to correspond perfectly to predicted behaviour in economic theory. If actual behaviour does not comply with predicted behaviour, Cartwright argues, then, ideally, we would like to have a full account of all forces and causes that jointly produced actual behaviour. This means that we would have to find some 'super'law (or unifying law), a law in which all relevant laws of tendencies and their interactions would be incorporated. Cartwright is sceptical, however, about the availability of such 'super'laws.[2] She thinks that there is no reason to believe that superlaws will ever be found.

We have seen that Mill held that the abstract truth of the laws of 'pure' economic theory is beyond reasonable doubt. But what does this mean? That Mill believed that the laws of 'pure' economic theory are true only in some possible, non-existent world? Are the laws true only in some imaginative world in which the cause under purview would not be counteracted or modified by other causes and forces (whereas, in reality, the cause would always be interfered with by other causes and forces)? This is the so-called modal or counterfactual interpretation of Mill's economic methodology that is generally acknowledged to be defensible on both textual and contextual grounds (see De Marchi 1986).

Yet for all their differences, Cartwright, Hausman and Mäki concur in the view that although Mill argues that the laws of tendencies are false at the phenomenal level, he takes them to denote something real. The laws of tendencies do not save the phenomena, they argue, but scientists believe nonetheless that they refer to causes or forces that are really operative in economies. What is more, scientists are said to be willing to accept the laws of tendencies only if they take the laws to reflect the working of some really existing cause or force. This introduces a commitment to a non-trivial kind of realism. For it entails not only the belief that causes and forces are operative in reality, but also the belief that what is expressed in the laws in a (pure) theory must be produced by really existing causes or forces. Following Mäki, I shall henceforth call this kind of realism *referential realism.*

Cartwright and Hausman seem to endorse the empiricist view that a statement that is false at the phenomenal level, a statement that is refuted by empirical evidence (or that would be refuted when subjected to an empirical test), cannot be true of anything. For they hold that even though the laws of tendencies can denote something real, their falsity (at the phenomenal level) cannot be denied. Mäki disagrees. He argues that truth should not be confused with 'the whole truth'. To accept that the laws of tendencies do not capture the whole truth does not imply, Mäki argues, that they cannot be partly (or partially) true. A law of tendencies may tell us the truth of the causal power of some object, even if the manifestation of this power is always disturbed by other coacting powers. The properties that are ascribed to the object in the law may be its real properties. Again, this view involves a particular kind of realism which Mäki calls *veristic realism.* Veristic realism maintains first of all that objects have real properties (or tendencies, or capacities) that influence their behaviour also when counteracted by other causes. And, second, it insists that what is said about an object in the laws of tendencies must be true of its real properties.

It can be defended, I think, that Mill's leaning towards the psychological law that humans prefer a greater over a smaller portion of wealth is consistent both with referential and veristic realism. He apparently believed that the law is true to a part of human nature. But what is the impact of this part compared with other parts in explaining the production and distribution of wealth? Hausman suggests that in Mill's view the desire for wealth predominates other longings and strivings in economic affairs.[3] It is a major cause that exerts considerable influence on economic behaviour. Whereas the impact of other, disturbing causes varies from case to case, the impact of the 'economic motive' is considered to be large and persistent. In this sense, this motive can be said to be essential in its own domain. Here, yet another kind of realism is involved, a kind that is dubbed *essentialist realism* by Mäki. Essentialist realism again entails two claims. The first claim is that among the causes or forces that are efficacious, there is one (or there are a few) that predominate the other ones in some specified domain. The second claim is that the laws of tendencies should relate to predominating causes and forces.

Finally, the last kind of realism that is tacitly embraced in Mill's methodology of economics is *methodological realism*. Mill somehow seemed to have believed it to be self-evident that since the desire for wealth is the dominating force governing economic behaviour this desire is and should be the first principle of economic theory. This reflects the methodological realist stance that a theory ought to represent and articulate the beliefs of the theorists formulating the theory. As Lawson puts it succinctly, the conjunction of methodological and essentialist realism entails that the main objective of economic science is:

> to abstract the real and the essential, to identify the real enduring generative structures and mechanisms that govern the flux of actual economic and social events.
>
> (Lawson 1989: 76)

Methodological realism is not as indisputable as it may seem at first glance. Methodological instrumentalists are willing to accept a theory that is not believed to be true. In contradistinction to methodological realists it is not demanded by methodological instrumentalists that only those theories are acceptable that express and articulate beliefs that are taken to be true.

We have now cleared the ground for a philosophical reconstruction of the main thrusts of the evolutionary arguments and approaches that I have discussed in the previous chapters.

3. THE SELECTION ARGUMENTS RECONSIDERED

In Chapter 2 I argued that the ultimate claim of the selection arguments, as espoused by Alchian, Friedman and Becker, relates to tendencies in industry behaviour. It is maintained by all of them that industries that initially are out of equilibrium are driven in the direction of the equilibria that are predicted by neoclassical theory. In this section it is ventured that such tendencies correspond to the laws of tendencies in J.S. Mill's sense. I shall also argue, however, that if we take the selection arguments seriously, the neoclassical laws of tendencies at stake are not the result of the insatiable desire of business men to make as much profits as possible, as Mill would have it, but to the operation of 'natural selection' in competitive markets.

Recall Alchian's (1950) paradigm example of a neoclassical tendency in industry behaviour: an increase in real wage rates in an industry leads to a decrease in its labour–capital ratio. As Alchian himself observes, this example needs to be qualified. For one thing, the profits that firms make (or the losses that they suffer) depend not only on their relative cost positions. Another obvious factor that determines their relative profitability

197

but that is abstracted from in the neoclassical tendency is their relative sales record, for example. The tendency therefore holds only *ceteris paribus*; it holds only if it is assumed that their relative sales records (and other variables that bear on the firms' profitability) do not change.[4]

Another qualification that is mentioned by Alchian relates to changes in the environment. Such changes may also disturb the process of 'natural selection'. Again, the implicit proviso in the neoclassical tendency is 'other things being equal'; the environment is assumed not to change in a way that would influence the predicted outcome. In short, then, it is not assumed that environmental factors and other factors that determine the firms' profitabilities do not influence the process of adaptation produced by 'natural selection'. It is assumed only that their values remain unaltered in studying the process.

Pointing out that the predicted tendencies are surrounded by vague *ceteris paribus* clauses falls short, however, of showing that they are laws of tendencies. To qualify as a law of tendency, it must be believed in addition that the tendency is produced by some real, essential cause or force. What predominating cause is taken to be responsible for the neoclassical tendency by the proponents of the selection arguments?

Mäki (1992) suggests that this overriding cause could be found in what is referred to in Friedman's maximization-of-expected-returns hypothesis: the desire of entrepreneurs to make as much profit as possible. The hypothesis could be read, Mäki argues, as a true representation of the essence or 'the fundamental structure' of firms. It would say then that the real essential underlying force behind firm behaviour is the motive of business men to maximize expected returns. This would not amount to a denial of other motives also guiding firm behaviour. It amounts to assigning a special status to the motive of achieving maximum profits. The desire for maximum profits is assumed to predominate other forces that may be operating also in shaping firm behaviour. This would be a perfectly legitimate reason, Mäki argues, for singling out and focusing on the desire for maximum profits in the theory of the firm.

It is this Millian reading, Mäki ventures, that would have rendered Friedman's defence of the maximization-of-expected-returns hypothesis coherent with traces of essentialist realism that can be found in the essay. As Mäki points out, Friedman argues that:

> A fundamental hypothesis of science is that appearances are deceptive and that there is a way of looking at or interpreting or organizing the evidence that will reveal superficially disconnected and diverse phenomena to be manifestations of a more fundamental and relatively simple structure.

> (Friedman 1953: 33)

Elsewhere, Friedman remarks that a meaningful scientific hypothesis asserts that certain forces are, and other forces are not, important in understanding a particular class of phenomena (Friedman 1953: 40). The phenomena to be predicted are said to behave as if they were to occur in a simplified world in which only those forces work that are asserted in the hypothesis. Inspired by these remarks, Mäki presents his own favoured interpretation of the 'maximization-of-returns' hypothesis: the hypothesis asserts what would happen if the force that is mentioned in the hypothesis, the desire to gain maximum profits, were the only force at work.

As is observed by Mäki himself, however, the problem with his essentialist realist Millian reading of Friedman's hypothesis is that it does not match with the interpretation that is given to it by Friedman himself. It cannot be denied that there are also instrumentalist elements to be found in Friedman's defence of the hypothesis. As we have seen in Chapter 2, Friedman argues that the issue of the real determinants of firm behaviour that was raised by the antimarginalists is a pseudo-issue really. Although Friedman does not seem to doubt that entrepreneurs are led by the desire to maximize profits, his acceptance of the 'maximization-of-expected-returns' hypothesis is not based on the belief that entrepreneurs are led by this desire. Friedman's defence of the hypothesis does not entail the claim that entrepreneurs are really or essentially after maximum expected returns. Indeed, to Friedman it does not entail any claim relating to the motives of business men at all. In short, Friedman seems to be an instrumentalist in that his acceptance of the hypothesis is not grounded in the belief that what the hypothesis says of firm behaviour is true (let alone that it captures the essence of firm behaviour).

Yet we are not bound to conclude, I think, that Friedman's defence of the hypothesis is incoherent with essentialist realism. As indicated in Chapter 2, an essentialist realist reinterpretation of the hypothesis can be given that is based on Friedman's own remarks. In this reinterpretation the hypothesis asserts nothing at all about motives, desires, deliberations or other mental states and processes of business men. Instead, the hypothesis is taken to assert what type of firms survive economic 'natural selection'. As Friedman puts it, acceptance of the hypothesis is based largely on the judgement that it summarizes appropriately the conditions for survival. It is Friedman's belief, first, that market economies essentially involve processes of economic 'natural selection', and, second, that only those firms survive in these processes that display behaviour which is consistent with the hypothesis, that underlies his acceptance of the hypothesis. Hence, the essentialism in Friedman's position is not to be found in 'personal' mental processes, I venture, but in 'impersonal' market forces. In giving his evolutionary underpinning, Friedman is consistent with Mäki's observation that a realist: 'insists on pursuing explanations for the instrumental success of nonbelieved theories in terms of theories that are believed' (Mäki 1992: 183).

This essentialist realist reinterpretation of the maximization-of-returns hypothesis is not strictly in agreement with Mill's methodology. Mäki seems to think that Friedman follows (or would have to follow) Mill all the way in believing not only that there is an essential, predominating cause in (political) economy, but also that this force relates to psychological qualities of 'human nature'. I take it that Friedman embraces only the first part of Mill's views. Friedman rejects the second part by arguing that the major force pertains to selective properties of competitive markets.

On this reading Friedman is a referential, veristic and an essentialist realist. Friedman's referential realism relates to his beliefs both that the notion of economic 'natural selection' denotes a real force in competitive markets and that neoclassical laws of tendencies are brought about by this force. Friedman is a veristic realist in that he believes both that the powers and properties that he attributes to this force are real and that they lead to outcomes that are predicted by neoclassical theory. And he is an essentialist realist because he takes economic 'natural selection' to be an essential, fundamental force in market societies. This does not mean that Friedman is a realist in every sense of the word, for Friedman cannot be said to be a methodological realist. He is a methodological instrumentalist. Friedman does not hold that a sound economic theory should express and explicate the basic beliefs of the economists who accept the theory. In this he differs from Enke who advances a selection argument similar to that of Friedman, but who concludes from this that marginal analysis should be replaced by 'viability analysis'. In Friedman's opinion (and also in Alchian's and Becker's opinion) there is no need to replace marginal analysis.

The foregoing places Friedman's well-known 'as if' methodology in a new light. Firms can be said to behave *as if* they maximize their expected returns, but not, as Mäki suggests, because all entrepreneurs are essentially engaged in attempts to maximize returns (whatever else they may be pursuing). If we look at the behaviour that firms actually display, Friedman argues, we may at first glance come to believe that firms behave in the ways they do because their entrepreneurs are rational maximizers. But a closer and more profound look reveals that the 'fundamental structure' in their behaviour is really moulded by processes of economic 'natural selection'. This reading of Friedman's *as if* methodology is strikingly similar to Dawkins' interpretation of his own *as if* representation of biological evolutionary processes (see chapter 7). In Dawkins' popularization of evolutionary game theory, individual organisms (that are taken to be programmed by selfish genes) are said to be behave *as if* they maximize their own fitness at the margin. Dawkins explains the notion of an evolutionarily stable strategy, for example, by saying that fitness is equalized at the margin; no organism can improve its fitness by (slightly) altering its behaviour then.

What Friedman's use of the *as if* construction (in relation to the 'maximization-of-returns hypothesis) has in common with Dawkins' is that seemingly rational individual behaviour is believed to be produced really by the force of natural selection. Neither Friedman, in his acceptance and use of the hypothesis, nor Dawkins, in his popularization of evolutionary game theory, engage in an explicit analysis of this force and of the processes that are governed by it. Apparently, they both appear to consider it to be perfectly legitimate in methodological respect to summarize the results of selection in terms of rational, maximizing choice without subjecting the processes of selection to explicit analysis.[5]

4. IN SEARCH OF AN ECOMOMIC TRANSMISSION MECHANISM

Mill held that giving explanations of phenomena (*explananda*) in economic theory consists in tracing these phenomena to fundamental economic causal factors (see Hausman 1994: 208). It must be shown that the force(s) that are pinpointed in economic theory are causally responsible for the occurrence of the phenomena to be explained. This notion of explanation accords well with the common sense view that to explain something is to explicate how it is brought about. In the field of philosophy of science this notion is in no way confined to Millians. It seems that a growing number of present-day philosophers of science want to come to grips with this root notion of causal explanation (see, for example, Salmon 1984 and 1990). In the context of our present discussion it is important to see that endorsing this root notion commits one to embrace methodological realism. Methodological instrumentalists, such as Friedman, are willing to accept theories without believing them. But a theory that is not believed in cannot provide the kind of explanation Mill and others are searching for. A theory can offer causal explanations only if we believe that the forces pinpointed in that theory are operating in reality.

Koopmans (1957) is probably the first who expressed a methodological realist stance toward Friedman's selection argument. For Koopmans in effect argues that if acceptance of the assumption of profit maximization is rooted in the belief that there is economic 'natural selection' going on, then we should postulate economic 'natural selection' itself and not profit maximization which it is said to imply. As argued in Chapter 4, Nelson and Winter (1982) can be regarded as the first systematic attempt to build an evolutionary theory based on this notion of economic 'natural selection'. One of the central tenets of Nelson and Winter's evolutionary theory is that making profits enables firms to expand, whereas suffering losses forces firms to contract.

In his early examinations of the selection arguments, Winter (1964, 1971 and 1975) already observed that this market force leads to determinate, predictable results only if individual firm behaviour shows some consistency over time. If firms employ the profits that they make in irregular and unpredictable ways, then nothing in general can be said about the aggregate effects that economic 'natural selection' produces. Initially, Winter seems to have treated the assumption of stable firm behaviour as some sort of *ceteris paribus* clause, as a stabilizing idealization needed to derive theoretical results. But later on this assumption appears to be uplifted in Nelson and Winter (1982) to a 'first principle', a principle having the same status as the principle of economic 'natural selection'.

Nelson and Winter argue at length that firms display routine behaviour. Firm behaviour is said not to be the outcome of rational choice, as 'orthodoxy' would have it, but of firm-specific, persistent routines. This view, that firm behaviour is governed by routines, is as essential to Nelson and Winter's evolutionary theory as is their belief that industry behaviour is moulded by 'natural selection'. We can safely assert, I think, that Nelson and Winter are dedicated to referential, veristic and essentialist realism with regard to both 'first principles'.

Nelson and Winter also insist on methodological realism. If routines are the real determinants of firm behaviour, they hold, then routines are to be dealt with in a sound theory of firm behaviour. In this respect they differ from Machlup and Friedman, who also acknowledge that there is routine firm behaviour, but who argue that there is no principled obstacle to analyse routine behaviour in terms of maximizing behaviour. Both Machlup in his account of the experienced automobile driver and Friedman in his account of the expert billiard player purport to show that what is unconscious skilful behaviour from the agents' point of view can be treated as maximizing behaviour from a theorist's point of view. There is no doubt that this can be done 'technically speaking'. Indeed, as argued in Chapters 4 and 8, in so far as behaviour is consistent over time, it can be dealt with theoretically either as routine (or rule-guided) or as maximizing behaviour.[6] But it can be questioned whether analysing routine behaviour as maximizing behaviour is a cogent way to proceed. Methodological realists answer this question in the negative. Just as Friedman's acceptance of the maximization-of-expected-returns hypothesis on evolutionary grounds is inadmissible to a methodological realist, so is Friedman's analysis of skilful behaviour in terms of maximizing.

Nelson and Winter take routines to be the economic counterpart of genes. Routines are believed to instruct firms in much the same way as genes instruct organisms. An obvious disanalogy is, however, that organisms pass their genes over to their descendants (in a well-understood inheritance process), while firms do not literally leave offspring. Nelson and Winter's contention that routines resemble genes is meant to signify only that if firms make (positive) profits and hence (can) expand,[7] their operating characteristics remain unaltered. It is only their scale of operation, their market share, that is altered. This is not to say that routines cannot be transmitted from one firm to another in Nelson and Winter's view. Firms can imitate other firms. But on Nelson and Winter's own understanding of routines imitation is impeded. They argue that the 'know how' that is embodied in routines is tacit. This means that the practical knowledge involved cannot be fully articulated and, hence, that is difficult to copy.

One of the things that Nelson and Winter want to show in their theory is that economic 'natural selection' can produce change in economic aggregates even if the properties of individual firm behaviour, their routines, do not change:

> This appraisal of organizational functioning as relatively rigid obviously enhances interest in the question of how much aggregate change can be brought about by selection forces alone.
>
> (Nelson and Winter 1982: 10)

I take this statement to invite an interpretation of Nelson and Winter's evolutionary project in terms of Millian laws of tendencies. Nelson and Winter do not believe that routines and selection are the only two forces that impinge on firms. In particular, Nelson and Winter believe that there are forces working on firms also that, if expedient, let them change their operating characteristics. But this in no way conflicts with their belief that routines and selection are real, essential determinants of industry behaviour. And as such, abstracting from changes in firms' routines does not imply that their enterprise cannot yield genuine insight into industry behaviour. On the contrary, Nelson and Winter appear to be convinced that doing so makes us understand the essentials of industry behaviour.

Nelson and Winter's 'first principles' can be compared, I think, with the two mechanisms that together produce Darwinian natural selection: the selection and the inheritance (or transmission) mechanism. The effects produced by the inheritance mechanism are expressed in the laws of Mendelian genetics. As argued in Chapter 5, these laws can be regarded as zero-force laws, as laws that would hold if no selection force was operating. This can be adequately rephrased, I think, by saying that these laws are Millian laws of tendencies that hold only *ceteris absentibus*. If organisms in a population differ in fitness, then introducing the selection mechanism implies a modification of the gene frequencies in a population predicted by Mendelian genetics. In the population's gene pool the genes of fitter organisms tend to supplant the genes of organisms with lower chances of having reproductive success. When reproduction is asexual, the joint operation of the inheritance and selection mechanism leads to changes in gene frequencies in the population's gene pool as described in *replicator dynamics*. Recall from chapter 7 that replicator dynamics roughly says that the growth rates of gene frequencies in a population's gene pool depend on the fitness of organisms relative to the population-weighted average fitness. As replicator dynamics can be said to state the effects of the composition of two causes, it is one of the rare instances in science of what Cartwright calls 'super'laws.

Darwinian natural selection can be expected to drive a population to an equilibrium (or to a stationary point) only if this process is not disturbed by changes in the environment. If environmental change occurs frequently, gene frequencies in a population's gene pool may fluctuate wildly without ever coming to rest. In this sense, natural selection can be said to bring about regular, patterned change in populations only *ceteris paribus*, under the assumption of stability of the relevant parameters.

Natural selection is not the only evolutionary force that may be at work. As Sober (1984) argues, change in populations may be generated also by evolutionary forces like mutation, migration and genetic drift that, if active, operate independently of the evolutionary force of natural selection. For reasons of simplicity I have placed these other evolutionary forces under the rubric of 'mutation mechanism' (see Chapter 5). In Darwinism the mutation mechanism must be regarded as a separate third mechanism besides the inheritance and the selection mechanism, because it is taken to work unresponsively to the survival needs of organisms. Genuinely novel genetic material in a population's gene pool can only be generated by the mutation mechanism.[8] Natural selection cannot produce new genetic material. It always impinges on already existing genetic material and it tends to eliminate rather than proliferate genetic material.

In evolutionary game theory this characteristic feature of natural selection is reflected in analyses of the (replicator) dynamics within a fixed strategy set. The predicted effects hold only *ceteris absentibus*, only if the mutation mechanism is assumed to be inoperative. If the mutation mechanism is introduced, new genetically programmed strategies may be brought about (and may thus lead to an extension of the strategy set), and altogether different results may obtain. So far, no 'super-super'law has been found that accounts for the combined workings of the inheritance, selection and mutation mechanism.[9]

After this short digression on three mechanisms governing biological evolution, it is time to return to economics. In the next section, I want to examine whether there is a third mechanism, a 'mutation' mechanism, to be found in economics. And if so, is its relation to the transmission and selection mechanism similar to that in biological evolution?

5. ECOMOMIC 'MUTATIONS'? ADAPTIVE LEARNING AS A SEPARATE EVOLUTIONARY MECHANISM

Nelson and Winter treat innovations as the economic equivalent of mutations. But whereas mutations are taken to be blind, gradual and (most of the time) deleterious for organisms in Darwinian natural selection, innovations are considered by Nelson and Winter to be the outcome of directed and deliberate search. This belief that search is failure induced, Nelson and Winter argue, makes their evolutionary theory 'unabashedly' Lamarckian. I have argued in Chapter 6, however, that Nelson and Winter's evolutionary theory is better viewed as involving two evolutionary mechanisms, economic 'natural selection' and adaptive learning, rather than one. Upon closer inspection, what is presented by Nelson and Winter as the missing economic mutation mechanism in a Lamarckian conception of economic evolution turns out to be a separate evolutionary mechanism working alongside economic 'natural selection'.

Adaptive learning can be said to entail a selection mechanism of its own. Rules of behaviour that so far have yielded satisfactory results are retained while rules that failed to do so are dropped. In the latter case search is triggered. Nelson and Winter take over Simon's idea that search is selective. Search activities are assumed to be guided by higher-order rules. 'Selective search' seems to contradict the firmly established view in evolutionary biology that mutations are blind. In adaptive learning, the 'mutation' mechanism does not operate independently of the 'selection' mechanism. 'Mutations' spring from search efforts which in turn are enticed by dissatisfactory results of using 'old' rules (that so far have yielded satisfactory results). But, as I concluded in Chapter 8 (after having compared Simon's 'selective search' with Popper's 'blind search'), 'selective' is not the opposite of 'blind'. It is the opposite of 'random'.

The selectivity in search activities rather reveals, I think, that adaptive learning resembles Darwinian natural selection in being 'backward looking' in two respects. Not only are past actual results decisive in the selection process, the 'material' adaptive learning works with is assumed to be 'old' material, that is material that has been accumulated in the past. As noted above, if the 'old' material that is put into practice no longer works satisfactorily, search for 'new' routines is started. Following Simon, Nelson and Winter assume that search for new routines is itself guided by already existing higher-order procedures. What is more, Simon argues that the 'new' material that is thereby found consists most of the time of recombinations of 'old' material.

Rules that are selected in processes of adaptive learning can be said to be replicated. But unlike genetic inheritance in Darwinian natural selection this type of 'replication' refers to an *intra*individual process. We have seen in Chapter 8 that adaptive learning can be said to be the driving force behind Hayek's notion of cultural evolution. As Hayek argues, *inter*individual transmission of rules of conduct in cultural evolution can come about as a result of imitation.[10] Imitation may be the result of a deliberate attempt to copy the 'success formula' of others. Or, as Hayek stresses, imitations may occur without the imitators even being aware of them. In both cases, however, it seems that imitated rules are eventually subjected to the selection test. 'The proof of the pudding is in the eating'; only if the imitated rules turn out to do well are they maintained.

Whereas economic 'natural selection' accounts for market share at the industry level, adaptive learning typically accounts for changes in 'individual' firm behaviour. Adaptive learning may alter the *beliefs* of firms and possibly also their *targets* (their aspiration levels). Their individual subjective aspiration levels determine what rules of behaviour 'survive', and not some objective industry-weighted average of profitability. Furthermore, if confronted with dissatisfactory results adaptively learning individuals must be able to identify in one way or other the rule(s) that are causally responsible for the failure. In economic 'natural selection' such a mediating recognition is not required. These differences between economic 'natural selection' and adaptive learning are reflected in different conceptions of *competition*.

From the perspective of economic 'natural selection', competition is a 'brute fact of life' due to scarcity of resources. Whether market participants value these resources or not, the resources that they appropriate determine their productive opportunities. Whatever the motives, goals and opinions of market participants, if their material means are exhausted, they will be eliminated (as a market participant; not necessarily physically) in due time. In this limited sense market participants can be said to compete for scarce resources. From this perspective adjustment processes in market processes run via changes in the market share of individual firms.

In contrast, in a Hayekian conception of competition, adjustment processes in markets are the outcome of discovery processes of individual market participants. What are adjusted are opinions and plans of individuals. As a result their former rules may be eliminated. To paraphrase Popper, individuals can let rules go in their stead. There may not be a 'common denominator' that, as a 'standard of selection', decides over the fate of rules. Individuals may have different targets. And each individual may decide for him- or herself whether to retain some rule or not and whether to change his or her aspiration level or not.

What dynamics is produced by adaptive learning? Quite a few evolutionary theorists who hold that adaptive learning is the primary (or even only) force governing economic evolution take it more or less for granted that adaptive learning yields the same (replicator) dynamics as natural selection.[11] Indeed, Witt (1993a) goes as far as to declare that replicator dynamics signifies a basic pattern that is characteristic of economic evolutionary theory *per se*. I have my doubts about this. In natural selection the weighted average fitness in a population is the common threshold value to all individuals. In adaptive learning there is no a priori reason to believe in the existence of a comparable threshold value that decides over the success or failure of the learning efforts of each individual. As Maynard Smith puts it, a common 'currency' similar to the one that governs natural selection (fitness) may be lacking in cultural evolution.

At any rate, adaptive learning (or search, as Nelson and Winter call it) can be regarded as a force or mechanism, I think, that works independently of selection in Nelson and Winter's evolutionary theory. And as it is an independent force or mechanism, it can interfere with selection, leading to other results than can be expected on the basis of selection alone. This reading seems to be underwritten by Nelson and Winter themselves:

> Search and selection are simultaneous, interacting aspects of the evolutionary process: the same prices that provide selection feedback also influence the directions of search. Through the joint action of search and selection, the firms evolve over time, with the condition of the industry in each period bearing the seeds of its condition in the following period.
>
> (Nelson and Winter 1982: 19)

The conception of Nelson and Winter's evolutionary theory as involving two independent evolutionary mechanisms modifying each other's effects is reinforced by the distinction Nelson and Winter make between selection and search effects and between the mechanisms responsible for them (see, for example, Nelson and Winter 1982: 169).

But how exactly do the two evolutionary mechanisms interact with each other? As in biological evolutionary theory, a 'super-super'law seems to be lacking here. This is not to say that no attempts have been made to analyse the joint operation of the two mechanisms. In Chapter 6, two attempts are discussed. In the first attempt, it is maintained that the force of selection does not work directly but only indirectly on the operating characteristics and decision rules of firms. Selection is thought of as working directly on higher-order learning or search rules.

The idea that search and learning efforts are guided by (higher-order) routines is also entertained by Simon and Nelson and Winter. But Nelson and Winter take another track in analysing the interplay of selection and search. In their evolutionary models Nelson and Winter assume that search is faster than selection. To be more precise, they assume that search of firms is terminated before the force of selection does its work. Selection is taken to operate on the end products of search. Nelson and Winter concede that this assumption is unrealistic. They argue that it would be more realistic to proceed from the assumption that the two mechanisms work concurrently. In Chapter 6 I argued that Nelson and Winter do not build their models on this realistic assumption presumably because they recognize that the problems that they would encounter by doing so are intricate if not insurmountable.

There is an unresolved tension in Nelson and Winter's evolutionary theory between their desire to give a realistic account of industry behaviour and their attempts to formulate analytical–tractable models. Their informal discussions of the basic constituents of economic evolutionary theory are much richer and more sophisticated than their formal treatments of the processes of economic evolution. This tension is not peculiar to Nelson and Winter. It is a tension, I shall argue in the next section, that seems to be indicative of the present state of the art in the emerging field of 'evolutionary economics'.

6. REALISTICNESS VERSUS TRACTABILITY

Nelson and Winter (1982) has inspired an increasing number of economists to analyse economic evolutionary processes explicitly. Rather than applying some preconceived static notion of equilibrium, these economists engage in modelling dynamic processes. It seems that one of Nelson and Winter's 'first principles', that economic agents are of a more or less fixed behavioural type, is taken over in all of these modelling efforts. Economic agents cannot change their operating characteristics overnight (there is some degree of behavioural *inertia*), even if they have a strong desire to do so. But apart from this shared understanding, many differences can be observed.

Perhaps exaggerating and simplifying a little, the models can be divided into two camps. On the one side there are evolutionary game theorists who typically assume that replicator dynamics adequately describes the population behaviour that evolutionary mechanisms produce.[12] Evolutionary game theorists typically are concerned with questions pertaining to the relation between economic evolutionary processes and (different notions of) equilibria, such as: do economic evolutionary processes converge on equilibria; if so, on what kind(s) of equilibria do such processes converge (see Van Damme 1987); and, in particular, does studying economic evolutionary processes offer a solution to the 'equilibrium selection problem'?[13] On the other side there are evolutionary economists who are more antagonistic to neoclassical equilibrium analysis than evolutionary game theorists.[14] Evolutionary economists typically want to dispense with notions of equilibrium altogether. Evolutionary economists tend to emphasize that real economies are open systems that continuously interact with changing environments, and also that there is endogenous systems change, that there are forces at work within those systems that take care of an unceasing stream of innovation.

Such differences in theoretical outlook are in no way peculiar to economics. In Chapter 7 we have seen that similar differences can be observed in evolutionary biology. There we have on the one hand theorists such as Dawkins who concentrate on 'orthodox' Darwinian natural selection that is assumed to bring about evolutionarily stable equilibria. On the other hand there are biologists like Gould who argue that 'orthodox'

Darwinian natural selection is just one 'agent' among others that are responsible for evolutionary change.

The philosophical framework that is developed in this chapter is also suited, I contend, to point out that the differences between the adversaries are in a sense less fundamental than is sometimes suggested. It seems to me that there is a shared understanding of methodological and ontological issues. Both evolutionary game theorists and evolutionary economists seem to share the view that economic theories should explicate the workings of evolutionary mechanisms in real economies. They also need not disagree on what underlying evolutionary mechanisms are at work in real economies. Evolutionary economists do not deny (or at least need not deny) that natural selection leads populations to converge on equilibria *ceteris absentibus* and *ceteris paribus*. And, conversely, evolutionary game theorists do not deny (or, again, need not deny) that such processes of convergence can be disturbed by changes from the outside or changes from within. In short, the two camps can be methodological and referential realists about the same generative mechanisms.

It can be defended also, I think, that the real difference between the opponents does not concern veristic realism either. That is, evolutionary economists could agree with evolutionary game theorists that population behaviour produced by natural selection abides with replicator dynamics *if* natural selection were the only force at work and *if* this force were to operate in a stable environment. Evolutionary game theorists need not hold that the two conditions under which population behaviour abides with replicator dynamics, are met in economic reality. As argued in section 2, the conditions can be thought of as being part of a thought experiment in which the force of natural selection is isolated theoretically. Evolutionary economists seem to argue that as the two conditions mentioned rarely if ever are met in economic reality, this theoretical exercise does not make sense. What they object to, in other words, is the theoretical strategy evolutionary game theorists follow in analysing complex processes of economic evolution. If replicator dynamics is almost always upset by disturbing forces and influences, evolutionary economists argue, why then conduct thought experiments in which all disturbances are swept under a hypothesized carpet?

But perhaps the differences between the two adversaries go further than this disagreement on the theoretical strategy to be followed. Sometimes it seems that evolutionary economists do not only think that there are more forces and influences at work than the analyses of evolutionary game theorists suggest. Sometimes it seems that they hold over and above this that other forces and influences are more important in strength or impact than the force of natural selection that features exclusively in evolutionary game theory. This then would indicate that the two adversaries are essential realists about different forces governing economic change. If this is correct,

I think that two forces and influences can be pinpointed that evolutionary economists put forward as having a greater impact on economic change than selection: endogenous ('internal') technological innovation and environmental ('external') change. Evolutionary economists tend to stress the relentless creation of novelty in the economic system and the instability of environmental variables. Whereas evolutionary game theorists seem to be preoccupied with processes of variation-destroying convergence, evolutionary economists are concerned mainly with factors that counteract such processes of convergence. One of these factors, endogenous innovation, is thought of as being responsible for processes of ('variation-inducing') divergence.

In response to the criticism of economists, evolutionary game theorists need not necessarily deny that the factors stressed by evolutionary economists play a crucial role in producing economic change. Instead, it could be argued by evolutionary game theorists that these admittedly crucial factors escape modelling efforts. Environmental change and the emergence of genuine novelty, they could argue, are by their very nature irregular and unpredictable.[15] And being unpredictable, these factors cannot be incorporated in formal models. If this argument cuts wood, the theoretical choice evolutionary theorists in economics have to make is the familiar one (among economists) between realisticness and tractability. *Realistic* is not to be confused here with *realist*. Whereas in the present interpretation 'realist' is inextricably tied up with isolation and abstraction (and hence with incompleteness), 'realistic' is taken here to be connoted with completeness, with accounts that are exhaustive in covering all causally relevant factors. A fully realistic model would take cognizance of all factors that (potentially) affect the processes and events under study. In this sense of 'realistic', then, if we want models that are both realistic and tractable, it seems we are faced with a dilemma: either we have a realistic but intractable account, or we have a tractable but unrealistic model. The pessimistic message would be that we cannot have it both ways.

Up till now I have tacitly assumed that evolutionary game theorists model processes that are governed by the force of selection. But evolutionary game theory is used increasingly, it seems, to analyse that other evolutionary mechanism: adaptive learning. Indeed, this seems to reflect a general trend of treating adaptive learning instead of (natural) selection as the most influential selective force behind economic evolution. Often the very same notions of evolutionarily stable equilibria and replicator dynamics that have been developed to study natural selection are entertained also to study adaptive learning.[16] As argued in the preceding section, given the differences between the two evolutionary mechanisms the legitimacy of the transfer of these notions is far from self-evident. What is at issue here is veristic realism about the properties of the mechanism of adaptive learning.

210

7. DIFFERENT CONDITIONS AND DIFFERENT UNITS OF EVOLUTION

The issue of what forces and mechanisms have the greater impact on the generation of economic change has to be sharply distinguished, I think, from two issues that also seem to be at stake in the confrontation between evolutionary game theorists and evolutionary economists. The first issue concerns the conditions under which the evolutionary mechanisms of selection and adaptive learning operate. If we assume, for the sake of argument, that replicator dynamics adequately describes the effects of both mechanisms, then the effects that eventually are produced by the mechanisms depend crucially on the conditions that (are assumed to) obtain. In evolutionary game theory, the conditions are reflected in the structure of the game the participants are assumed to be playing. The structure of the game determines to a great extent whether the outcome is optimal or efficient for the population as a whole. There is a fairly wide range of games, both of the (impure) coordination and of the cooperation (or mixed-motive) type, in which populations may get stuck in suboptimal evolutionarily stable strategies.

Indeed, optimal equilibria can be expected to result (without qualifications) only if the situation individuals find themselves in is of the pure coordination type. Only in those situations do the interests of individuals coincide completely with that of the population or group taken as a whole. What is best for the group is then also best for the individuals that make up the group and vice versa. In pure coordination games the relation between individuals and the groups of which they are part is similar to that between organs and the comprising organism. In Chapter 8 I have defined organicism as the view that at levels higher than the organism, parts relate to each other and to the comprising whole in the same way as organs relate to each other and to the organism of which they are part. I argued that Hayek held such an organicistic view on cultural evolution in groups. What is valuable in Hayek's view, I argued, is the emphasis on the *interdependency* of the functioning of individuals (the 'parts'). When individuals change their behaviour, this may change the cultural environment, both for others and for themselves, which, in turn, may affect the overall performance of the group. What is dubious in Hayek's view is his assumption that all individuals have the same interest in coordinating their plans in one unique and optimal equilibrium. This is what makes Hayek believe that eventually the group will settle on optimal rules.

Organicism should be distinguished, I argued in Chapter 8, from group selection. What the two have in common is the view that what evolves is best for some encompassing whole, be it an organism or a group. But whereas organicism entails a particular view on the relation between parts and wholes, group selection entails a particular view on the entities that

211

evolutionary mechanisms work on. To say that there is group selection is to say that evolutionary mechanisms impinge on groups. Here we come to the second issue that is to be distinguished from the issue of what mechanisms are most essential in generating economic change. Both evolutionary game theorists and evolutionary economists believe that there is individual selection going on. But beyond this there seems to be persistent disagreement. Generally speaking, evolutionary economists seem to be less hostile to the notion of group selection than evolutionary game theorists.[17] Evolutionary economists tend to believe, it seems, that there is multi-level evolution going on (see, for example, Hodgson 1993b).

The intuitively appealing idea of interdependency can be nicely illustrated, I argued, by the notion of frequency-dependent selection in evolutionary game theory. The paradigm example of frequency-dependent selection is the Hawk–Dove (HD) game. In the HD-game it depends on the relative proportions of H- and D-strategists in the population whether selection favours H-strategists or D-strategists. Again, under the pressure of selection the population will settle at a suboptimal equilibrium. This suboptimal equilibrium can be replaced by an optimal one only if the mutation mechanism takes care of entry of the right type of mutant strategies in the population. As there is no a priori reason to believe that the mutation mechanism will produce an optimal strategy, outcomes can be said to be contingent or conditional on behavioural 'input'. What evolves is crucially dependent on the available behavioural types in the population. In this sense, and under these conditions, history can be said to matter.

History also matters, and even more so, when there is path dependency (see, for example, Arthur 1988 and 1989 and David 1985). Some evolutionary economists tend to elevate path dependency to the status of a first principle of evolutionary economics (see, for example, Hall 1994).[18] I think that this is unjustified. Path dependency obtains when historical small events decide over the course of evolution. When there are increasing returns, for example, some technology may establish itself that is inferior in respect to efficiency with some rival technology, for no other reason than that the inferior technology happens to have been tried out by more firms than those that tried out the superior one. The process in which the inferior technology establishes itself is irreversible in the sense that when this process is well under way the inferior technology can no longer be outcompeted by the superior one. Also related are so-called lock-in effects. Once an inferior technology or institution has established itself as the standard in an industry, the industry is locked in this standard. This is similar to a population that gets stuck in the suboptimal Nash equilibrium in impure coordination games (as discussed in Chapter 8, section 7).

Path dependency and lock-in effects can be said to be phenomena that obtain under particular conditions. Evolutionary economists such as Arthur and David do not question the 'standard' operation of evolutionary mechanisms. Their analyses presuppose that new technologies and institutions can get a foothold in some population only if they outcompete rivals that are also tried out. What evolutionary economists question is that the conditions are met *de facto* that are necessary to obtain 'standard' results: only efficient technologies and institutions evolve. The issue that is at stake here is what conditions obtain in economic reality. This is an issue that is to be resolved (in principle, at least) by conducting empirical research. What I want to stress here is that path dependency and lock-in effects are not on the same footing as the evolutionary mechanisms that both camps, evolutionary game theorists and evolutionary economists alike, take to be operating. It is the presumed working of evolutionary mechanisms, and not the results that they generate under particular conditions, that are rightly to be regarded, I think, as 'first principles' of economic evolutionary theory.

8. AN AGENDA FOR FURTHER RESEARCH

There are many points, I have argued, that evolutionary game theorists and evolutionary economists (and indeed anyone who is sympathetic to the idea of 'economic evolution') could agree on. The ontological issue, for example, of what sorts of processes are captured under the rubric of 'economic evolution' is not (or at least need not be) controversial: there is *multi-mechanism, multi-level* economic evolution going on in economic reality. Economic evolution can take place at different levels of description and analysis. Firms either may expand or are forced to contract, depending on their actual performance. One level above, industries may thrive and prosper or may disappear completely. And one level below, individual persons may be more or less successful in propagating their character traits (see Chapter 7) and in transmitting their behavioural dispositions (Chapter 8). Different evolutionary mechanisms may be involved in these processes of economic evolution. In this book two evolutionary mechanisms have been distinguished: economic 'natural selection' and adaptive learning. Economic evolution at both the level of firms and that of individual persons can be said to be governed (at least partly) by the interplay of these two evolutionary mechanisms.

In the terms of the philosophical framework that is developed in this chapter, the foregoing implies a shared referential and essentialist realist understanding of economic evolution. 'Economic evolution' is taken to refer to the same type of dynamic processes and the same two evolutionary mechanisms are considered to be essential in guiding these processes. This is not to say that all advocates of evolutionary theorizing in economics believe that the two mechanisms mentioned are *the* (most) essential forces producing economic evolution. But they all seem to concur with the view that understanding the workings of evolutionary mechanisms is a *sine qua non* for a proper understanding of processes of economic evolution. In addition, advocates of evolutionary theorizing in economics can also be called methodological realists, for they hold that processes of economic evolution should be modelled explicitly.

Beyond this basis of agreement, however, disagreement reigns. As noted in section 6, there is disagreement on how to proceed theoretically: given that economic evolution is a multi-level and multi-mechanism phenomenon, does it make sense to achieve theoretical closure by isolating (in a thought experiment) one mechanism working at one level? Whatever one is inclined to answer, it should be clear by now that acceptance of any of the types of realism discussed here does not prejudge this issue. Arguments to the contrary (see, for example, Hodgson 1993b and Foss 1994) seem to rest on a confusion of 'realism' with what I have called 'realisticness'. Only those who are wedded to realisticness are committed to reject analyses of economic evolution in which causally relevant factors are subtracted theoretically.

Other points of disagreement relate to veristic realism concerning the dynamics adaptive learning produces and to the conditions under which economic evolution is assumed to take place. And it is here, I contend, that more research is needed most. The first issue to be tackled is whether adaptive learning produces replicator dynamics. In this book I have raised several doubts about this. The issue cannot be decided, I think, on a priori grounds. But, to say the very least, the doubts raised warrant further empirical research. Only empirical research can tell whether processes of adaptive learning (approximately) display the regular pattern, if any, that is described by the equations of replicator dynamics. And only after we have found this out can we tell what notion of equilibrium, if any, is appropriate. Further empirical research on this subject is thwarted by the fact that in actual processes the working of the mechanism of adaptive learning may be disturbed by other factors and forces. But maybe experimental economics is capable of isolating the mechanism materially. If so, experimental economics could in principle be of much avail in finding out what dynamics fits what problem situations. Structural deviations from 'standard' replicator dynamics should not be treated as outright refutations of this specific type of dynamics, but rather as phenomena in want of further explanation (see, for example, Crawford 1991).

As it stands there are many things in adaptive learning that we only have a dim understanding of. For example, how do individuals form categories of situations that they perceive as similar (see Vanberg 1993)? In the likely case that adaptively learning individuals entertain a repertoire of rules (and not just one rule), this is an important question. For how does an adaptively learning individual 'judge' (or 'sense') that a 'new' situation resembles 'old' situations (in relevant respects) when the individual follows the rule(s) again that worked reasonably well in the 'old' situations? And if several rules go into one and the same token of behaviour, and if the token fails to be successful, what rule(s) are blamed for it (see Loasby 1991)? Yet another issue concerns the specifics of search behaviour that can be triggered in such a situation. Do adaptively learning individuals tend to search in the near vicinity of the rules that they have followed so far, or do they often experiment with radically different rules? In other words, are 'mutations' of a gradualist type (as in biological evolution) or of a 'saltationist' type (involving leaps and jumps)? More clarification is sorely needed also, I think, of the crucial 'replication' mechanism of imitation. Studying these phenomena will take us into the field of psychology, a field that economists such as Williamson appear to be reluctant to enter.

The second issue pertains to the *conditions* under which evolutionary mechanisms work. 'Conditions' will here be taken to comprise the basic structure of situations (as in the structure or type of games), the rules that govern the interaction of agents ('the rules of the game') and the specification of the initial set of rules ('the strategy set'). Throughout the book we have seen that outcomes of the evolutionary process are highly sensitive to the specific conditions that are assumed to obtain. Again, recall Hayek's organicism. If indeed market participants relate to markets as organs do to the organisms they are part of, then Hayek would be right that the 'invisible hand' can be expected to yield optimal outcomes. But, as Coase made clear, the problem we have to face then is how to account for the existence of organizations (as 'islands of conscious control') within markets. In Williamson's transaction cost economics organizations exist because markets cannot solve contract compliance problems as efficiently as organizations can. In the post-contractual period, the interests of individual contractants do not coincide completely. Given this condition (and Williamson's assumption of opportunism), optimal outcomes can only come about when 'invisible hands-off governance' (the market) is replaced by 'visible hands-on governance' (organization).[19]

Williamson's account of the existence of firms resembles the view of those who argue (like Schotter) that optimal cooperative behaviour in the Prisoners' Dilemma can be sustained only by an external authority. Later game-theoretic attempts by Axelrod and Sugden to show that uniform cooperation can evolve spontaneously even in cooperation games like PD only confirm the crucial importance of the specification of conditions. For, as we have seen in Chapter 8, their attempts can succeed only if the 'rules of the evolutionary game' are changed. Conditions, now in the sense of specified initial strategy sets, have been shown to be crucial also in Chapter 7. It depends on the strategy set specified whether ESSs that are optimal evolve. Likewise, in games with an impure coordination structure we need to know the initial steps taken by agents in order to tell whether 'lock-in effects' result. Again, as in the case of the dynamics that adaptive learning produces, the right way to proceed theoretically does not seem to be to interpret first some persistent phenomenon as some equilibrium and then to infer from this the conditions of the problem situation that it helped to solve (as in Schotter 1981). The right way to proceed rather seems to be the other way around: to investigate first what conditions obtain (and what dynamics is produced), and only then what can be expected to evolve.

In short, what is needed is a more profound and detailed analysis of the workings of adaptive learning under a wider variety of conditions. Or, to put it in the philosophical terms of Chapter 5, functional explanation (as well as equilibrium and invisible hand explanation) has to give way to causal process analysis. This implies, I think, that economic evolutionary theory will find psychological and historical issues on its way to maturity. Perhaps at some time evolutionary theorizing seemed to be especially attractive to economists because it held out the hope of getting around troublesome psychological and historical issues. But now it has become clear that this was a chimera. Psychological and historical issues will have to be tackled even by those who are willing to accept an economic evolutionary theory in which all forces and factors but one are subtracted.

NOTES

1 INTRODUCTION

1 Witness for example the appearance of new periodicals such as *Journal of Evolutionary Economics* and *Journal of Social and Evolutionary Systems.*

2 Lately a process can be observed, however, of 'evolutionary economics' and 'new institutional economics' developing into two separate strands of theory. See Chapter 9.

3 The reader is also warned right from the outset that this book does not contain discussions of the relevance of notions like 'dissipative structures' and of non-equilibrium thermodynamics (as introduced and analysed by Prigogine and Stengers) for economics.

4 In Klamer and Leonard (1994) the need for distinctions between different roles of metaphors and analogies is acknowledged. Metaphors reflecting basic background beliefs are called constitutive (or root) metaphors by Klamer and Leonard.

2 SELECTION ARGUMENTS *PRO* AND *CONTRA* THE NEOCLASSICAL THEORY OF THE FIRM

1 Of course, when firms consist of two or more members, this supposition is not self-evident. This observation can be said to lie at the heart of the so-called new theory of the firm. See Chapter 3.

2 It may not be too difficult to find out the demand function of a group of oligopolies in an industry, taken as a whole.

3 In other situations, in situations of pure monopoly and of monopolistic competition, for example, there are no principled obstacles for entrepreneurs to get to know their demand functions. Hall and Hitch argue, however, that there may be other reasons (such as the longing for a quiet life) that may prevent entrepreneurs from getting the relevant information.

4 See, for example, the discussion of Nelson and Winter's evolutionary theory in Chapter 4. It should also be mentioned that Harrod gives an account of another empirical finding of Hall and Hitch's (that entrepreneurs think of prices based on the 'full cost' principle as 'fair' prices, as prices that ought to be charged) that closely resembles Ullmann-Margalit's (1977) game-theoretic account of Prisoners' Dilemma (PD) norms (see Chapter 8).

5 Machlup rightly points out that the factor 'variations in profits or losses' comprises all the others.

6 Indeed, Machlup argues that: 'economic theory, static as well as dynamic, is essentially a theory of adjustment to change' (Machlup 1946: 521).

7 This point seems to be acknowledged in Machlup (1967).

8 In Machlup (1967), it is no longer argued that the neoclassical theory of the firm is a theory of individual firm behaviour. It is now argued that the 'neoclassical firm' is just a theoretical construct to predict tendencies in industry behaviour.

9 Recall that this is one of the neoclassical hypotheses that is challenged by Lester (1946) and defended by Machlup (1946).

10 Alchian also expresses some doubts on this point, however. At the end of this section, I shall discuss these doubts.

11 See also Archibald (1959) and (1987).

12 Even in the insightful and comprehensive study of Hirsch and De Marchi (1990), Friedman's selection argument is not given the attention that it deserves.

13 This is confirmed by Alchian (personal communication, September 1993). Friedman was a referee of Alchian's paper, but Friedman did not see a draft of the paper before 1949/50.

14 As a matter of fact, this title gives us a clue as to why Friedman wrote his essay at all. It seems that Friedman was a little bit weary of extensive discussions of methodological principles. But he seems to have engaged in such discussions himself, because Marshallian economics was criticized from two sides: first the criticism that its assumption of perfect competition is unrealistic, and second, the antimarginalist criticism (which he took to be less important than the first one, see Friedman 1953: 15–16).

15 In an otherwise instructive paper, Musgrave (1981) misses this point completely. Musgrave takes the profit-maximizing assumption to be a 'domain assumption', that determines the domain of applicability of a theory. In this reading, the antimarginalists would have been right after all in arguing that if firms are not profit-maximizers, the theory of the firm is inapplicable.

16 In Nagel (1963), it is taken for granted that the 'evidence' Friedman refers to is empirical evidence that either supports or falsifies the 'maximization-of-expected-returns' hypothesis.

17 Langlois also suggests that 'profit-maximizing behaviour' is: 'an intermediate term in the marginalist explanation of price and quantity changes' (Langlois 1986b: 246).

18 The production opportunity set of firms is defined by Becker as the region of possible actions of firms within which profits are non-negative.

19 See Chapter 8 for an elaboration of this point.

20 In his reply to Kirzner, Becker (1962b) concedes that he has not shown that all the market implications of rational behaviour would be reproduced by all or most irrational behaviour.

21 See Chapter 9, sections 2 and 3, for a further discussion of such tendencies in terms of J.S. Mill's laws of tendencies.

22 I think that this can be regarded as an 'innocuous general statement' the economists involved believe in, as Caldwell (1992) puts it.

23 Of course, when firms recognize that making positive profits is a *sine qua non* for survival, this may help them survive. But this is not a *panacea* for success.

3 BREAKING OPEN THE BLACK BOX

1 Coase argues that Knight's well-known explanation in terms of uncertainty is not satisfactory basically for the same reason: it is not pointed out by Knight

why the price mechanism does not suffice and why entrepreneurial control is needed.

2 Of course, the 'Coase Theorem' is also a milestone in the development of the property rights approach (see Coase 1960).

3 In particular, the assumption of profit maximization is replaced by the assumption of utility maximization. Most of the time, property rights theorists assume that there are non-pecuniary sources of utility (besides pecuniary sources). The classical reference here is Becker (1957). In Williamson (1964), this assumption is operationalized to deal with the discretionary behaviour of managers in corporations. Williamson's operationalization is taken over by many property rights (see, for example, Alchian 1965) and agency costs (see Jensen and Meckling 1976) theorists.

4 Putterman's assertion that Jensen and Meckling rejoin corporate management with the 'profit motive' is not correct, however. Jensen and Meckling argue that deviation from 'profit maximization' is minimized by an interplay of efficient markets, not that this interplay annihilates any deviation from 'profit maximization'.

5 I shall concentrate here on the basic assumptions and on some of the characteristic hypotheses in Williamson's transaction cost economics (neglecting many other interesting aspects).

6 See Alchian (1984), in which it is also argued that all these different terms denote the same contract formation and enforcement problem.

7 A similar view is presented in Simon (1951).

8 Williamson argues that his own transaction cost economics differs from the property rights approach in this respect (see, for example, Williamson 1990: 67).

9 See also section 5.

10 This seems to imply that not even the fundamental issue has been resolved conclusively of what 'organizations' and 'markets' (and *hybrids*, possible intermediate forms) signify.

11 Recently, Williamson has argued that economizing on the sum of production costs and transaction costs is a more general statement of his hypothesis (see, for example, Williamson 1990: 67).

12 The truth or falsity of synthetic (or contingent) statements does not depend only on their syntactic composition and on the meanings of their constituent terms. Their truth or falsity depends also, and crucially, on the prevailing state of affairs in reality.

13 I shall postpone the examination of this claim to Chapter 5, where I will deal extensively with Darwinian natural selection.

14 This assumption that Jensen extracts from Alchian's selection argument is more akin to Friedman's intermediate claim than to Alchian's own ultimate claim. Alchian did not conclude (as Friedman and Jensen do) that the behaviour of each and every surviving economic unit approximates maximizing behaviour.

15 For a similar account, see Langlois (1984: 26). See also Milgrom and Roberts (1992) for a defence of 'efficiency' as a 'positive principle' in the study of economic organization.

16 Williamson refers to Simon (1991) who argues that 'a mythical visitor from Mars' would notice that the greater part of economic life takes place within organizations and not between organizations in markets, whereas economists have focused on the latter. What Williamson does not mention, however, is that Simon criticizes new institutional economics for relying too much on neo-classical concepts whilst ignoring key organizational mechanisms like docility and identification.

17 Mueller also argues that Williamson's work is 'miles ahead of these Panglossian applications of the transaction costs approach' (Mueller 1986: 834). Mueller's

reasons for arguing this are that Williamson addresses problems of monopoly, of managerial discretion and of worker alienation and dignity.

18 But to say that one organization form is more efficient than another is to say that no individual agent is worse off in the first form than in the second.

19 It should be borne in mind, however, that Williamson subscribes to 'weak-form selection', whereas the other authors discussed seem to embrace 'strong-form selection'.

20 Williamson relates this idea to Kuhn. In my opinion, however, this idea, as well as Williamson's ideas on 'main case propositions', resembles more Lakatos's ideas than Kuhn's.

21 In section 4, we have seen that Jensen (1983) can be said to pursue such a strict Lakatosian line.

4 MODELLING THE SELECTION ARGUMENT

1 In an otherwise sympathetic book review, Baumol remarks that: 'my main complaint against the book is the amount of space wasted in denouncing neoclassical approaches' (Baumol 1983: 581).

2 Winter (1964) is an abbreviated version of the (unpublished) doctoral dissertation Winter wrote at Yale University.

3 This objection to Friedman's argument was raised also in Archibald (1959). A second objection Archibald raised was that 'profit maximization' need not imply positive profits. 'Profit-maximizing' firms therefore need not survive.

4 A capital utilization rule is a function of the ratio of price (P) and the unit variable cost of production (c).

5 As Brian Loasby has rightly pointed out to me (personal communication), *all* behaviour in non-equilibrium situations is to be called non-orthodox, since there is no orthodox theory of optimization outside equilibrium.

6 According to Nelson and Winter, we encounter the 'prototypical' question of positive economic theory here: 'what is . . . the sign of the response of intensity of use of an input to a rise in its price?' (Nelson and Winter 1982: 169).

7 See also: 'the qualitative predictions of orthodox comparative statics analysis may well describe the typical patterns of firm and industry response in the dynamic, evolving economy of reality' (Nelson and Winter 1982: 175).

8 In addition, neoclassical theory considers 'standard' responses to be self-evident, that is the possibility of exceptions (in which the responses are 'perverse') is not taken seriously.

9 Orthodox appreciative theory is also called *working paper orthodoxy* in Winter (1991).

10 Although Nelson and Winter seem to take the results of Hall and Hitch seriously, they appear to consider their method of empirical research, the mailing of questionnaires, to be unreliable (see, for example, Nelson and Winter 1982: 92).

11 Similarly, it is argued by Teece that: 'core business skills need to be constantly exercised to retain corporate fitness' (Teece 1988: 265).

12 A firm's resistance to change can thus be seen to have a 'rational' basis. See also Winter (1986: 175 and 182).

13 Actually, there are many different ideas about this distinction in Nelson and Winter (1982). Sometimes Nelson and Winter suggest that routine behaviour and deliberate choice are not mutually excluding 'options', but that they are complementary. For example, they argue that deliberate choice determines what large-scale plan to initiate and that skills and routines are required to

perform smaller-scale tasks within the plan (Nelson and Winter 1982: 84–5). This idea seems to be compatible with 'orthodoxy'.

14 Nelson and Winter seem to acknowledge this point. They remark that as routines may be keyed in complex ways to signals in the environment, routine behaviour does not imply literal identity of behaviour over time. But this remark is dissonant to their overall treatment of routines.

15 The strange thing is that this is noticed by Nelson and Winter themselves. They acknowledge that in 'Friedman's sophisticated and carefully hedged position', 'choice' does not entail that firms go through explicit calculating deliberation (Nelson and Winter 1982: 91 and 67–8).

5 FUNCTIONAL EXPLANATION

1 In Rosenberg (1985), it is also argued that functional claims in biology are all ultimately explained by the mechanism of natural selection. But unlike Elster, Rosenberg does not hold that functional claims are always justified by natural selection.

2 It must be added, however, that genetic recombination in sexual reproduction may be a source of incessant variation in genetic material.

3 The same idea seems to be entailed in Elster's notion of a 'local maximum trap' (see, for example, Elster 1989: 72).

4 Dr Pangloss stands for Leibniz in Voltaire's 'Candide', a persiflage on Leibniz' metaphysics. Leibniz seemed to be committed to the view that we live in the best of all possible worlds.

5 A classic criticism of panadaptationism is Gould and Lewontin (1979).

6 There is functionalism also in psychology, for example. I will not deal with this type of functionalism here.

7 In Elster (1983), Elster argues that he is convinced by Hardin (1980) that there are more examples of valid functional explanations in social science. In Vromen (1992a), I have argued, however, that Hardin's examples are not convincing. In his examples, Hardin exploits an ambiguity in Elster's representation: the actors producing X need not belong to group Z.

8 This idea seems to be captured also in Nozick's (1974) notion of invisible hand explanations.

9 The view that firms are satisficers can be read into Alchian (1950). But whether Alchian would subscribe to this view or not, I have argued in Chapter 2, section 4, that it is not part of his selection argument.

6 TWO EVOLUTIONARY MECHANISMS

1 It is rightly stressed by Metcalfe (1989) that a replacement of neoclassical theory by evolutionary economic theory involves a shift from typological to population thinking.

2 Hodgson argues that 'genotype' stands for rules of action in Nelson and Winter's theory and 'phenotype' for the actions themselves (Hodgson 1994: 416). In evolutionary theory, however, the phenotype of an organism does not refer to its behaviour, but to its behavioural traits (that are more akin to rules of action) and its morphological features.

3 See Teece (1988) for an attempt to integrate both contractual and propriety issues (from a transaction cost perspective) and technological issues (from an evolutionary perspective) in one encompassing framework. But in the end

Teece seems to subscribe to Williamson's intuition that the (in)efficiency of a firm's organization form decides its viability (Teece 1988: 267).

4 In Winter (1986) 'routine' is presented as a 'catchall', a generic term that encompasses not only decision rules and standard operating procedures, but also organization forms (among other things). I reject this 'conceptual strategy'. As it blurs important differences, it simply is not informative. I shall henceforth understand 'routines' in the more restrictive sense of (technological) decision rules and operating procedures.

5 This is akin to the context-dependence objection Sober brings forward against 'genic selection' (see Sober 1984: 313). Genic selection will be discussed in Chapter 7.

6 In devising this example, I was inspired by 'Simpson's paradox'. See Sober (1987).

7 See also Metcalfe (1989: 61).

8 This seems to conflict with Winter's (1986) assertion that it is, 'of course', a fundamental commitment to an economic evolutionary theory that routines of firms are persistent.

9 Simon argues that it makes no sense to speak of 'optimal' simplifications, because the costs and benefits of gathering new relevant information are not known in advance by the decision maker. A similar argument against the view that satisficing is just a form of maximizing (taking search costs into account) is offered in Winter (1964).

10 Simon refers to Festinger's work on cognitive dissonance. See, for example, Simon (1956: 137, note 6).

11 The feedback mechanism in adaptive learning is emphasized also, for example, in Cyert and March (1963), Levitt and March (1988) and Cross (1983).

12 Indeed, Simon calls 'choice' *ir*rational when it is dominated by affective mechanisms like emotions and instincts, not if it is produced by intellective mechanisms. Therefore, although Simon holds that rational choice does not imply optimization, in his view rational choice does imply the process of reasoning or deliberation (see, for example, Simon 1964).

13 I owe many of the points that follow to van Parijs (1981). I wonder, however, whether van Parijs would agree that Simon's notion of adaptive learning can be called an evolutionary mechanism. See van Parijs (1992).

14 In Simon (1978), it is argued that in Williamson's work on transaction costs interesting functional analyses are given of existing organization forms. Simon seems to approve of Williamson's analyses primarily because they are explicitly based on 'bounded rationality'.

15 Simon's contention that 'maximizing' is silent on the decision-making processes individuals go through is affirmed in Latsis' (1976) account of the neoclassical theory of the firm in terms of *situational determinism*.

16 As a matter of fact, the Hayekian conception of 'competition' that is defended in Kirzner's (1962) criticism of Becker is much more akin to Simon's notions of bounded rationality and adaptive learning than Becker's (1962a) paper. For a further discussion see Chapters 8 and 9.

17 Selection for higher-order learning rules is modelled in the economic realm, for example, in Blume and Easley (1992), and in the biological realm, for example, in Harley (1981).

18 In Loasby (1991), it is also argued that higher-level rules are better viewed as decision-premises than as complete specifications of (search) behaviour.

19 See Chapter 4, section 2. Recall that this was one of Penrose's points of criticism of Alchian's selection argument also (see Chapter 2, section 4).

7 ALTRUISM AND UNITS OF SELECTION

1 This is not to say, however, that 'group selection' is discarded by all (socio)-biologists. Some hold that both individual selection and group selection occur. The results are said to depend then on the relative 'mortality rates' of individuals and groups. See also Hodgson (1993b).

2 The replicator dynamics is formalized by Taylor and Jonker (1978) and Zeeman (1980).

3 This way of representing the game deviates from the standard representation with pairs of payoffs. As the HD-game is symmetrical, however, no information is lost in giving this deviating representation.

4 In recent years several models have been developed in which all of these assumptions have been relaxed.

5 It is assumed, for example, that having some role and playing some strategy are independent of each other (there is no *pleiotropy* between the genes influencing role and those influencing strategy), so that a B-strategist plays H and D with equal frequencies. Furthermore, it is assumed that in contests between two Bs, if one plays H then the other plays D.

6 It is easy to verify that just as B is the only ESS in the HDB-game, X is the only ESS in the HDX-game. If a population were to consist of X-strategists, then resources would shift from owner to intruder in every contest.

7 Again, it is assumed that there is no pleiotropy. See note 5.

8 This is demonstrated in Vromen (forthcoming). In the more realistic HDBA-game, it is assumed that assessors have to incur assessment costs c, and that larger individuals have a chance x, $\frac{1}{2} < x < 1$, to win contests if it comes to fighting. For low values of c and high values of x, A is a suboptimal ESS in this game.

9 Maynard Smith (1982: 5) concedes that too much effort is put into seeking an optimum and not enough into defining the strategy set. Maynard Smith argues, for example, that the strategy set in the Hawk–Dove game is ridiculously naive.

10 Dawkins is not the first one who defends the claim that the gene is the unit of selection. He is indebted to Williams (1966). But Dawkins' provocative presentations have attracted more attention.

11 'Genes' are defined by Dawkins (1976) in a functional way as those parts of the genomes of individuals that are long lived enough to serve as units of selection.

12 Maynard Smith calls entities that can evolve adaptations by natural selection *units of evolution.*

13 Houthakker argues that 'although nature may have no discernible motives, it may nevertheless operate in the same way as if it had a motive' (Houthakker 1956: 187).

14 It has been observed by many that these problems within firms can be represented in a game-theoretic format. Notice, however, that proponents of the new theory of the firm argue that these internal problems are mitigated by external market pressures (see Chapter 3).

15 Axelrod (1990) is another example. As Axelrod takes his own account to be based on 'strategic reasoning' rather than genetic inheritance, I shall discuss Axelrod in Chapter 8.

16 See for example: 'I have shown that altruism may actually increase personal fitness because of its effect on the behaviour of others' (Becker 1976: 824).

17 See Chapter 6. Of course, it is possible to argue that Kid finds out about Daddy's true degree of altruism in an evolutionary trial and error type of learning process. But then an evolutionary theory would have to model this process explicitly.

18 Similar speculations have been entertained by many distinguished economists. See for example Coase (1976 and 1978), Demsetz (1988: 275) and Alchian (quoted in Zerbe 1982).
19 In Chapter 8 I shall deal more extensively with the PD-game.
20 'Meme' is derived from *mimeme*, Greek for imitation.
21 In Harley (1981), animal learning is assumed to be governed by stable *meta*strategies. Harley shows that there is a relatively simple learning rule that will take the individuals to a DSS that is identical to the ESS.

8 THE CULTURAL EVOLUTION OF BEHAVIOURAL DISPOSITIONS

1 Popper refers to Hayek (1967).
2 Simon argues that 'cues signaling progress play the same role in the problem-solving process that stable intermediate forms play in the biological evolutionary process' (Simon 1962: 472).
3 See also Campbell (1987) where it is argued in Popperian vein that search is blind only in so far as it goes beyond already achieved wisdom.
4 Simon does not seem to be prepared to defend the view that if we move up the hierarchy, there are 'limiting-case' rules at each level that would automatically select 'the thing to be done'. If domain-specific routines do not work well, Simon (1992) argues, individuals may well resort to 'open-ended' means–end analysis.
5 A major stumbling block is that Hayek's remarks are far from unequivocal. Some of his remarks are rather obscure, others are ambiguous if not inconsistent.
6 One could also prefer to say that the market itself is an institution.
7 See also the notion of hidden-hand explanation in Nozick (1974).
8 We have found this view on competition also in Kirzner's (1962) criticism of Becker (1962a). See Chapter 2.
9 In an otherwise excellent paper, Vanberg (1993) wrongly attributes this view to Hayek.
10 This accords with the views on cultural evolution that are put forward in Cavalli-Sforza and Feldman (1981) and Boyd and Richerson (1985).
11 Hayek (1976: 78) frankly admits that imitation denotes a process of which we know very little.
12 See for example: 'what may be called the natural *selection* of rules will operate on the basis of the greater or lesser efficiency of the resulting *order of the group*' (Hayek 1967: 67).
13 See Chapter 6, section 6.
14 If a population gets stuck in (R,R), *lock-in effects* can be said to obtain (see David 1985 and Arthur 1988, 1989). For a further discussion of 'lock-in effects' and the related notion of *path dependency*, see Chapter 9.
15 Lewis' notion of a convention does not seem to allow for any choice. Like Hayek's 'negative rules', however, Lewis' conventions restrict behaviour without removing all choice (Lewis 1969: 51).
16 Hayek (1964: 7–8) acknowledges that in some situations the enforcement of rules by the government may be required to get optimal results.
17 Taking Axelrod's numerical example of the PD-game (see matrix 5), a population of tit for tatters can resist an invasion of defectors only if the discount parameter $w > \frac{1}{2}$ (see Maynard Smith 1982: 203). Other crucial assumptions are that confrontations are always pairwise and that the overall performance is the decisive criterion for success (it is not an 'elimination tournament').

18 See Chapter 7.

19 Axelrod's presentation of Maynard Smith's definition of invadibility is incorrect (Axelrod 1990: 217, note 1 of Chapter 3).

20 See, for example, the strategies 'Punisher' and 'Bully' in Hirshleifer and Martinez Coll (1988) and 'Pavlov' in Nowak and Sigmund (1993).

21 For example, Robson's (1992) 'secret handshake mutant', which is assumed to possess secret signals that only other mutants of the same type possess, seems to be too contrived to be taken seriously. The funny thing is that Robson shows that the introduction of another incredible mutant, the 'sucker punch', annihilates the advantages of the secret handshakers, thereby restoring the original inefficient 'all D' outcome.

22 It can be calculated that only if the proportion of tit for tatters in the population x exceeds $(1 - w)/(3w - 1)$ can tit for tatters invade a population of 'all D'. We have seen in note 17 that only for $w > \frac{1}{2}$ is 'tit for tat' a stable strategy. When $w = \frac{2}{3}$, for example, x must exceed $\frac{1}{3}$, which of course is pretty large for a group of mutants entering a large population.

23 Labelling asymmetry refers to some perceived distinction in roles that the individuals play. Outcome asymmetry goes further. It refers to differences in payoffs that the individuals have when occupying different roles.

24 It may be objected that this is a result that is peculiar to the specific numerical example given in matrix 2. In other numerical examples the frequencies of meeting individuals playing H or D change. But the problem is that the 'dumb' M-strategists do not know from what time on they are to compare the new frequencies with the old ones, since they 'miss' the invasion of the P-strategists.

25 See also Sugden (1990). In Sugden (1986 and 1989), a Humean account is given of the transition of conventions that are followed on the condition only that others follow them too, into norms, that are followed more or less unconditionally. According to Hume and Sugden, the transition is produced by human desire to get the approval of others.

26 Or perhaps it is more appropriate to say that many 'background' institutions are implicitly assumed in evolutionary game theory. See also Field (1984).

9 A REALIST RECONSTRUCTION OF ECONOMIC EVOLUTIONARY THEORY

1 The same methodological view can also be expressed by saying that economies are conceived of as 'closed systems' in 'pure economic theory'. See also Lawson (1992). This should not be confused with the ontological view, however, that economies really are closed systems. For a further discussion see section 6.

2 See Cartwright (1983: 12). The problem at stake here is discussed by Mill under the heading of 'composition of causes'.

3 Cartwright seems to disagree. She argues that to Mill: 'causes did not divide themselves into major and minor' (Cartwright 1989: 176).

4 Alchian's use of the qualifying phrase 'to that extent' (Alchian 1950: 217) shows his awareness of this *ceteris paribus* clause.

5 An important difference of course is that whereas the traditional or standard interpretation of population behaviour in evolutionary biology is in terms of Darwinian natural selection, the traditional or standard understanding of industry behaviour in neoclassical economics is in terms of rational individual action.

6 Nelson and Winter do not believe that all firm behaviour is regular and

predictable. They add stochastic elements to their theory in order to account for irregular and unpredictable behaviour.

7 Whether firms invest (part of) their profits is also determined by investment rules in Nelson and Winter's theory.

8 Of course, when there is sexual reproduction, new genetic material can be said to be produced continuously also by the inheritance mechanism. But as this new material consists of recombinations of 'old' material, I do not call this new material genuinely novel.

9 But see, for example, Kandori *et al.* (1993) for an attempt to derive general results from models that incorporate incessant mutations.

10 As argued in section 4, Nelson and Winter are sceptical of the possibilities for interfirm transmission of routines via imitation for the reason that the knowledge of firms, that is embodied in their routines, is tacit.

11 See, for example, Banerjee and Weibull (1994) and Binmore and Samuelson (1994). In contrast, Friedman (1991) and Mailath (1992) are much more careful in this respect (witness, for example, Mailath's warning that 'there is nothing in economics to justify the replicator dynamics' (Mailath 1992: 268)).

12 What I have in mind here is a theoretical tradition starting with Cornell and Roll (1981) and continuing with, for example, Hansen and Samuelson (1988), Schaffer (1989), Binmore and Samuelson (1992 and 1994) and Banerjee and Weibull (1992 and 1994).

13 Sometimes it seems that resort is taken to an evolutionary interpretation of games for the reason that the 'standard', 'educative' interpretation seems to be unable to solve these problems. See, for example, Binmore (1987, 1988).

14 Evolutionary economists seem to be inspired more by the work of Schumpeter, Veblen and, more recently, of Prigogine and Stengers. I am thinking in particular of the papers in Dosi *et al.* (1988), Saviotti and Metcalfe (1991), Day and Chen (1993) and Witt (1993b).

15 This is acknowledged by some evolutionary economists. See, for example, Witt (1993a).

16 It must be added, however, that lately evolutionary game theorists have become more sensitive to differences between biological and social evolution and the different types of dynamics that are involved. See, for example, Friedman (1991) and Weibull (1994).

17 The willingness of evolutionary economists to accept the notion of group selection seems to be more inspired by their reluctance to embrace methodological individualism than by the belief that what evolves in reality is best for groups taken as a whole. Indeed, it seems that in general evolutionary economists precisely want to argue for the opposite claim that what evolves in reality is not best (or at least not always best) for groups taken as a whole.

18 One sometimes cannot get away without the *déjà vu* feeling that evolutionary economists are eager to arrive at 'non-standard' results (efficient equilibria are the exception rather than the rule), while evolutionary game theorists have an overriding concern to derive 'standard' results from 'non-standard' evolutionary models.

19 If we take the interplay of evolutionary mechanisms working at different levels into account, this conclusion may well have to be altered. It has been observed by property rights and agency costs theorists (see Chapter 3) that selection at the levels of individuals may mitigate opportunistic behaviour in markets. Employees can improve their market position by building a good reputation. And Frank argues that committed, non-opportunistic persons fare well in individual selection (see Chapter 7).

BIBLIOGRAPHY

Alchian, A.A. (1950) 'Uncertainty, evolution, and economic theory', *Journal of Political Economy* 58: 211–21.

—— (1953) 'Biological analogies in the theory of the firm: comment', *American Economic Review* 43: 600–3.

—— (1965) 'The basis of some recent advances in the theory of management of the firm', *Journal of Industrial Economics* 13: 30–41.

—— (1984) 'Specificity, specialization, and coalitions', *Journal of Institutional and Theoretical Economics* 140: 34–49.

Alchian, A.A. and Demsetz, H. (1972) 'Production, information costs, and economic organization', *American Economic Review* 62: 777–95.

—— (1973) 'The property rights paradigm', *Journal of Economic History* 33: 16–27.

Allen, P.M. (1988) 'Evolution, innovation and economics', in G. Dosi *et al.* (eds) *Technical Change and Economic Theory*, London: Pinter, pp. 95–119.

Archibald, G.C. (1959) 'The state of economic science', *The British Journal for the Philosophy of Science* 10: 58–69.

—— (1987) 'The theory of the firm', in J. Eatwell *et al.* (eds) *The New Palgrave: A Dictionary of Economics*, London: Macmillan Press, pp. 357–62.

Arthur, W.B. (1988) 'Competing technologies: an overview', in G. Dosi *et al.* (eds) *Technical Change and Economic Theory*, London: Pinter, pp. 590–607.

—— (1989) 'Competing technologies, increasing returns and lock-in by historical events', *Economic Journal* 99: 116–31.

Axelrod, R. (1990) *The Evolution of Co-operation*, London: Penguin Books. (First published in 1984 by Basic Books Inc., New York.)

Banerjee, A. and Weibull, J. (1992) 'Evolution and rationality: some recent game-theoretic results', unpublished paper.

—— (1994) 'Evolutionary selection and rational behavior', in A. Kirman and M. Salmon (eds) *Rationality and Learning in Economics*, Oxford: Basil Blackwell.

Barlow, G.W. and Silverberg, J. (eds) (1980) *Sociobiology: Beyond Nature/Nurture?*, Boulder, Colorado: Westview Press.

Baumol, W.J. (1959) *Business Behavior, Value and Growth*, New York: Macmillan Press.

—— (1982) 'Contestable markets: an uprising in the theory of industry structure', *American Economic Review* 72: 1–15.

—— (1983) 'Book review of Nelson, R.R. and Winter, S.G. (1982)', *Journal of Economic Literature* 21: 580–1.

Becker, G.S. (1957) *The Economics of Discrimination*, Chicago: University of Chicago Press.

—— (1962a) 'Irrational behavior and economic theory', *Journal of Political Economy* 70: 1–13.

—— (1962b) 'A reply to I. Kirzner', *Journal of Political Economy* 70: 82–3.

—— (1974) 'A theory of social interactions', *Journal of Political Economy* 82: 1063–93.

—— (1976) 'Altruism, egoism, and genetic fitness: economics and sociobiology', *Journal of Economic Literature* 14: 817–26.

Berle, A. and Means, G. (1932) *The Modern Corporation and Private Property*, New York: Commerce Clearing House.

Bianchi, M. (1993) 'Hayek's spontaneous order: the correct *vs.* the corrigible society', unpublished paper.

Binmore, K. (1987) 'Modelling rational players: part I', *Economics and Philosophy* 3: 179–214.

—— (1988) 'Modelling rational players: part II', *Economics and Philosophy* 4: 9–55.

Binmore, K. and Samuelson, L. (1992) 'Evolutionary stability in repeated games played by finite automata', *Journal of Economic Theory* 57: 278–305.

—— (1994) 'An economist's perspective on the evolution of norms', *Journal of Institutional and Theoretical Economics* 150: 45–63.

Blume, L. and Eastey, D. (1992) 'Evolution and market behavior', *Journal of Economic Theory* 58: 9–40.

Boyd, R. and Richerson, P.J. (1985) *Culture and the Evolutionary Process*, Chicago: University of Chicago Press.

Caldwell, B. (1982) *Beyond Positivism: Economic Methodology in the Twentieth Century*, London: Allen & Unwin.

—— (ed.) (1984) *Appraisal and Criticism in Economics: A Book of Readings*, Boston: Allen & Unwin.

—— (1992) 'Commentary on "human molecules"' (by A. Nelson), in N. De Marchi (ed.) *Post-Popperian Methodology of Economics. Recovering Practice*, Boston: Kluwer Academic Publishers, pp. 135–49.

Campbell, D.T. (1987) 'Evolutionary epistemology', in G. Radnitzky and W.W. Bartley III (eds) *Evolutionary Epistemology, Rationality, and the Sociology of Knowledge*, La Salle, Illinois: Open Court, pp. 47–89. (First published in 1974.)

Cartwright, N. (1983) *How the Laws of Physics Lie*, Oxford: Clarendon Press.

—— (1989) *Nature's Capacities and their Measurement*, Oxford: Clarendon Press.

Cavalli-Sforza, L.L. and Feldman, M.W. (1981) *Cultural Transmission and Evolution*, Princeton, New Jersey: Princeton University Press.

Chandler, A. Jr (1962) *Strategy and Structure*, Cambridge, Masachusetts: MIT Press.

Clark, N.G. and Juma, C. (1988) 'Evolutionary theories in economic thought', in G. Dosi *et al.* (eds) *Technical Change and Economic Theory*, London: Pinter, pp. 197–218.

Coase, R.H. (1938) *The Firm, the Market and the Law*, Chicago: University of Chicago Press, pp. 33–55.

—— (1960) 'The problem of social cost', *Journal of Law and Economics* 3: 1–44.

—— (1976) 'Adam Smith's view of man', *Journal of Law and Economics* 19: 529–46.

—— (1978) 'Discussion', *American Economic Review (Papers and Proceedings)* 68: 244–5.

—— (1991) 'The nature of the firm: influence', in O.E. Williamson and S.G. Winter (eds) *The Nature of the Firm: Origins, Evolution and Development*, Oxford: Oxford University Press, pp. 61–74.

Cornell, B. and Roll, R. (1981) 'Strategies for pairwise competitions in markets and organizations', *Bell Journal of Economics* 12: 201–13.

Crawford, V.P. (1991) 'An "evolutionary" interpretation of Van Huyk, Battalio, and Beil's experimental results on coordination', *Games and Economic Behavior* 3: 25–59.

Cross, J.G. (1983) *A Theory of Adaptive Economic Behavior*, Cambridge: Cambridge University Press.

Cummins, R. (1975) 'Functional analysis', *Journal of Philosophy*, 72: 741–64. Reprinted in E. Sober (ed.) (1986) *Conceptual Issues in Evolutionary Biology: An Anthology*, Cambridge, Masachusetts: MIT Press, pp. 386–407.

Cyert, R.M. and March, J.G. (1963) *A Behavioral Theory of the Firm*, Englewood Cliffs, New Jersey: Prentice Hall.

David, P. (1985) 'Clio and the economics of QWERTY', *American Economic Review (Papers and Proceedings)* 75: 332–7.

Dawkins, R. (1976) *The Selfish Gene*, Oxford: Oxford University Press.

—— (1980) 'Good strategy or evolutionarily stable strategy?', in G.W. Barlow and J. Silverberg (eds) *Sociobiology: Beyond Nature/Nurture?* Boulder, Colorado: Westview Press, pp. 331–67.

Day, R.H and Chen, P. (eds) (1993) *Nonlinear Dynamics and Evolutionary Economics*, New York/Oxford: Oxford University Press.

Day, R.H. and Tinney, E.H. (1968) 'How to co-operate in business without really trying: a learning model of decentralized decision making', *Journal of Political Economy* 76: 583–600.

De Marchi, N.B. (1986) 'Mill's unrevised philosophy of economics: a comment on Hausman', *Philosophy of Science* 53: 89–100.

Demsetz, H. (1967) 'Toward a theory of property rights', *American Economic Review* 57: 347–59.

—— (1988) *Ownership, Control and the Firm: The Organization of Economic Activity. Volume 1*, Oxford: Basil Blackwell.

—— (1991) 'The theory of the firm revisited', in O.E. Williamson and S.G. Winter (eds) *The Nature of the Firm: Origins, Evolution and Development*, Oxford: Oxford University Press, pp. 159–78.

Diesing, P. (1971) *Patterns of Discovery in the Social Sciences*, Chicago: Aldine Atherton.

Dosi, G., Freeman, C., Nelson, R., Silverberg, G. and Soete, L. (eds) (1988) *Technical Change and Economic Theory*, London: Pinter.

Dow, G.K. (1987) 'The function of authority in transaction cost economics', *Journal of Economic Behavior and Organization* 8: 13–38.

Dugger, W. (1983) 'The transaction cost analysis of Oliver E. Williamson: a new synthesis?', *Journal of Economic Issues* 17: 95–114.

Dupré, J. (ed.) (1987) *The Latest on the Best: Essays on Evolution and Optimality*, Cambridge, Masachusetts: MIT Press.

Egidi, M. and Marris, R. (eds) (1992) *Economics, Bounded Rationality and the Cognitive Revolution*, Aldershot: Edward Elgar.

Elster, J. (1979) *Ulysses and the Sirens: Studies in Rationality and Irrationality*, Cambridge: Cambridge University Press.

—— (1983) *Explaining Technical Change: A Case Study in the Philosophy of Science*, Cambridge: Cambridge University Press.

—— (1989) *Nuts and Bolts for the Social Sciences*, Cambridge: Cambridge University Press.

Enke, S. (1951) 'On maximizing profits: a distinction between Chamberlin and Robinson', *American Economic Review* 41: 566–78.

Faber, M. and Proops, J.L.R. (1991) 'Evolution in biology, physics and economics: a conceptual analysis', in P.P. Saviotti and J.S. Metcalfe (eds) *Evolutionary Theories of Economic and Technological Change*, Chur/Reading (etc.): Harwood Academic Publishers, pp. 58–87.

Fama, E. (1980) 'Agency problems and the theory of the firm', *Journal of Political Economy* 88: 288–307.

Fama, E. and Jensen, M.C. (1983a) 'Separation of ownership and control', *Journal of Law and Economics* 26: 301–26.

—— (1983b) 'Agency problems and residual claims', *Journal of Law and Economics* 26: 327–50.

Field, A.J. (1984) 'Microeconomics, norms and rationality', *Economic Development and Cultural Change* 32: 683–711.

Foss, N.J. (1994) 'Realism and evolutionary economics', *Journal of Social and Evolutionary Systems* 17: 21–40.

Frank, R.H. (1988) *Passions within Reason: The Strategic Role of the Emotions*, New York: W.W. Norton & Company.

Friedman, D. (1991) 'Evolutionary games in economics', *Econometrica* 59: 637–66.

Friedman, M. (1953) 'The methodology of positive economics', in *Essays in Positive Economics*, Chicago: University of Chicago Press.

Friedman, M. and Savage, L.J. (1948) 'The utility analysis of choices involving risk', *Journal of Political Economy* 56: 279–304.

Furubotn, E.G. and Pejovich, S. (1972) 'Property rights and economic theory: a survey of recent literature', *Journal of Economic Literature* 10: 1137–62.

Ghiselin, M.T. (1974) *The Economy of Nature and the Evolution of Sex*, Berkeley, California: University of California Press.

—— (1978) 'The economy of the body', *American Economic Review (Papers and Proceedings)* 68: 233–7.

Gould, S.J. (1980) 'Sociobiology and the theory of natural selection', in G.W. Barlow and J. Silverberg (eds) *Sociobiology: Beyond Nature/Nurture?*, Boulder, Colorado: Westview Press, pp. 257–69.

Gould, S.J. and Lewontin, R.C. (1979) 'The spandrels of San Marco and the Panglossian paradigm: a critique of the adaptationist programme', *Proceedings of the Royal Society London* 205: 581–98. (Reprinted in E. Sober (ed.) (1986) *Conceptual Issues in Evolutionary Biology: An Anthology*, Cambridge, Massachusetts: MIT Press, pp. 252–70.)

Granovetter, M. (1985) 'Economic action and social structures', *American Journal of Sociology* 91: 481–510.

Hacking, I. (1983) *Representing and Intervening: Introductory Topics in the Philosophy of Natural Science*, Cambridge: Cambridge University Press.

Hall, P. (1994) *Innovation, Economics and Evolution: Theoretical Perspectives on Changing Technology in Economic Systems*, New York/London (etc.): Harvester Wheatsheaf.

Hall, R.L. and Hitch, C.J. (1939) 'Price theory and business behavior', *Oxford Economic Papers* 2. (Reprinted in T. Wilson and P.W.S. Andrews (eds) (1951) *Oxford Studies in the Price Mechanism*, Oxford: Clarendon Press.)

Hamilton, W.D. (1964) 'The genetical theory of social behavior', *Journal of Theoretical Biology* 7: 1–32.

Hammond, J.D. (1991) 'Early drafts of Friedman's methodology essay', unpublished paper.

Hannan, M.T. and Freeman, J. (1989) *Organizational Ecology*, Cambridge, Massachusetts: Harvard University Press.

Hansen, R.G. and Samuelson, W.F. (1988) 'Evolution in economic games', *Journal of Economic Behavior and Organization* 10: 107–38.

Hardin, R. (1980) 'Rationality, irrationality and functionalist explanation', *Social Science Information* 19: 755–72.

Harley, C.B. (1981) 'Learning the evolutionarily stable strategy', *Journal of Theoretical Biology* 89: 611–33.

Harrod, R.F. (1939) 'Price and cost in entrepreneurs' policy', in *Oxford Economic Papers* 2: 1–11.

Hausman, D.M. (1992) *The Inexact and Separate Science of Economics*, Cambridge: Cambridge University Press.

—— (1994) 'Kuhn, Lakatos and the character of economics', in R.E. Backhouse (ed.) *New Directions in Economic Methodology*, London: Routledge.

Hayek, F.A. (1948) 'The meaning of competition', in *Individualism and Economic Order*, Chicago: University of Chicago Press.

—— (1960) *The Constitution of Liberty*, London: Routledge & Kegan Paul.

—— (1964) 'Kinds of order in society', *The Individualist Review* 3: 3–12.

—— (1967) *Studies in Philosophy, Politics and Economics*, London: Routledge & Kegan Paul.

—— (1968) 'Competition as a discovery procedure'. Reprinted in F. A. Hayek (1978) *New Studies in Philosophy, Politics, Economics and the History of Ideas*, London: Routledge & Kegan Paul, pp. 254–65.

—— (1973) *Law, Legislation and Liberty. Vol. 1: Rules and Order*, London: Routledge & Kegan Paul.

—— (1976) *Law, Legislation and Liberty. Vol.2: The Mirage of Social Justice*, London: Routledge & Kegan Paul.

—— (1978) *New Studies in Philosophy, Politics, Economics and the History of Ideas*, London: Routledge & Kegan Paul.

—— (1988) *The Fatal Conceit: The Errors of Socialism*, London: Routledge.

Hempel, C.G. (1965) *Aspects of Scientific Explanation*, New York: Free Press.

Hirsch, A. and De Marchi, N. (1990) *Milton Friedman: Economics in Theory and Practice*, New York: Harvester Wheatseaf.

Hirshleifer, J. (1976) 'Shakespeare *vs*. Becker on altruism: the importance of having the last word', *Journal of Economic Literature* 14: 500–2.

—— (1977) 'Economics from a biological viewpoint', *Journal of Law and Economics* 20: 1–52.

—— (1978) 'Competition, cooperation, and conflict in economics and biology', *American Economic Review (Papers and Proceedings)* 68: 238–43.

—— (1982) 'Evolutionary models in economics and law: cooperation versus conflict strategies', in R.O. Zerbe Jr (ed.) *Research in Laws and Economics* 4, Greenwich, Connecticut/London: JAI Press Inc. pp. 1–60.

—— (1985) 'The expanding domain of economics', *American Economic Review* 75: 53–68.

—— (1987a) *Economic Behavior in Adversity*, Brighton, Sussex: Wheatsheaf Books.

—— (1987b) 'On the emotions as guarantors of threats and promises', in J. Dupré (ed.) *The Latest on the Best: Essays on Evolution and Optimality*, Cambridge, Massachusetts: MIT Press, pp. 307–26.

—— (1993) 'The affections and the passions: their economic logic', *Rationality and Society* 5: 185–202.

Hirshleifer, J. and Martinez Coll, J.C. (1988) 'What strategies can support the evolutionary emergence of cooperation', *Journal of Conflict Resolution* 32: 367–98.

Hodgson, G.M. (1993a) 'The Mecca of Alfred Marshall', *Economic Journal* 103: 406–15.

—— (1993b) *Economics and Evolution: Bringing Life Back into Economics*, Cambridge: Polity Press.

—— (1994) 'Optimisation and evolution: Winter's critique of Friedman revisited', *Cambridge Journal of Economics* 18: 413–30.

Hogarth, R.M. and Reder, M.W. (eds) (1987) *Rational Choice: The Contrast between Economics and Psychology*, Chicago: University of Chicago Press.

Houthakker, H.S. (1956) 'Economics and biology: specialization and speciation', *Kyklos* 9: 181–9.

Hull, D.L. (1982) 'The naked meme', in H.C. Plotkin (ed.) *Learning, Development and Culture*, New York: John Wiley & Sons, pp. 273–327.

—— (1988) 'A general analysis of selection processes', in *Science as a Process*, Chicago: University of Chicago Press.

Jensen, M.C. (1983) 'Organization theory and methodology', *Accounting Review* 58: 319–39.

Jensen, M.C. and Meckling, W. (1976) 'Theory of the firm: managerial behavior, agency costs, and ownership structure', *Journal of Financial Economics* 3: 305–60.

Kandori, M., Mailath, G.J. and Rob, R. (1993) 'Learning, mutation, and long run equilibria in games', *Econometrica* 61: 29–56.

Kirzner, I.M. (1962) 'Rational action and economic theory', *Journal of Political Economy* 70: 380–5.

Klamer, A. (1983) *Conversations with Economists*, Totowa, New Jersey: Rowman & Allenheld.

Klamer, A. and Leonard, T.C. (1994) 'So what's an economic metaphor?', in P. Mirowski (ed.) *Natural Images in Economics*, Cambridge: Cambridge University Press.

Klein, B., Crawford, R.G. and Alchian, A.A. (1978) 'Vertical integration, appropriable rents, and the competitive contracting process', *Journal of Law and Economics* 21: 297–326.

Koopmans, T.C. (1957) *Three Essays on the State of Economic Science*, New York: McGraw-Hill.

Langlois, R.N. (1984) 'Internal organization in a dynamic context: some theoretical considerations', in M. Jussawalla and H. Ebenfield (eds) *Communication and Information Economics*, Amsterdam: North-Holland, pp. 23–49.

—— (ed.) (1986a) *Economics as a Process: Essays in the New Institutional Economics*, Cambridge: Cambridge University Press.

—— (1986b) 'Rationality, institutions, and explanation', in R.N. Langlois (ed.) *Economics as a Process: Essays in the New Institutional Economics*, Cambridge: Cambridge University Press, pp. 225–55.

Latsis, S.J. (1976) 'A research programme in economics', in S.J. Latsis (ed.) *Method and Appraisal in Economics*, Cambridge: Cambridge University Press, pp. 1–41.

Lawson, T. (1989) 'Abstraction, tendencies and stylised facts: a realist approach to economic analysis', *Cambridge Journal of Economics* 13: 59–78.

—— (1992) 'Realism, closed systems and Friedman', *Research in the History of Economic Thought and Methodology* 10: 149–69.

Lester, R.A. (1946) 'Shortcomings of marginal analysis for wage-employment problems', *American Economic Review* 36: 63–82.

—— (1947) 'Marginalism, minimum wages, and labor markets', *American Economic Review* 37: 134–48.

Levitt, B. and March, J.G. (1988) 'Organizational learning', *Annual Review of Sociology* 14: 19–40.

Lewis, D.K. (1969) *Convention: A Philosophical Study*, Cambridge, Massachusetts: Harvard University Press.

Loasby, B.J. (1991) *Equilibrium and Evolution: An Exploration of Connecting Principles in Economics*, Manchester: Manchester University Press.

Lucas, R.E. (Jr) (1987) 'Adaptive behavior and economic theory', in R.M. Hogarth and M.W. Reder (eds) *Rational Choice: The Contrast between Economics and Psychology*, Chicago: University of Chicago Press, pp. 217–42.

McCloskey, D. (1985) *The Rhetoric of Economics*, Madison, Wisconsin: University of Wisconsin Press.

Machlup, F. (1946) 'Marginal analysis and empirical research', *American Economic Review* 36: 519–54.

— (1947) 'Rejoinder to an antimarginalist', *American Economic Review* 37: 148–54.

— (1967) 'Theories of the firm: marginalist, behavioral, managerial', *American Economic Review* 57: 1–33.

Mailath, G.J. (1992) 'Introduction: symposium on evolutionary game theory', *Journal of Economic Theory* 57: 259–77.

Mäki, U. (1989) 'On the problem of realism in economics', *Ricerche Economiche* 43: 176–98.

— (1992) 'Friedman and realism', *Research in the History of Economic Thought and Methodology* 10: 171–95.

— (1994) 'Isolation, idealization and truth in economics', in B. Hamminga and N. De Marchi (eds) *Idealization VI: Idealization in Economics*, Amsterdam/Atlanta, Georgia: Rodopi.

Mäki, U., Gustafsson, B. and Knudsen, C. (eds) (1993) *Rationality, Institutions and Economic Methodology*, London: Routledge.

Manne, H. (1965) 'Mergers and the market for corporate control', *Journal of Political Economy* 73: 110–20.

Marshall, A. (1920) *Principles of Economics* (Eighth Edition), London: Macmillan Press.

Matthews, R.C.O. (1984) 'Darwinism and economic change', *Oxford Economic Papers (Supplement)* 46: 91–117.

Maynard Smith, J. (1982) *Evolution and the Theory of Games*, Cambridge: Cambridge University Press.

— (1987) 'How to model evolution', in J. Dupré (ed.) *The Latest on the Best: Essays on Evolution and Optimality*, Cambridge, Massachusetts: MIT Press, pp. 119–31.

Menger, C. (1985) *Investigations into the Method of the Social Sciences with Special Reference to Economics*, New York: New York University Press. First published (in German) in 1883.

Metcalfe, S. (1989) 'Evolution and economic change', in A. Silberston (ed.) *Technology and Economic Progress*, Basingstoke, Hampshire: Macmillan Press, pp. 54–85.

Milgrom, P. and Roberts, P. (1992) *Economics, Organization and Management*, Englewood Cliffs, New Jersey: Prentice Hall.

Mill, J.S. (1967) 'On the definition of political economy; and on the method of investigation proper to it', in *Essays on Economics and Society (Collected Works IV)*, London: Routledge & Kegan Paul. (First published in 1836.)

— (1973) *A System of Logic (Collected Works VII–VIII)*, London: Routledge & Kegan Paul. (First published in 1844.)

Mirowski, P. (1986) 'Institutions as a solution concept in a game theory context', in P. Mirowski (ed.) *The Reconstruction of Economic Theory*, Boston: Kluwer Academic, pp. 241–63.

— (1989) *More Heat than Light*, Cambridge: Cambridge University Press.

Mueller, D.C. (1986) 'Review of "The Economic Institutions of Capitalism"', *The Antitrust Bulletin* Fall: 827–34.

Musgrave, A. (1981) '"Unreal assumptions" in economic theory: the F-twist untwisted', *Kyklos* 34: 377–87. Reprinted in B. Caldwell (ed.) (1984) *Appraisal and Criticism in Economics: A Book of Readings*, Boston: Allen & Unwin.

Nagel, E. (1961) *The Structure of Science*, London: Routledge & Kegan Paul.

— (1963) 'Assumptions in economic theory', *American Economic Review* 53: 211–19.

Neale, W.C. (1987) 'Institutions', *Journal of Economic Issues* 21: 1177–206.

Nelson, R.R. (1986) 'Evolutionary modelling of economic change', in J.E. Stiglitz and G.F. Mathewson (eds) *New Developments in the Analysis of Market Structure*, Basingstoke, Hampshire: Macmillan Press, pp. 450–71.

Nelson, R.R. and Winter, S.G. (1982) *An Evolutionary Theory of Economic Change*, Cambridge, Massachusetts.: Belknap Press of Harvard University Press.

Nowak, M.A. and Sigmund, K. (1993) 'A strategy of win-stay, lose-shift that outperforms tit-for-tat in the Prisoner's Dilemma game', *Nature* 364: 56–8.

Nozick, R. (1974) *Anarchy, State and Utopia*, New York: Basic Books.

van Parijs, Ph. (1981) *Evolutionary Explanation in the Social Sciences: An Emerging Paradigm*, Totowa, New Jersey: Rowman and Littlefield.

—— (1991) *Le Modèle Economique et ses Rivaux: Introduction à la Pratique l'épistémologie des Sciences Sociales*, Genève/Paris: DROZ.

—— (1992) 'Le paradigme rationaliste et ses compagnons: Réponse à Vromen et Favereau', *Recherches Economique de Louvain* 58: 37–50.

Penrose, E.T. (1952) 'Biological analogies in the theory of the firm', *American Economic Review* 42: 804–19.

—— (1953) 'Rejoinder', *American Economic Review* 43: 603–9.

Popper, K.R. (1934) *Die Logik der Forschung*, translated into *The Logic of Scientific Discovery*, London: Hutchinson.

—— (1963) *Conjectures and Refutations*, London: Routledge & Kegan Paul.

—— (1972) *Objective Knowledge: An Evolutionary Approach*, Oxford: Clarendon Press.

—— (1987) 'Campbell on the evolutionary theory of knowledge', in G. Radnitzky and W.W. Bartley III (eds) *Evolutionary Epistemology, Rationality, and the Sociology of Knowledge*, La Salle, Illinois: Open Court, pp. 115–20. (First published in 1974.)

Putterman, L. (1986) 'The economic nature of the firm: overview', in L. Putterman (ed.), *The Economic Nature of the Firm: A Reader*, Cambridge: Cambridge University Press, pp. 1–29.

Radnitzky, G. and Bartley, W.W. III (eds) (1987) *Evolutionary Epistemology, Rationality, and the Sociology of Knowledge*, La Salle, Illinois: Open Court.

Robson, A.J. (1992) 'Evolutionary game theory', in J. Creedy *et al.* (eds) *Recent Developments in Game Theory*, Aldershot: Edward Elgar, pp. 165–78.

Rosenberg, A. (1985) *The Structure of Biological Science*, Cambridge: Cambridge University Press.

—— (1988) *Philosophy of Social Science*, Oxford: Clarendon Press.

Salmon, W.C. (1984) *Scientific Explanation and the Causal Structure of the Word*, Princeton, New Jersey: Princeton University Press.

—— (1990) *Four Decades of Scientific Explanation*, Minneapolis, Minnesota: University of Minnesota Press.

Saviotti, J.P. and Metcalfe, J.S. (eds) (1991) *Evolutionary Theories of Economic and Technological Change: Present Status and Future Prospects*, Chur/Reading (etc.): Harwood Academic Publishers.

Schaffer, M.E. (1989) 'Are profit-maximizers the best survivors? A Darwinian model of economic natural selection', *Journal of Economic Behavior and Organization* 11: 29–45.

Schelling, T.C. (1960) *The Strategy of Conflict*, Cambridge, Massachusetts: Harvard University Press.

—— (1978) *Micromotives and Macrobehavior*, New York: W.W. Norton & Company.

Schotter, A. (1981) *The Economic Theory of Social Institutions*, Cambridge: Cambridge University Press.

—— (1985) *Free Market Economics: A Critical Appraisal*, New York: St Martin's Press.

Schweber, S.S. (1968) 'Darwin and the political economists: divergence of character', *Journal of the History of Biology* 13: 195–289.

Selten, R. (1991) 'Evolution, learning and economic behavior', *Games and Economic Behavior* 3: 3–24.

Simon, H.A. (1951) 'A formal theory of the employment relationship', *Econometrica* 19: 11–23.

—— (1955) 'A behavioral model of rational choice', *Quarterly Journal of Economics* 69: 99–118.

—— (1956) 'Rational choice and the structure of the environment', *Psychological Review* 63: 129–38.

—— (1959) 'Theories of decision-making in economics and behavioral science', *American Economic Review* 49: 253–83.

—— (1962) 'The architecture of complexity', *Proceedings of the American Philosophical Society* 106: 467–82.

—— (1964) 'Rationality', in J. Gould and W.L. Kolb (eds) *A Dictionary of the Social Sciences*, New York: Macmillan Publishing Company, pp. 573–4.

—— (1976) 'From substantive to procedural rationality', in S.J. Latsis (ed.) *Method and Appraisal in Economics*, Cambridge: Cambridge University Press.

—— (1978) 'Rationality as a process and as product of thought', *American Economic Review* 68: 1–16.

—— (1979) 'Rational decision making in business organizations', *American Economic Review* 69: 493–513.

—— (1982) *Models of Bounded Rationality (Vol. 2: Behavioral Economics and Business Organization)*, Cambridge, Massachusetts: MIT Press.

—— (1983) *Reason in Human Affairs*, Oxford: Basil Blackwell.

—— (1991) 'Organizations and markets', *Journal of Economic Perspectives* 5: 25–44.

—— (1992) 'Scientific discovery as problem solving', in M. Egidi and R. Marris (eds) *Economics, Bounded Rationality and the Cognitive Revolution*, Aldershot: Edward Elgar, pp. 102–19.

Sober, E. (1983) 'Equilibrium explanation', *Philosophical Studies* 43: 201–10.

—— (1984) *The Nature of Selection: Evolutionary Theory in Philosophical Focus*, Cambridge, Massachusetts: MIT Press.

—— (ed.) (1986) *Conceptual Issues in Evolutionary Biology: An Anthology*, Cambridge, Massachusetts: MIT Press.

—— (1987) 'What is adaptationism?', in J. Dupré (ed.) *The Latest on the Best: Essays on Evolution and Optimality*, Cambridge, Massachusetts: MIT Press, pp. 105–18.

Stigler, G.J. (1947) 'Professor Lester and the marginalists', *American Economic Review* 37: 154–7.

Sugden, R. (1986) *The Economics of Rights, Co-operation and Welfare*, Oxford: Basil Blackwell.

—— (1989) 'Spontaneous order', *Journal of Economic Perspectives* 3: 85–97.

—— (1990) 'Convention, creativity and conflict', in Y. Varoufakis and D. Young (eds) *Conflict in Economics*, New York: Harvester Wheatsheaf, pp. 68–90.

Taylor, P. and Jonker, L. (1978) 'Evolutionarily stable strategies and game dynamics', *Mathematical Biosciences* 40: 145–56.

Teece, D.J. (1988) 'Technological Change and the nature of the firm', in G. Dosi, *et al.* (eds) *Technical Change and Economic Theory*, London: Pinter.

Trivers, R. (1971) 'The evolution of reciprocal altruism', *Quarterly Review of Biology* 46: 35–57.

Ullmann-Margalit, E. (1977) *The Emergence of Norms*, Oxford: Clarendon Press.

—— (1978) 'Invisible-hand explanations', *Synthese* 39: 263–91.

—— (1990) 'Revision of norms', *Ethics* 100: 756–67.

Vanberg, V. (1986) 'Spontaneous market order and social rules: a critical examination of F.A. Hayek's theory of cultural evolution', *Economics and Philosophy* 2: 75–100.

—— (1993) 'Rational choice, rule-following and institutions: an evolutionary perspective', in U. Mäki *et al.* (1993) *Rationality, Institutions and Economic Methodology*, London: Routledge, pp. 171–200.

Vanberg, V. and Buchanan, J.M. (1988) 'Rational choice and moral order', *Analyse & Kritik* 10: 138–60.

Van Damme, E. (1987) *Stability and Perfection of Nash Equilibria*, Berlin: Springer-Verlag.

—— (1994) 'Evolutionary game theory', *European Economic Review* 38: 847–58.

Veblen, Th. (1898) 'Why is economics not an evolutionary science?', *Quarterly Journal of Economics* 12: 373–97.

Vromen, J.J. (1987) 'Conflicting methodological principles and the realism debate', *Proceedings of the Eleventh Wittgenstein Symposium*, Vienna: Pichler-Verlag.

—— (1992a) 'Bedrieglijk functionalisme in de "Chicago school of economics"', in E. Heijerman and P. Wouters (eds) *Crisis van de Rede? Perspectieven op Cultuur*, Assen/Maastricht: Van Gorcum, pp. 28–36.

—— (1992b) 'Evolutionary approaches in economics', *Recherches Economique de Louvain* 58: 3–20.

—— (1993) 'The spontaneous evolution of *de facto* property rights', unpublished paper.

Weibull, J.W. (1994) 'The "as if" approach to game theory: three positive results and four obstacles', *European Economic Review* 38: 868–81.

Whitehead, A.N. and Russell, B. (1910) *Principia Mathematica*, Cambridge: Cambridge University Press.

Williams, G.C. (1966) *Adaptation and Natural Selection*, Princeton, New Jersey: Princeton University Press.

Williamson, O.E. (1964) *The Economics of Discretionary Behavior: Objectives in a Theory of the Firm*, Englewood Cliffs, New Jersey: Prentice Hall.

—— (1975) *Markets and Hierarchies: Analysis and Antitrust Implications*, New York: The Free Press.

—— (1985) *The Economic Institutions of Capitalism*, New York: The Free Press.

—— (1987) 'Transaction cost economics', *Journal of Economic Behavior and Organization* 8: 617–25.

—— (1988) 'Economics and sociology: promoting a dialog', in G. Farkas and P. England (eds) *Industries, Firms and Jobs: Sociological and Economic Approaches*, New York: Plenum, pp. 159–85.

—— (1990) 'A comparison of alternative approaches to economic organization', *Journal of Institutional and Theoretical Economics* 146: 61–71.

—— (1991a) 'The logic of economic organization', in O.E. Williamson and S.G. Winter (eds) *The Nature of the Firm: Origins, Evolution and Development*, Oxford: Oxford University Press, pp. 90–116.

—— (1991b) 'Economic institutions: spontaneous and intentional governance', *Journal of Law, Economics and Organization* 7: 159–87.

—— (1993) 'The economic analysis of institutions and organisations: in general and with respect to country studies', *Economics Department Working Papers* 133, Paris: OECD.

Williamson, O.E. and Winter, S.G. (eds) (1991) *The Nature of the Firm: Origins, Evolution and Development*, Oxford: Oxford University Press.

Wilson, E.O. (1975) *Sociobiology*, Cambridge, Massachusetts: Harvard University Press.

Winter, S.G. Jr (1964) 'Economic "natural selection" and the theory of the firm', *Yale Economic Essays* 4: 225–72.

—— (1971) 'Satisficing, selection, and the innovating remnant', *Quarterly Journal of Economics* 85: 237–61.

—— (1975) 'Optimization and evolution in the theory of the firm', in R.H. Day and T. Groves (eds) *Adaptive Economic Models*, New York: Academic Press, pp. 73–118.

—— (1986) 'The research program of the behavioral theory of the firm: orthodox critique and evolutionary perspective', in B. Gilad and S. Kaish (eds) *Handbook of Behavioral Economics*, Greenwich, Connecticut: JAI Press Inc, pp. 151–88.

—— (1987a) 'Natural selection and evolution', in J. Eatwell *et al.* (eds) *The New Palgrave: a Dictionary of Economics*, London: Macmillan, pp. 614–17.

—— (1987b) 'Comments on Arrow and Lucas', in R.M. Hogarth and M.W. Reder (eds) *Rational Choice: The Contrast between Economics and Psychology*, Chicago: University of Chicago Press, pp. 243–50.

—— (1991) 'On Coase, competence and the corporation', in O.E. Williamson and S.G. Winter (eds) *The Nature of the Firm: Origins, Evolution and Develop- ment*, Oxford: Oxford University Press, pp. 179–95.

Witt, U. (1991) 'Reflections on the present state of evolutionary economic theory', in G.M. Hodgson and E. Screpanti (eds) *Rethinking Economics: Markets, Technology and Economic Evolution*, Aldershot: Edward Elgar, pp. 83–102.

—— (1993a) 'Evolutionary economics: some principles', in U. Witt (ed.) *Evolution in Markets and Institutions*, Berlin: Springer-Verlag, pp. 1–16.

—— (ed.) (1993b) *Evolution in Markets and Institutions*, Berlin: Springer-Verlag.

Wynne-Edwards, V.C. (1962) *Animal Dispersion*, Edinburgh: Oliver & Boyd.

Zeeman, E.C. (1980) 'Population dynamics from game theory', in *Proceedings from the International Conference on Global Theory of Dynamical Systems*, Evanston, Illinois: Northwestern University Press.

Zerbe, R.O. Jr (ed.) (1982) *Research in Law and Economics* 4, Greenwich, Connecticut/ London: JAI Press Inc.

INDEX

238